D0982975

DATE DUE

Immigration

Immigration

Other Books in the Turning Points Series:

Turning | Points
IN WORLD HISTORY

Immigration

Jeff Hay, *Book Editor*

Bonnie Szumski, *Editorial Director*
Scott Barbour, *Managing Editor*

Greenhaven Press, Inc., San Diego, California

Every effort has been made to trace the owners of copyrighted material. The articles in this volume may have been edited for content, length, and/or reading level. The titles have been changed to enhance the editorial purpose.

No part of this book may be reproduced or used in any form or by any means, electrical, mechanical, or otherwise, including, but not limited to, photocopy, recording, or any information storage and retrieval system, without prior written permission from the publisher.

Library of Congress Cataloging-in-Publication Data

Immigration / Jeff Hay, book editor.
        p.   cm. — (Turning points in world history)
    Includes bibliographical references and index.
    ISBN 0-7377-0638-4 (pbk. : alk. paper) —
ISBN 0-7377-0639-2 (lib. bdg. : alk. paper)
    1. United States—Emigration and immigration—History.
2. Immigrants—United States—History. I. Hay, Jeff. II. Turning points (Greenhaven Press)

JV6450 .I556 2001
304.8'73—dc21   00-052800
                                                                              CIP

Cover photo: © Superstock
Library of Congress, 42, 87, 118, 186

© 2001 by Greenhaven Press, Inc.
P.O. Box 289009, San Diego, CA 92198-9009

Printed in the U.S.A.

Contents

Americans. An anti-Catholic movement emerged that tried to make life difficult for these newcomers.

Chapter 2: The Second Great Wave: European Emigration from 1880 to 1924

Chapter 3: Emigration from Asia

from Asia. They believed these workers would be more docile and, most importantly, cheaper than Americans.

Chapter 4: Emigration from Mexico

Chapter 5: The Open Door Closes

Foreword

Certain past events stand out as pivotal, as having effects and outcomes that change the course of history. These events are often referred to as turning points. Historian Louis L. Snyder provides this useful definition:

> A turning point in history is an event, happening, or stage which thrusts the course of historical development into a different direction. By definition a turning point is a great event, but it is even more—a great event with the explosive impact of altering the trend of man's life on the planet.

History's turning points have taken many forms. Some were single, brief, and shattering events with immediate and obvious impact. The invasion of Britain by William the Conqueror in 1066, for example, swiftly transformed that land's political and social institutions and paved the way for the rise of the modern English nation. By contrast, other single events were deemed of minor significance when they occurred, only later recognized as turning points. The assassination of a little-known European nobleman, Archduke Franz Ferdinand, on June 28, 1914, in the Bosnian town of Sarajevo was such an event; only after it touched off a chain reaction of political-military crises that escalated into the global conflict known as World War I did the murder's true significance become evident.

Other crucial turning points occurred not in terms of a few hours, days, months, or even years, but instead as evolutionary developments spanning decades or even centuries. One of the most pivotal turning points in human history, for instance—the development of agriculture, which replaced nomadic hunter-gatherer societies with more permanent settlements—occurred over the course of many generations. Still other great turning points were neither events nor developments, but rather revolutionary new inventions and innovations that significantly altered social customs and ideas, military tactics, home life, the spread of knowledge, and the human condition in general. The developments of writing, gunpowder, the printing press, antibiotics, the electric light, atomic energy, television, and the computer, the last two of which have recently ushered in the world-altering information age, represent only some of these innovative turning points.

Each anthology in the Greenhaven Turning Points in World History series presents a group of essays chosen for their accessibility. The anthology's structure also enhances this accessibility. First, an introductory essay provides a general overview of the principal events and figures involved, placing the topic in its historical context. The essays that follow explore various aspects in more detail, some targeting political trends and consequences, others social, literary, cultural, and/or technological ramifications, and still others pivotal leaders and other influential figures. To aid the reader in choosing the material of immediate interest or need, each essay is introduced by a concise summary of the contributing writer's main themes and insights.

In addition, each volume contains extensive research tools, including a collection of excerpts from primary source documents pertaining to the historical events and figures under discussion. In the anthology on the French Revolution, for example, readers can examine the works of Rousseau, Voltaire, and other writers and thinkers whose championing of human rights helped fuel the French people's growing desire for liberty; the French *Declaration of the Rights of Man and Citizen*, presented to King Louis XVI by the French National Assembly on October 2, 1789; and eyewitness accounts of the attack on the royal palace and the horrors of the Reign of Terror. To guide students interested in pursuing further research on the subject, each volume features an extensive bibliography, which for easy access has been divided into separate sections by topic. Finally, a comprehensive index allows readers to scan and locate content efficiently. Each of the anthologies in the Greenhaven Turning Points in World History series provides students with a complete, detailed, and enlightening examination of a crucial historical watershed.

Introduction

In the seventeenth and eighteenth centuries, colonial North America was sparsely settled by Native Americans and by small groups of Europeans clinging to their towns on the Atlantic coastline along with their African slaves. The only major settlements were far to the south, in Spanish Mexico. The Spanish, French, Dutch, and English had all claimed sovereignty over what they saw as the empty spaces of North America. But it was not until after the Seven Years' War, also known as the French and Indian War, fought from 1756 to 1763, that control passed definitively to the English. Only a short time later, from 1775 to 1783, the mostly English and Scots-Irish colonists fought to free themselves from British control and establish the United States of America.

Meanwhile, Europe had begun to experience a population explosion. New agricultural techniques, better health care, and more effective sanitation allowed more children to survive to adulthood and have healthier children of their own. By 1800 the populations of many western European countries were expanding too quickly for all the new people to find work and support themselves.

The open spaces of North America offered a solution. The United States spent much of the first half of the nineteenth century acquiring new territory, until the nation stretched from the Atlantic to the Pacific Oceans. And throughout most of the nineteenth century and into the twentieth, wave after wave of European immigrants crossed the Atlantic to fill America's open spaces.

Until the period of mass immigration began, the United States remained largely an outpost of British culture. But immigration turned America into what many have called, using the words of a Jewish American poet, a melting pot of peoples from all over the world. At first, Irish and German Catholics, German businessmen and intellectuals, and Scandinavian farmers and fishermen added elements of their lives to American culture. Later, Italians, Poles, Greeks, Russians, Jews, and many others made their contributions to the melting pot. Over time, many of these groups intermarried, creating a white America that is, in fact, a combination of all European nationalities.

Immigration also had a significant effect on the "old countries" of Europe. The frequent departure of emigrants meant, first of all, that more work was available for those who remained at home. Moreover, immigrants in America often sent money to their relatives in Europe along with reports about their lives. Some immigrants, in fact, were "birds of passage" who traveled back and forth across the Atlantic between their home villages and their jobs in America.

Emigration was also one means by which European nations expanded their influence across the globe during the nineteenth century, often called the age of imperialism. Emigration gave many nations a voice in America they might not have had when the United States had a mostly British heritage. In addition, while most European emigrants went to America, others took the same idea to other areas: Australia, New Zealand, Canada, Argentina, Brazil, or Chile.

Smaller numbers of Chinese, Japanese, Filipino, and other Asians also sought opportunities in the United States. Their experiences often paralleled those of European emigrants. Asian newcomers had many successes. Despite prejudice against them, they frequently sent money home, and numerous Asian "birds of passage" considered their stays in the United States to be only temporary. From south of the border, sizable numbers of Mexicans also sought opportunities as temporary and permanent immigrants. Although these groups were small compared to European totals, Asians and Mexicans also added a great deal to the developing United States and were precursors to later immigrants.

Immigration is an ongoing as well as a very controversial story. Today, huge numbers of immigrants continue their journey to America, mostly from Asia and Latin America. Many Americans wonder whether today's immigration is similar to that of the past. Will immigrants assimilate? Will they intermarry? Does America attract skilled self-starters who will contribute to society, or those who could not make it at home? Is the idea of the melting pot accurate? Is America too crowded to allow continued immigration? Do immigrants take jobs away from Americans?

All of these questions were asked in the past, particularly as America decided to restrict immigration in the 1920s. An examination of past immigration to the United States can help expand understanding of this important aspect of American, European, and world history and shed light on an ongoing phenomenon.

Turning Points in World History: Immigration to the United States provides an overview of the important aspects of immigration from 1830 to 1924. The articles included in this volume examine both the push factors—conditions in Europe, Asia, and Mexico that led to immigration—as well as the various pull factors—reasons immigrants were drawn to the United States. The book examines where immigrants settled, what sort of work they did, and ways in which they combined American culture with their own. It also describes American feelings toward immigrants and immigration. The readings are supplemented by an appendix of primary source documents that offer various perspectives on immigration, from letters home to personal reminiscences to arguments over immigration policy. In addition, a historical essay at the beginning and a chronology at the end of the book place the articles and documents in context.

Mass immigration has helped to define the United States and reflects developments in other parts of the world. The selections in this volume are intended to introduce students to the multifaceted history of immigration and its effects on a wide variety of regions and peoples as well as the lessons that history might have for the modern world.

A Brief History of Immigration to the United States

On February 22, 1912, the anniversary of George Washington's birth, a young Italian immigrant named Alicia Gasperetti stepped ashore on New York's Ellis Island after a long journey from Genoa, Italy, in a third-class compartment. She was one of millions of Italians, Poles, Greeks, Russians, and others who emigrated from Europe to the United States in the period from 1885 to 1924. They all hoped to create a better life for themselves and their families and were willing to work hard and sacrifice in order to succeed in America.

Gasperetti remembered being very happy to see the Statue of Liberty at the end of her journey. The statue, a gift from the French Third Republic, was dedicated in 1886. Inscribed on its base was a phrase from a poem by Emma Lazarus that read, "Give me your tired, your poor/Your huddled masses yearning to breath free . . . /I lift my lamp beside the golden door!" Both the statue and the poem have come to symbolize America's openness to immigrants seeking political freedom or greater prosperity.

When Gasperetti saw the Statue of Liberty for the first time and disembarked to be processed as a new immigrant on Ellis Island, she was eighteen years old. Within a year, she was married and working as a seamstress, making three dollars a week and living in a small apartment in Manhattan. Her son, however, became a university professor. In many ways her experience was typical of the millions of immigrants to the United States: With hard work, not only they but their children could have the greater education and the chance of prosperity that were unavailable in their homelands.

A Nation of Immigrants

The United States, as President John F. Kennedy wrote in the early 1960s, is a nation of immigrants. Aside from Native

Americans, the country is populated entirely by people who have migrated from some other part of the world and their descendants. Most of these migrants came to America voluntarily, the major exception being the hundreds of thousands of African slaves who were brought forcibly.

Immigrants have come to the United States from all over the world and for a wide variety of reasons. Some sought religious or political freedom. Others have come seeking prosperity or, at the very least, the chance to survive. The countries they left behind were sometimes stable and prosperous, sometimes chaotic and poor. Any accurate study of immigration makes it clear that no generalization is entirely true.

Today, immigrants continue to depart their home countries for the United States. More immigrants have come since 1965, when the last major change in immigration legislation took place, than at any other period in American history. Yet these newer immigrants are following a well-worn path. The United States has been attracting immigrants in large quantities since 1830.

A Mostly British Population

Before 1830 the population of the United States was mostly of British descent. The first permanent European settlement was established by Englishmen in 1607 at Jamestown, Virginia. The second major settlement, the Plymouth Colony in Massachusetts, was also set up by English migrants. English and Scots Irish—Scottish Protestants who had settled in Ireland in the mid-1600s—made up most of the non-African newcomers to colonial America in the seventeenth and eighteenth centuries. Moreover, these British settlers practiced a single religion, Protestant Christianity. Small congregations of Roman Catholics and Jews did not alter the fact that early America was overwhelmingly Protestant as well as British.

Other Europeans were certainly attracted to colonial America. Small communities of German, Swiss, French, Spanish, Swedish, and Dutch migrants existed throughout the colonial era. They had, however, little influence on American politics or culture. Since the original thirteen colonies were part of the British Empire, the English language and British ways determined the course of development in America.

Of course, dwindling communities of Native Americans as well as large numbers of African slaves and a much smaller number of free African Americans lived in America. But they had even less influence on mainstream American life. Although Americans freed themselves from direct British control in the American Revolution (1775–1783) and fought the British again in the War of 1812, Britain and America were closely tied by bonds of language, culture, religion, politics, and trade.

In the 1830s immigration began to challenge the overwhelmingly British character of American life. Waves of immigrants brought huge numbers of Europeans, Asians, and Latin Americans to the United States, and each new immigrant group added its own language, religion, and customs to the American mix. Indeed, aside from the period from 1921 until 1965, when a number of restrictions were in force, immigrants have kept coming in sizable numbers.

The flow of immigrants from 1830 until 1921 was remarkably constant. One measure, that of the foreign population, finds that between 10 and 15 percent of the population throughout that period was born outside the United States. However, the period might also be divided into two major waves of immigration based largely on the immigrants' countries of origin or ethnicity.

The first wave of immigrants lasted from approximately 1830 until 1880, when the largest groups of emigrants came from Ireland, the German states (Germany was not a unified nation until 1871), and the Scandinavian countries of Sweden, Norway, and Denmark. During the same era a substantial number of Chinese migrants sailed across the Pacific to California, and many Mexicans became Americans as a result of border changes.

The second wave was from 1880 to the 1920s. During this era emigrants came not only from Ireland, Germany, and Scandinavia but also from Italy, Greece, and eastern Europe. Many eastern European Jews, from Poland and Russia, joined the migration. Japanese and, later, Filipinos came across the Pacific. Also, for the first time large numbers of Mexicans crossed their northern border voluntarily.

The Expanding United States

The immigrants who made up the first wave arrived in a nation that had room for them. The mid–nineteenth century was a time of great expansion for the United States both territorially and economically. War, purchase, and negotiation added territory from Texas to the Pacific coast. These new lands, as well as the previously added territories in the Mississippi River valley, Great Lakes, and plains regions, were put to work by farmers as land could be had cheaply or, in some areas, for free. The California Gold Rush of 1849 and the growth of trade with China brought huge development to California and other areas in the far west.

A transportation revolution followed the territorial expansion. First, canals and rivers were used to transport goods and people using new steam-powered ships. More importantly, railroads began to connect America in an ever-growing network. By the 1860s railroad lines not only crisscrossed the nation east of the Mississippi River, but also connected the Atlantic Ocean with the Pacific. Often, rail lines were built using inexpensive immigrant labor. Irishmen built many of the eastern lines while California railroad builders such as Charles Crocker of the Central Pacific Line contracted to bring over cheap labor from China.

Meanwhile, new cities began to grow as transport hubs and to serve the economic needs of the expanding nation. In the middle of the country, Cincinnati, Chicago, St. Louis, and Milwaukee became important centers of settlement, trade, services, and transportation. Further west, Denver and San Francisco served similar purposes.

Economic expansion took place in the older cities of the East Coast as well. The Industrial Revolution, which began in England in the late 1700s, started to take effect in the United States in the 1820s and 1830s. Factories powered by steam were able to produce goods, particularly textiles in this era, more quickly and cheaply than hand labor could. Industry required workers not only to handle the machines but also to transport, load, and unload both raw materials and finished products. Miners were needed to dig the coal that powered the steam machines. Moreover, industrialism created a new class of educated office workers and shopkeepers.

Immigrants could be found everywhere in the expanding United States of the mid-1800s. Irish laborers not only built railroads but also became an important part of the working class of East Coast cities such as Boston, New York, Providence, Philadelphia, and Baltimore. There, they worked in factories and loaded and unloaded ships and trains. Over time, Irish immigrants took minor government jobs or opened their own shops, taverns, and restaurants. Many Irishwomen found work as domestic servants in the houses of the newly rich. In some cities there seemed to be more Irish than anyone else. According to the 1850 census, one-third of Boston's workers were Irish.

These immigrants left their homes for a number of reasons beyond economic opportunity. Europe, for example, experienced a population explosion throughout the 1800s as its population more than doubled, from 190 to 400 million. In many areas there was simply not enough land or work for all of these people, and emigration became the only outlet for the landless or unemployed. Ireland's population, for instance, doubled in a few decades in the late 1700s and early 1800s. Many Irishmen were forced to emigrate, as the only alternative was to stay home and starve.

The potato blight of the 1840s made matters worse. The potato was the staple food of Ireland's peasant farmers, and in 1845 and 1847, the potato crop went bad. In the ensuing famine, perhaps 1 million people died of starvation or disease. Another 1.5 million emigrated. Many went to England, Canada, and Australia, but the greatest number traveled to the United States. Altogether, nearly 3 million Irish people came to the United States between 1830 and 1880.

German emigrants, who generally were better off and better educated than the Irish, often moved into the new territories of the Midwest, where substantial German communities, with their own German-speaking churches, schools, and newspapers, emerged as early as the 1840s. Other Germans gravitated toward cities such as Cincinnati, St. Louis, or Milwaukee, where they started businesses such as breweries or transport companies. Smaller numbers of Germans dispersed as far as Texas or the Pacific Northwest. German communities were often self-contained as well as culturally active. Theater companies, singing societies, and political organizations abounded. Germans were also very interested in education; the kindergarten is a German institution.

German emigrants, unlike the mostly penniless Irish, sought more than an escape from starvation. They wanted, instead, a chance at prosperity. While the German states suffered rapid population growth as well as the potato blight, Germany remained one of Europe's wealthier areas. Emigrants left Germany for the chance to own land or start their own businesses.

Political instability also inspired some Germans to emigrate. Germany was in transition from a collection of as many as three hundred independent principalities, kingdoms, and city-states to a single, unified nation. In the midst of this process, in 1848, a series of revolutions shook Germany (as well as much of the rest of Europe). While a few German political radicals sought exile in the United States, more Germans left simply to seek out a more stable country in which to find prosperity and peace. Many of these "forty-eighters," as they were called, were extremely well-educated, which was unusual for any immigrants throughout the 1800s. A total of nearly 3 million Germans left for America between 1830 and 1880.

Scandinavian emigrants also moved west from the Atlantic coast, often settling in areas where the climate or landscape reminded them of home. Swedish, Norwegian, and Danish farmers established homesteads in Midwestern or Great Plains states such as Wisconsin, Minnesota, and Iowa. Norwegian fishermen settled the Pacific Northwest. Scandinavians were also supportive of education; in the early 1860s Swedish immigrants founded Gustavus Adolphus and Augustana Colleges, which were the first institutions of higher learning west of the Mississippi.

Most of the Scandinavian emigrants were poor farmers or fishermen although they, too, tended to be better off than their Irish counterparts. They left due to the overcrowding and chronic poverty of their home provinces. Like the Germans, most Scandinavians sought prosperity rather than simple survival. There were many fewer Scandinavians than Germans or Irish, nearly one-half million by 1880.

The California Gold Rush of 1849 attracted migrants from all over the world, including substantial numbers of Chinese men who hoped to strike it rich and return home. While a few Chinese found gold and continued to work in the mines, most started service businesses such as laundries or restaurants in the boomtowns of San Francisco and Sacramento. While some Americans, such as Charles Crocker, sought cheap Chinese labor for railroads, others sought it in agriculture. In some areas in early California, 85 percent of farmworkers were Chinese men.

Chinese emigrants sought escape from overcrowding and instability. The Opium War between Britain and China (1839–1842) had opened China to foreign trade and influence, and one result was that the Chinese government now allowed labor agents to contract and export migrant workers. Others took advantage of the new openness to head for the California gold fields. Most of the Chinese who emigrated in this era came from the Guangdong province in southern China. Not only was this area feeling the greatest amount of Western influence, it also had never been effectively incorporated into the Manchu regime that governed China. Finally, the Taiping Rebellion of the 1850s helped bring about widespread chaos and starvation. California, or "Gold Mountain" as some Chinese referred to it, offered an opportunity that did not seem to exist at home. Despite the chaos in China, however, many of the Chinese immigrants planned to return home after working in the United States.

The territorial expansion of the United States had also added a substantial population of Mexican Americans to the nation's expanding ethnic mix. After the American victory in the Mexican-American War of 1846, both nations signed the Treaty of Guadalupe Hidalgo. The treaty, along with the

Gadsden Purchase of 1853, officially added Texas, New Mexico, Arizona, Utah, Nevada, and California to America's possessions. The Mexicans who inhabited those areas simply had the borders changed around them and found themselves, all of a sudden, American rather than Mexican residents. Altogether, around seventy-five thousand people found their nationality changed in this manner.

During this era most Mexican Americans remained a poor, rural underclass. Although the Treaty of Guadalupe Hidalgo had promised to protect their land claims, most Mexican Americans lost their land to unscrupulous American speculators. While a few wealthy *Tejanos* or *Californios* melded into the elites of Texas and California, most Mexicans were stuck on the fringes of society. Many Americans, in fact, thought that Mexicans were comparable to the rapidly disappearing Native American population and treated them with similar disdain.

American Reactions to Immigrants

The American reaction to all of these newcomers varied, and no federal restrictions existed to limit their numbers. Many Americans argued that immigration was necessary because the expanding United States needed all of the immigrants it could contain. Farmers and settlers were required, they claimed, in the newly opened areas west of the Mississippi, and industrial workers were needed in the East. Railroad executives were only one group among many who sought to recruit workers from overseas. Land speculators, transport companies, and even state and territorial governments often sought to attract overseas immigrants with promises of land and prosperity. Meanwhile, immigrants who had already arrived often sent letters back to their home villages advertising the opportunities available in the United States. In hundreds of villages in Ireland, Germany, Sweden, Norway, and China, "America fever" took hold.

Foreign immigration, however, also inspired a nativist movement of a sort never seen before 1830, when most Americans traced their origins to Britain. Nativists believed that America was best preserved for "natives," by which they meant people who had been born there. Consequently, they argued that immigration should be banned or restricted. Nativists were also afraid of possible "foreign" influences, ranging from unfamiliar religions to strange food and holidays.

Nativist sentiment in the period between 1830 and 1880 was mainly directed toward the two groups who seemed especially foreign to Americans: Roman Catholics and the Chinese. The majority of Irish and approximately one-third of German emigrants were Catholics, and they had constructed sizable numbers of new Catholic churches and schools as they settled in America. Many Protestants, for their part, still had the traditional distrust of Catholics that European Protestants had carried with them since the 1500s. They felt that Catholics worshiped the church itself rather than God, and they were afraid that Catholics in America would be more loyal to the pope than to the president.

Dislike for the Irish in general strengthened the anti-Catholic sentiment. Even though Ireland was part of the United Kingdom, many in Britain often considered the Catholic Irish to be dirty, backward, and superstitious, and that attitude could be found in America as well. Some looked on with fear or regret as cities like New York and Boston began to fill up with poor Irish emigrants. Often, employers refused to hire workers simply because they were Irish. Signs could be seen posted on the doors of clubs, restaurants, and shops that proclaimed "no Irish allowed."

Catholic churches and schools were attacked as early as the 1830s, and priests and nuns were accused of lechery and corruption. In 1834, for instance, a mob burned down a Catholic convent outside of Boston. A book published in 1837, Maria Monk's *Awful Disclosures of the Hotel Dieu Nunnery of Montreal*, incited more anti-Irish violence. The book described how, among other things, priests seduced nuns and killed the babies that resulted. The book, as well as its sequel, sold hundreds of thousands of copies.

The Know-Nothings

The anti-Catholic movement culminated in the formation of the American Party, also known as the Know-Nothings, in 1845. Adopting as their slogan "Americans should rule America," the Know-Nothings emerged as a legitimate political force in the mid-1850s. They argued that immigrants represented a threat to America because of their heavy drinking and also due to crime and overcrowding in big cities. They also claimed that immigrants voted illegally, and wanted to extend the period required for immigrants to become naturalized American citizens from fourteen to twenty-one years.

Although the Know-Nothing party had some electoral successes in 1854, it failed to capitalize on them. The party faded away as America began to turn its political attention to the strains that resulted from the American Civil War (1861–1865). For the time being, no restraints were put on immigration, and, indeed, new immigrants proved their loyalty to their new homes by fighting well, on both sides, during the Civil War.

After the war, the Fourteenth Amendment to the Constitution was ratified. It established that all persons born in the United States were fully naturalized American citizens. While the amendment was designed to guarantee citizenship for the newly freed African slaves, it also made naturalization automatic for millions of immigrant children.

Excluding Chinese Immigrants

On the West Coast, anti-Chinese sentiment grew strong as larger numbers of immigrants, both Chinese and European, settled the region. European emigrants grew to resent the Chinese because, rather than blending into American life, they preferred to stay within their own communities. The Chinese Six Companies, a network of aid associations and businesses in the San Francisco Bay Area, appeared to operate like a shadow government, some claimed, and commanded far more loyalty from Chinese emigrants than the American government. Others argued that the Chinese were simply too foreign, too different, to ever be true Americans. Furthermore, many claimed, the Chinese were willing to work for wages that were too low, which kept white Americans from finding jobs.

In the 1870s, for the first time since America's nineteenth-century expansion began, the country began to suffer economic pains in the form of rising unemployment in industry, agriculture, and the railroads. In this context, white Americans grew to resent Chinese workers even more than before. Dennis Kearney, a naturalized Irish immigrant, formed the Workingmen's Party in San Francisco to lobby for the end of Chinese immigration. In Washington, D.C., lawmakers expressed fears that the Chinese were a threat to America's racial purity and social order, and they designed legislation to limit Chinese immigration.

Finally, in 1882, President Rutherford B. Hayes signed into law the Chinese Exclusion Act. It ended all Chinese immigration to the United States for ten years and prevented resident Chinese from becoming naturalized citizens. In 1892 the act was extended for another ten years, and in 1902 it was extended indefinitely. For the first time, the federal government of the United States had stepped in to restrict immigration. Meanwhile, the Chinese community on the West Coast was left to grow older without wives and families, as few Chinese women had joined the thousands of men who had journeyed across the Pacific to Gold Mountain.

The Second Wave of Immigration

Although Chinese immigration ended, large numbers of Irish, German, and Scandinavian emigrants continued to come to America during the second great wave of immigration. These communities, however, had grown familiar in America over the decades, and Irish, German, and Scandinavian migrants were no longer "foreign." Instead, these groups had become familiar parts of the American ethnic landscape, with the earlier immigrants largely assimilated into American life. Second-generation "ethnics," the children of the actual immigrants, tended to be wealthier than their parents, speakers of English rather than German or Swedish, and comfortable with America's political structure. Moreover, intermarriage among the early immigrant groups had grown common, making ethnic lines even more difficult to perceive.

The second wave of immigration, from approximately

1880 until the 1920s, is best defined according to the new groups that were foreign to the assimilated Americans of that era. From Europe came Italians, Greeks, Poles, Czechs, and Russians, among others. In addition, hundreds of thousands of European Jews joined the migration. From Asia, Japanese immigrants began to replace the excluded Chinese, along with smaller numbers of Filipinos and Koreans. Internal problems in Mexico inspired many Mexicans to cross their northern border in the first large wave of Mexican migration. Other immigrants came in smaller numbers from the Arab Middle East, Turkey, India, the Caribbean, and Canada. Most of these newcomers were not Protestant, practicing religions ranging from Catholicism to Judaism, Orthodox or Nestorian Christianity, Buddhism, or Sikhism. Indeed, the entire world was able to take advantage of the fact that, aside from the Chinese Exclusion Act, the United States had no meaningful immigration restrictions. In the period from 1890 until 1917, to give a sense of the total, nearly 18 million new immigrants entered the country.

These new immigrants came to a nation that was no longer expanding territorially—aside from the additions of Hawaii, the Philippines, Puerto Rico, and Guam—but was undergoing rapid industrial and economic development. The so-called second Industrial Revolution of the late 1800s had added electricity, chemicals, and the internal combustion engine to the coal, steam, textiles, and railroads of the first Industrial Revolution. Artificial fertilizers and machines made farming more productive and food more plentiful. In the cities, where most immigrants lived, a new economy based not only on industry but also on retail stores and other services had begun to flourish. Indeed, at the turn of the twentieth century the American economy was growing more quickly than that of any other nation on Earth, except perhaps Germany.

Overcrowding, Political Instability, and Religious Oppression

As in the first wave, most of the second-wave immigrants came in search of prosperity. The European population explosion of the 1800s reached southern and eastern Europe by the end of the nineteenth century. In many areas, peasant farmers could no longer earn a living from their traditional lands and set out for big cities such as Warsaw, Rome, or Vienna. Often, this was the first step toward immigration to the United States since European cities themselves offered few opportunities, full as they were of newcomers from rural areas.

The impulse to leave Europe for economic reasons was strengthened by other local conditions. Most Italian emigrants, for example, came from the southern part of the country, which was much poorer than the north. Rich Italians from the industrialized north often considered southern Italians to be backward and stupid and paid little attention to the economic development of the south. Moreover, southern Italy was struck by a series of earthquakes and crop failures in the first decade of the twentieth century, inspiring still more peasants to try their luck elsewhere. Not only did over 3 million Italians immigrate to the United States, another 2 million left for Argentina and Brazil.

Poland in that era was part of the Russian Empire, and many Poles sought to escape Russian oppression as well as Russia's persistent economic backwardness. Furthermore, the Russians had begun, in 1881 after the assassination of Czar Alexander II, an active persecution of the millions of Jews who lived in Poland and Russia. Almost all Jews were forced to reside in a specific area known as the Pale of Settlement. There, they were prevented from pursuing agriculture, industry, or any of the professions and languished in poverty. Finally, Russian leaders looked with approval as Russians staged pogroms, or violent anti-Semitic attacks. Many Jews, in response, set out for the United States. Scholars of immigration have had difficulty counting both Polish and Jewish emigrants since neither was considered a separate nationality. Poles came from Russia, Austria-Hungary, and Germany, and they were often counted as emigrants from those countries while Jews were often counted as Russian emigrants. Estimates are that over 1 million Poles and 2 million Jews entered the United States in the early 1900s.

Other Europeans sought to escape political instability, which was at its most troublesome in the huge, unwieldy

Austro-Hungarian Empire. The empire contained substantial populations of Austrians, Hungarians, Poles, Czechs, Slovaks, Serbs, Croatians, and others. At the dawn of the twentieth century, the empire was being torn apart as different groups asserted their nationalist instincts. Frequent wars, bombings, and assassinations added to the insecurity caused by overcrowding and unemployment. Between 1901 and 1910, over 2 million emigrants came from Austria-Hungary.

A Skilled and Self-Selected Group

In this period European emigrants tended to gravitate toward the large cities of the Northeast and Midwest. Half, in fact, settled in only four states: New York, Massachusetts, Pennsylvania, and Illinois. In a repeat of the 1840s and 1850s, Boston and New York became immigrant cities. Each had its large immigrant communities; now, however, there were not only Irishtowns or Germantowns but also Little Italys, Russiantowns, and Jewish quarters. Farther west, Pittsburgh and Chicago attracted huge numbers of eastern Europeans to work in the coal mines, steel mills, transport companies, and slaughterhouses.

The new immigrants worked in industry or in jobs requiring craft skills. Few European emigrants in this era wanted to become farmers. Not only had American land grown scarcer and more expensive, the emigrants had left Europe hoping to get away from the drudgery and poverty of farmwork. Indeed, many historians argue that it was the availability of inexpensive immigrant labor that allowed American industry to expand so successfully in the first decades of the twentieth century. In some industries, new emigrants from southern and eastern Europe accounted for as much as half the labor force.

Moreover, many of these new immigrants were not the poorest of the poor in their homelands. They were people who possessed not only the initiative to emigrate but also the money to pay for the journey and to start them off in the New World. A number of them, in fact, were skilled craftsmen or practiced a trade such as fishing, which could easily adapt to America.

Jewish immigrants often opened small businesses rather than work for wages in factories. Many of them turned to the textile trade. From initial work in sweatshops assembling clothing, they moved toward retailing their merchandise first from street carts, then from shops. In New York City at the beginning of the twentieth century, the clothing business, from manufacturing to sales, was dominated by Jewish immigrants. From clothing, Jewish newcomers moved to other businesses, ranging from banking to entertainment.

Processing Immigrants on Ellis Island

The first stop for almost all but the wealthiest of the European emigrants was Ellis Island in New York Harbor. In 1892 the federal government turned Ellis Island into a clearinghouse for immigrants. They were taken there directly from the ships that had brought them across from Europe. At Ellis Island, they were registered and their health was evaluated as legislation passed in 1891 required inspectors to deny entry to people suffering from contagious diseases as well as those likely to turn into public wards.

The registration process required immigrants to describe their origins, occupations, literacy levels, families, and their intended destination in America. Registration was hardly an exact science since the inspectors often lacked language skills and were otherwise overburdened. They often mistook the immigrants' homelands, registering them as Russians perhaps when they were really Poles or Italian when they were Greek. In addition, immigrants were often renamed. Few of the newcomers were literate enough to write their names in their own languages. Moreover, immigration inspectors found many Norwegian, Swedish, German, Italian, Yiddish, Greek, and Slavic names unpronounceable and took the opportunity to Americanize them. The German or Yiddish "Weisskopf," for instance, might simply become "White."

Few immigrants were refused entry due to disease, but many were detained due to ill health. Diseases such as tuberculosis and smallpox were common, and victims were quarantined on Ellis Island until they recovered. Frequently, however, given the huge numbers of immigrants, inspectors simply let them through. Most immigrants did not even stay overnight on Ellis Island, moving instead to the crowded immigrant quarters of Manhattan and Brooklyn before, perhaps, embarking for their final destination in America.

From Asia and Mexico

Japan, like much of Europe, was also experiencing rapid growth and urbanization. In the 1880s, in the midst of an economic depression, the government of Japan sought to decrease the burden on its nation's labor force by allowing some Japanese to emigrate. They looked for stable, literate, and hard-working candidates. Consequently, most of the Japanese who came to the United States were selected by their government. At first, many of the Japanese left for jobs in the pineapple and sugarcane fields of the Hawaiian Islands. In the 1890s more left for the American mainland. Japanese farmers, in fact, achieved great success in agriculture, often with new crops and on marginal lands. Soon, many Japanese moved from the fields to mines and railroads or to domestic work. Little Tokyos emerged in Los Angeles and Seattle, where Japanese merchants opened businesses serving other Japanese. The expansion of these Japanese communities ended, however, when Japanese emigration was stopped in 1907.

The Call to End Immigration

Nativism and antiforeigner attitudes were widespread throughout the second wave of immigration. As cities filled with new immigrants, calls grew louder for the American government to end, or at least modify, its practice of open immigration.

The Japanese were the first group subjected to these stronger nativist sentiments. In addition to simple racism, nativist fears appear to have grown out of Japanese successes, particularly in agriculture. Many white Americans grew jealous as Japanese farmers grew prosperous. Furthermore, not only did many believe it was impossible for Japanese people to assimilate into American life, more and more Americans grew concerned about the growing political and economic power of Japan itself, and they believed, somehow, that Japanese emigrants might be representatives of this powerful Asian nation. Indeed, Japan, within a very short period, had become the industrial and military equal of Great Britain or Germany, and in 1904–1905 it defeated the vast Russian Empire in the Russo-Japanese War. Newspapers and periodicals began to warn of a "yellow peril" that threatened to engulf America and the world.

A Yellow Peril

Calls to restrict Japanese emigration came as early as 1892, when Dennis Kearney, who had led the struggle against the Chinese earlier, declared that "the Japs must go." After 1900, as American nationalism grew more vehement, measures against the Japanese took direct forms. In 1906, for instance, the San Francisco Board of Education tried to establish segregated schools for all Asian students. The Japanese community protested, and the Japanese government lodged a formal protest in Washington, D.C.

The result was an informal settlement known as the Gentleman's Agreement, which took effect in 1907. President Theodore Roosevelt agreed to disallow any attempts by Americans to segregate Japanese emigrants. The Japanese, for their part, stopped allowing Japanese people to immigrate to America, except for the wives of men already there. It also allowed prospective wives to join their husbands in the United States, resulting in the "picture bride" phenomenon, by which Japanese people agreed to marriages across the Pacific based on nothing more than a small black-and-white photograph. The Gentleman's Agreement was the second measure, after the Chinese Exclusion Act of 1882, to restrict immigrants based on national origin.

According to a mysterious logic, however, Americans sought a new Asian labor force to take the place of the excluded Chinese and Japanese. They found it in the Philippines, which, in 1898, had become an American possession. Filipino laborers made their way both to Hawaii and to the mainland, although their numbers were small until the 1920s and 1930s. In an effort to extend civilization to those

who some Americans referred to as "our little brown brothers," Filipino students were also encouraged to study at
American schools and universities. A number of these *pensionados* returned to the Philippines to become leaders in
business and education.

The Largely Invisible Border Between Mexico and the United States

Unlike the other major immigrant groups, Mexicans could
cross the border back into their home country easily. Many
Mexicans saw themselves as sojourners. They traveled
throughout the United States to find work and also returned
to Mexico to visit their home villages, often with money and
American products. Those who chose to settle more permanently in the United States found established Mexican communities where Spanish was spoken, familiar food was eaten,
and Mexican holidays were observed. For Mexicans, in fact,
the border between the two countries meant little.

Not only did Mexicans perform farm labor, but they also
worked as manual laborers everywhere from construction to
restaurants and hotels. Smaller groups moved to Chicago
and Detroit, where they worked in industry. Other Mexicans
took jobs as domestic servants. American employers liked
Mexican workers and often sought these migrants out using
border-based labor contractors. Employers claimed they
were cheaper and more reliable than many other groups of
workers. Often, Mexicans worked for half what white workers earned, regardless of the job.

Mexicans began migrating across the border in large
numbers only after 1900. Many Mexican peasants had been,
first, forced off the land by large land developers and then
trapped in unemployment in the cities. Moreover, the semi-
dictatorial regime of Porfirio Díaz (1876–1911) had focused
on developing Mexico's south, further impoverishing the
rural north. Finally, although a revolution toppled Díaz in
1911, the ensuing conflict left Mexico in a state of civil war.
To as many as 1.5 million Mexicans, perhaps one-tenth of
the population, prospects north of the border appeared
more promising than the chaos and poverty at home.

Racism and Eugenics

The anti-Japanese movement was only one manifestation of the growing nativism of the late 1800s and early 1900s. It was, in fact, directed toward most of the new immigrants. The era, again, was one of increasingly vehement nationalism. Using false interpretations of such scientific discoveries as Charles Darwin's theory of evolution, many people began to argue that nations and races, like individuals, were trapped in a struggle for survival. In this struggle, they argued, only the fittest would survive. A nation or race could not allow itself to be "thinned out" with large numbers of immigrants.

In 1894 these ideas entered the mainstream of American culture with the formation of the Immigration Restriction League, organized by a group of young Harvard graduates. A spokesman for the League claimed that America's strongest "stock" was British, German, or Scandinavian, and that Jews, Italians, and Slavs were "historically down-trodden, atavistic, and stagnant." The Immigration Restriction League grew to be the strongest force behind the anti-immigration movement.

Another well-known statement of pro-Nordic beliefs was Madison Grant's popular *The Passing of the Great Race*, published in 1916. Grant claimed that the European stock that had built America was in danger of being watered down with Jewish and Mexican emigrants as well as "half-breeds."

Grant was among many who subscribed to a false science known as eugenics, which claimed that there were biological differences between the races, and even biological subdivisions that divided Europeans into Teutonic northern Europeans; Alpine peoples from France, Austria, and northern Italy; and Mediterraneans from southern Europe. David Starr Jordan, president of Stanford University, claimed with no hesitation in a 1902 book that Teutonic Europeans were racially superior to not only Africans or Asians but also to their European cousins.

Not only was America in danger of racial dilution through intermarriage, according to eugenicists, it faced the danger of huge numbers of immigrants who, they believed, tended to have larger families than other Americans. They claimed that if widespread immigration was to continue, Teutonics would be swamped by other groups, who were much more likely to be weak or criminal. Such beliefs explain why, when Americans finally adopted broad-based immigration restrictions in the 1920s, the laws were designed to permit emigrants from northern and western Europe while restricting emigrants from the rest of the world.

Objections to Inexpensive Immigrant Labor

Nationalism and racism, however, were not the only reasons why many Americans wanted to restrict immigration. The era was also one of a growing labor movement in which working people clamored for higher pay and better working conditions. Immigrants, many believed, kept wages down by being willing to work for far less than fully assimilated Americans would. In effect, labor activists argued, immigrants kept food out of the mouths of American workers. Indeed, these labor leaders often conflicted with industrialists and agricultural employers on the immigration issue. Until the 1920s, an era of strong anti-immigrant activity, employers lobbied for continued open immigration, which they argued kept wages down and reduced the risk of strikes and labor unrest.

Others wanted to restrict immigration on political grounds. Immigrants, nativists claimed, could not grasp America's democratic principles due either to ignorance or the authoritarian traditions of their homelands. Nativists were also afraid that a number of political radicals could be found in the crowds on Ellis Island. Indeed, Leon Czolgosz, the son of emigrants from Poland, assassinated President William McKinley in 1901. Czolgosz reportedly belonged to the anarchist movement, which had carried out a number of assassinations and bombings and advocated the destruction of all government institutions. In addition to anarchists, some claimed, open immigration threatened to open America to revolutionary Communists.

Still other nativists claimed that immigrants were more likely to be criminals, more likely to carry dangerous diseases, and more likely to become state dependents than other Americans. But what finally turned the majority of Americans, or at least their representatives in Congress, into opponents of immigration was American participation in World War I.

World War I and "100 Percent Americanism"

World War I had broken out in August 1914. It was the result of long-term nationalist conflict among the major European powers. The conflict pitted Great Britain, France, and Russia against Germany, Austria-Hungary, and Turkey. While the United States remained aloof from the conflict at first, President Woodrow Wilson finally convinced the nation that the war would "make the world safe for democracy" and America joined the British and their allies in 1917. American involvement proved to be decisive, and the Germans and their allies finally surrendered in November 1918.

America's entry into World War I inspired the country with the need to create a sense of national purpose and unity, which was to be built around traditional American customs and values, such as the use of the English language and respect for American institutions. There was little tolerance, in this context, for huge communities of "foreign" immigrants speaking their various languages and clinging to their unfamiliar ways. German Americans, in particular, felt the pinch, as many believed that German emigrants, who were still coming in large numbers in the early 1900s, might be more loyal to the enemy than to their adopted country. German communities and individuals were often attacked by those who advocated "100 percent Americanism."

American officials also grew concerned about the health and educational levels of immigrants during World War I, as many immigrants, or their children, were inducted into the armed forces. Tests seemed to prove that immigrants were less intelligent than other inductees as well as more inclined to be weak or sick. These tests simply gave more ammunition to those who claimed that America was being diluted by open immigration. Indeed, in 1917 Congress mandated, over President Wilson's veto, a literacy test for almost all new immigrants.

Soon after World War I ended, and in the face of immigrant ships full of escapees from a devastated Europe, the U.S. Congress began to enact legislation restricting immigration. Americans, fed up with foreign conflicts and in favor of isolation, applauded the measures.

New Quotas and Restrictions

The first law restricting immigration was passed in 1921. It set the pattern for later legislation by basing allowable immigration on a system of national quotas. Each nation that sent immigrants to the United States was annually allowed to send only 3 percent of their immigrant population already in America according to the census of 1910. As a hypothetical example, if, for instance, the 1910 census had counted 10,000 emigrants from Poland (in reality there were many more), after 1921 only 300 Poles could enter the United States every year. Altogether, only 375,000 immigrants were to be allowed annually.

The National Origins Act, as it was known, was modified in 1924, becoming markedly more open to emigrants from Nordic or Teutonic countries while seeking to limit emigration from southern and eastern Europe. Annual quotas were restricted to 2 percent of the foreign-born population based on the 1890 census. In 1890, of course, the foreign-born populations of Italians, Poles, Jews, Greeks, and others who made up the second wave were quite small, and their immigration quotas were correspondingly low. Thanks to the first wave of European emigration, the 1890 populations of Germans, Scandinavians, and Irish were larger, and emigration from these areas was less restricted, although the total of immigrants allowed annually was reduced to 164,000 people.

The legislation was again modified in 1929, and it was this law that remained in place, with a few changes, until 1965. The modification was again based on a national origins system that tried, dubiously, to measure ethnicity in America dating back to 1790, when the first census was conducted. Every nation was given a quota of allowable immigrants up to a total of 156,987 per year.

The quotas were again designed in favor of Great Britain, Germany, Scandinavia, and Ireland, all countries that were unlikely to use their full quota of immigrant visas. In one year, for instance, Great Britain used less than one-third of its over 65,000 visas; Ireland used fewer than half of its nearly 18,000. On the other hand, Poland was allowed 6,488 visas, Italy 5,666, and Greece 308. Not only were those quotas easily filled, huge backlogs of applicants awaited the next round.

The immigration restrictions of the 1920s mostly affected European emigrants. Chinese and Japanese emigrants had already been excluded altogether. Filipinos, since they were American subjects, could not be excluded, although they were denied full American citizenship. No restrictions at all were placed on emigrants from North American countries. Canada, in any case, sent few immigrants aside from small groups of French Canadians who migrated with the harvests.

The demand for cheap labor from Mexico increased as emigration from other areas dwindled. However, both government and employers began to view Mexicans as mostly temporary migrants, and they took efforts to force them to return to Mexico rather than settle permanently in a nation where, it was believed, Mexicans would never fit in.

Still a Nation of Immigrants

Even though immigration was restricted in the 1920s, it did not stop altogether. Between 1929 and 1945, for instance, a period of depression and war, well over 1 million immigrants came to the United States. After the end of World War II in 1945, new categories of immigrants, such as highly skilled experts or political refugees, kept America's borders open.

A new wave of widespread immigration began, however, in 1965 when the United States again changed its immigration laws. The complicated Immigration Act of 1965, signed into law by President Lyndon B. Johnson with the Statue of Liberty and Ellis Island as his backdrop, effectively ended the national quotas of the 1920s. While the total of immigration visas was capped at 290,000 per year, a number of groups were exempted from the caps, particularly the family members of immigrants already in the country. An unforeseen effect of the act was to tilt immigration in favor of Asia and Latin America and away from Europe.

The framers of the act also failed to realize the huge numbers of immigrants the new legislation would allow. Since 1978, for instance, no fewer than 300,000 immigrants have arrived annually. In the late 1980s and early 1990s, over 1 million came per year. Indeed, at the turn of the twenty-first century, America is in the midst of another wave of immigration. It is a familiar experience in American history.

Chapter 1

The First Great Wave: European Emigration from 1830 to 1880

Turning Points
IN WORLD HISTORY

Seeking Economic Opportunity in the United States

Leonard Dinnerstein and David M. Reimers

The first major wave of immigrants to the United States began around 1830. Most of the newcomers came from three regions in Europe: Ireland, the German states (Germany was not unified as a nation until 1871), and the Scandinavian nations of Norway, Sweden, and Denmark.

According to Leonard Dinnerstein and David M. Reimers, authors of the following selection, the emigrants left home seeking to escape poverty at home, believing that jobs and land were available in the growing United States. Among the most dramatic of the circumstances that inspired immigrants in this era was the potato blight of the late 1840s. Across much of western Europe, the potato, which was a staple food for the poor, suffered a mysterious disease that rendered the crop inedible. Ireland, in particular, lost over a million people to starvation and disease in addition to the million-plus who emigrated.

The authors go on to point out that immigration to the United States lessened during periods of trouble, such as the American Civil War (1861–1865) or the economic depression of 1873 to 1879.

Leonard Dinnerstein is professor of history at the University of Arizona. David M. Reimers is professor of history at New York University. Both are experts on immigration and ethnicity in the United States.

The Irish were the first group of impoverished Europeans to leave their homeland in the nineteenth century. The Irish Poor Law of 1838, the enclosure movement on the land, and

Excerpted from Leonard Dinnerstein and David M. Reimers, *Ethnic Americans*, 4th ed. Copyright © 1999 by Columbia University Press. Reprinted by permission of the Copyright Clearance Center on behalf of the copyright holder.

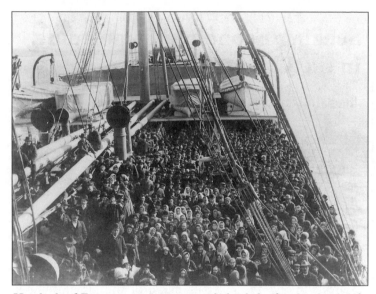

Hundreds of European emigrants crowd the deck of a ship headed for New York harbor. Many newcomers were fleeing a potato famine that afflicted western Europe during the late 1840s.

finally the great famine at the end of the 1840s, when blight ravaged the potato crops and brought untold misery and starvation to millions, combined to increase emigration. A French observer who had visited both America and Ireland before the Great Hunger said the condition of the Irish was worse than that of black slaves, and concluded: "There is no doubt that the most miserable of English paupers is better fed and clothed than the most prosperous of Irish laborers." As hundreds of thousands starved to death during the famine, one of the few lucrative trades left in Tipperary was the sale of coffin mountings and hinges. One man lamented, "Every day furnished victims, and the living hear, and endeavor to drive from their minds, as soon as they can, the horrifying particulars that are related. I have this day, returning to my house, witnessed more than one person lying in our district at this moment unburied. I have known of bodies here remaining in the mountainous parts, neglected for more than eight days." Many of the destitute went to England and some to South America, but more than a million came to the United States. The majority of these people remained in the port cities of New York and Boston, where they landed, because they were too poor to move any farther; but others traveled west. As conditions improved in Ireland in the middle of the 1850s, emigration subsided, but another potato rot in 1863 and still another famine in the 1880s swelled the Irish emigration statistics. Almost 4 million Irish came to the United States in the nineteenth century. Their impact in this country has far exceeded both their numbers and their percentage of the population.

Within nineteenth-century immigrant groups, only among the Irish did women predominate. The famine and the shortage of land left many of them with dim prospects for marriage. Many decided not to marry or to postpone marriage, and to support themselves. They went to the cities, frequently finding jobs as domestic servants. But why stop in Dublin, many asked, when stories of America made emigration sound like such a better choice? So they headed for New York and Boston and other cities, where they readily found jobs in domestic service.

For contemporary Americans such work has a low status, but this was not necessarily the case for Irish women. In contrast with grim prospects at home or jobs in sweat shops, domestic service offered food and a clean place to live. Thus the Irish women became the ubiquitous "Bridget," the domestic worker employed by each middle-class family. Some of these women eventually married and left their jobs, but others remained single. Many opened bank accounts and provided passage money to bring their brothers and sisters to the United States.

German and Scandinavian Emigrants Join Irish Ones

Along with the Irish came the Germans. But unlike the Irish, they continued to be the largest ethnic group arriving in all but three of the years between 1854 and 1894. Before the end of the century more than 5 million Germans reached the United States; in the twentieth century another 2 million came. The exodus, at first primarily from the rural and agricultural southern and western regions of Germany, fits the general pattern of immigration. Crop failures, high rents, high prices, and the changeover to an industrial economy stimulated the move. Conditions were not as bad as in impoverished Ireland, but they were bad enough. One observer told of the "poor wretches" on the road to Strasbourg: "There they go slowly along; their miserable tumbrils— drawn by such starved dropping beasts, that your only wonder is, how can they possibly reach Havre alive." Relatives and friends who went first to America wrote glowing letters, for the most part, and this in turn stimulated further waves. Rich farmers who saw a bleak future in Germany, poor ones who had no future, peasants and paupers whom the state paid to leave, a handful of disappointed revolutionaries after 1848, and an assortment of artisans and professionals came in the 1840s and 1850s.

In late 1854 reports circulated in the German states of large numbers of shipwrecks and cholera epidemics at sea that resulted in death rates as high as 50 percent. At about the same time, nativist agitation in the United States reached a peak and the American economy turned downward. These factors slowed immigration in the late 1850s. Then came the Civil War, which deterred people already beset with their own troubles from emigrating.

Between 1866 and 1873, however, a combination of American prosperity and European depression once again increased German emigration totals. Congressional passage of the 1862 Homestead Act granting free land to settlers, the convulsions in the German states owing to [chancellor Otto von] Bismarck's wars in the 1860s, the high conscription rate, and low wages at home also prompted German emigration. When the United States suffered a severe depression between 1873 and 1879, immigration figures were correspondingly depressed. But when the American economy improved, anxious Europeans once again descended on American shores. Germans who believed that prosperity would never be theirs at home left in record numbers; in 1882 more than 250,000 passed through the immigration stations here. The American depressions of the late 1880s and 1893–1894 cut emigration sharply, but by then an improved industrial economy in Germany provided greater opportunities than in the past, and fewer Germans felt compelled to seek their fortunes in the New World.

Scandinavians—the largest northwestern European group, after the British, Germans, and Irish, to populate America in the nineteenth century—increased their numbers in the United States markedly after the Civil War. The first group of nineteenth-century Scandinavians arrived in the autumn of 1825, when about 50 Norwegians settled in Kendall, New York, about 30 miles southwest of Rochester. In 1841 a Swedish colony developed in Pine Lake, Wisconsin. During the next decades, Scandinavians continued to come, but never in the numbers that either the Irish or the Germans did. For example, Scandinavian immigration totaled only 2,830 in 1846 and not much more in 1865. After 1868, however, annual immigration from Norway, Sweden, Denmark, and Finland passed the 10,000 mark. Jacob Riis, social reformer and friend of Theodore Roosevelt, for example, left Denmark for America in 1870. Like so many other immigrants, he arrived with little but "a pair of strong hands, and stubbornness enough to do for two; [and] also a strong belief that in a free country, free from the dominion of custom, of caste, as well as of men, things would somehow come right in the end." Other Danes and Scandinavians obviously agreed, for annual immigration from Scandinavia did not fall below 10,000 until the disruptions caused by World War I. In the 1920s, when other Europeans resumed their exodus, the Scandinavians joined them.

Immigrants Came for Economic Reasons

As in the case of the Irish and the Germans, Scandinavian immigration can be correlated to a large extent with economic conditions at home and in the United States. Sweden enjoyed a period of good crop production between 1850 and 1864; the years between 1865 and 1868, however, culminated in a great famine that coincided with particularly bountiful times in the United States. During those years, the numbers of emigrants increased sharply, doubling from 1865 to 1866 and tripling from 9,000 in 1867 to 27,000 in 1868.

The exodus from Norway of a large percentage of the nation's entire population at that time can be explained almost wholly by the industrial transformation and the consequent disruptions at home. Norwegian migration can be grouped into three significant periods: from 1866 to 1873, when 111,000 people came; from 1879 to 1893, when the figures went over 250,000; and from 1900 to 1910, when the numbers totaled about 200,000.

Industrialism came earlier in Denmark than in either Norway or Sweden, and the rural upheaval sent people into the cities and towns. But there were simply not enough jobs for those willing to work, and many artisans and skilled laborers sought opportunities in America. Wisconsin was the first state to attract Danes in any substantial number, but subsequently large contingents could be found in Iowa and Illinois as well. Before 1868 families generally emigrated from Denmark as units, but thereafter unmarried, young adult male immigrants exceeded married ones by an almost 3:1 margin. A plurality of these Danes were farmhands, but there was also a sprinkling of small landholders, craftsmen, and unskilled factory laborers. By 1920 United States census figures recorded 190,000 Danish-born.

Although economic factors overshadowed all others for the Scandinavians, it would be misleading to overlook social difficulties as motivating forces, except in the case of the Danes, who had no serious political or religious problems. In Sweden and Norway church and state were aligned, and both dissenters and nonconformists were penalized. There was no universal suffrage, and tightened conscription laws bothered many young men and their families; one scholar noted a particularly high proportion of emigrants among those eligible for military service in Sweden in the 1880s. Swedes in particular also abhorred the hierarchy of titles and the rigidly defined class system. After living in the United States, one Swede wrote home that his "cap [is not] worn out from lifting it in the presence of gentlemen. There is no class distinction between high and low, rich and poor, no make-believe, no 'title-sickness,' or artificial ceremonies. . . . Everybody lives in peace and prosperity."

Letters from America

Another compelling, perhaps decisive, reason was something called "American fever." After Europeans left their homelands, they wrote to their compatriots and described the wonders of America, or the "land of Canaan." Nowhere did these letters have a greater impact than in the Scandinavian countries. They were passed carefully from family to family, published intact in the local newspapers, and discussed avidly from pulpits on Sundays. The influx of favorable mail inspired whole villages with the fervent desire to emigrate to America. Not all the letters from the United States glowed with praise, however, and many complained of the adjustment to the New World. But as one emigrant succinctly put it, "Norway cannot be compared to America any more than a desert can be compared to a garden in full bloom."

The Irish, the Germans, and the Scandinavians constituted the main group of non-English European immigrants before the 1890s, but others also chose to emigrate to the New World. Between 1815 and 1850 the predominantly rural Welsh endured severe agricultural discontent as the nation began industrializing. A depression hit Wales after 1815. The winter of 1814 had been the coldest in memory; and in 1816, "the year without summer," Wales began to feel the effect of a population explosion. By mid-century the region's inhabitants, like those in the rest of Europe, had doubled in number. The high birth rate, the increase in illegitimate births, and the pauperization of the peasants compounded the discontent. By comparison, the United States, to which an individual could sail for £2 or £3 from Liverpool in 1836, seemed to be a pot of gold at the end of the rainbow. The availability of land, the growth of American industry—especially in iron making and mining, where many Welshmen could use their skills—and the increasing number of "American letters" tempted those most inclined to seek a better life. . . .

The Need for Immigrant Workers

The physical and economic growth of the United States in the nineteenth century made it mandatory for Americans to turn to the new settlers for cheap labor to plow fields, build canals and railroads, dig mines, and run machinery in fledgling factories. Without the newcomers the vast riches of the nation could not have been exploited quickly. Major efforts and inducements were made to lure Europeans, French Canadians, Chinese, and, later, Latin Americans to the United States. Their strong backs and steadfast enterprise were necessary to turn American dreams into American accomplishments. At the forefront of these efforts were the state and territorial governments, the railroads, and the various emigrant-aid societies, which were buttressed by federal legislation.

Just as the Atlantic seaboard states had made efforts in the colonial period to attract settlers, so in the nineteenth century practically every state and territory of the American West, plus several others, sought to entice select groups of Europeans to their area. More people meant more schools and post offices, larger federal appropriations for internal improvements, larger markets for goods, faster economic development, "and the speedy arrival of the eagerly desired railroad."

The Business of Encouraging Immigration

Carl Wittke

According to Carl Wittke, the author of the following excerpt, Europeans were encouraged to immigrate to the United States in the nineteenth century for a variety of reasons. One of the most important, he suggests, were letters sent back from previous immigrants. Although not all reports from America were positive, many reported that America, indeed, seemed a land of abundance and opportunity. To further embolden potential newcomers, others wrote guidebooks to life in America and pointed out that newcomers could often settle in communities of earlier immigrants. In such communities, customs would be not quite as foreign, and sometimes old-country languages such as German or Swedish would still be spoken.

However, Wittke suggests, the encouragements of shipping companies, railroad firms, and land agents were even more important. Such businesses, of course, saw immigrants as potential customers. Moreover, the governments of new states and territories in the Midwest and Pacific Northwest sought settlers to help fill the new lands. These governments, in addition to their own promotion efforts, worked with businesses to encourage ever-more newcomers from Europe.

Carl Wittke was a professor of American history at Ohio State University, Oberlin College, and Case Western Reserve University, where he was also vice president.

In the nineteenth century, and with increasing volume after 1830, the tide of emigration set in again from Europe. Wave

Excerpted from Carl Wittke, *We Who Built America: The Saga of the Immigrant* (Englewood Cliffs, NJ: Prentice-Hall, 1939).

after wave rolled over the cities and prairies of the New America. The Irish, the Germans, and the Scandinavians, in more or less sharply defined but overlapping streams, poured into the United States; and these major groups, together with several minor ones, constitute the "old emigration" from western and northern Europe, in contradistinction to the newer groups that came in the last quarter of the century from the south and east. Each deserves detailed treatment. In each case, specific causes, to be treated later, operated to start the emigrant tide on its way across the Atlantic and to keep it flowing steadily for decades. Aside from the universal desire for adventure and greater opportunity, there were certain causes for emigration common to all these groups; and it must be remembered that much of the European emigration was artificially stimulated and encouraged by interests in America desirous, for one reason or another, of bringing in a larger population.

Positive Reports from America

First of all, . . . the earlier population movements were influenced by the "America letters", "the literature of the unlettered" written home by those who had ventured out first and whose accounts of the New Canaan were eagerly awaited and devoured by those who had remained behind. Christopher Saur's "America letters" praising "the goodness I have heard and seen" were printed and reprinted many times in Germany during the latter half of the eighteenth century, in order to induce people to come to Pennsylvania. What the United States after 1776 symbolized to the liberty-loving, thwarted, and exploited Irishman can readily be imagined, especially when the glowing accounts that reached the Irish countryside assured the readers that "there is a great many ill conveniences here, but no empty bellies." In 1818, an enthusiastic reporter described the region around Wheeling in extravagant terms that must have been irresistible. He wrote:

> I believe I saw more peaches and apples rotting on the ground than would sink the British fleet. I was at many plantations in Ohio where they no more knew the number of their hogs than myself. . . . The poorest family has a cow or

two and some sheep . . . good rye whiskey; apple and peach brandy, at 40 cents a gallon. . . . The poorest families adorn the table three times a day like a wedding dinner—tea, coffee, beef, fowls, pies, eggs, pickles, good bread; and their favorite beverage is whiskey or peach brandy. Say, is it so in England?

Gottfried Duden's rosy picture of Missouri, which he painted as a budding center for German culture in the American West, had a tremendous effect on a young Germany just passing through its period of *Sturm und Drang* ["storm and stress," an influential literary and cultural movement]. The "America fever" was a highly communicable disease, spread by thousands of letters that reached the little cottages of peasant and burgher in Ireland, Germany, and Scandinavia.

Ole Rynning's *America Book*, first published in 1838, describing an America where wages were high, prices low, land excellent, religion and government free, and servant girls without outside work to do save milking the cows had a large circulation in Norway and went through several editions. "America letters" to Sweden depicted a land where "the hogs eat their fill of raisins and dates" and, "when they are thirsty, they drink from ditches flowing with wine." Sober Scandinavians would hardly be swept off their feet by such extravagant inventions; but they were duly impressed by reports of Iowa's supply of corn, hogs, and pumpkins, and by the report that all doors could be left unlocked because there were no beggars in America, that the climate was healthier and more invigorating than in their native Sweden, and that there were no artificial class distinctions, ceremonies, or "title-sickness" in the new land across the sea. "There are no large estates," wrote one Swedish-American, "whose owners can take the last sheaf from their dependents and then turn them out to beg." Ministers and churches were said to be less worldly in America, and "there is ceaseless striving to spread the healing salvation of the Gospel." Hired men and maids ate at the same table with their employers and wore clothes of the same style. "Neither is my cap worn out," added another, "from lifting it in the presence of gentlemen." Small wonder that enthusiastic newcomers wrote: "We see things here that we could never describe, and you would never believe them if we did. I would not go back to Sweden if the whole country were presented to me." "It is no disgrace to work here," wrote a Swede in 1841. "Both the gentleman and the day laborer work. No epithets of degradation are applied to men of humble toil. . . . I do not agree . . . that in order to appreciate the blessings of monarchy, one must live in a democracy."

Not all of the letters that came from immigrants in America were, of course, as optimistic and laudatory as those just cited. The Swedish pastor, Gustaf Unonius, cynically observed that "the American competes with the mosquitoes to bleed the emigrant." Some "America letters" expressed bitter regret for having yielded to the lure of the New World. "Do not expect to find roasted pigs, with knives and forks in their backs, ready for anyone to eat," wrote an immigrant from Buffalo, in 1851. "The work is very hard, as you have to accomplish in one day here what you get three days to do in Norway." There were other letters of disillusionment and frustration, but the great majority were enthusiastic descriptions of a land of unlimited opportunity, in contrast with what was available to the poor at home. They were read and reread by the simple, credulous people to whom they were originally addressed, then widely circulated among relatives and friends, and often read by the entire village. They were discussed in the home, at the market place, in church, and at the county fair; and were often printed for wider circulation in the newspapers. One or two such "America letters" were sufficient stimulus to spread the "America fever" through an entire parish.

Businesses Encouraged Immigration

Ship companies and organizations interested in land speculation did their part to keep the America fever burning at the proper temperature. Advertisements in American newspapers reveal a veritable flock of emigration agents; immigrant bankers dealing in remittances, steamship, and railroad tickets; and dealers in foreign exchange, each of whom had his special reasons for keeping the immigrant tide flowing in a steady, unbroken stream to the United States. Land agencies, with acreage for sale in Texas, Missouri, Wisconsin, and other parts of the West, advertised their bargains in newspapers published at the Eastern ports of arrival. A New England Land Company, incorporated under Iowa law, offered to assist emigrants to reach the western Eldorado it had for sale and to arrange for an easy payment plan. Such offers frequently received editorial endorsement from the papers in which the advertisements appeared. An "Irish Pioneer Emigration Fund" brought in Irish servant girls. There was a Foreign Emigration Association in Maine in the 1860's to bring over servant girls under the Contract Labor Law of 1864. The American Emigrant Company, the Columbia Emigrant Agency, and the American Emigrant Aid and Homestead Company were other organizations interested in bringing immigrants to Chicago and the West. . . .

In the middle of the [nineteenth] century, the Middle West needed population above everything else. To attract desirable immigrants was the overpowering ambition of practically every new state in this region. State after state began to enact legislation to encourage and stimulate migration to its borders. The attractions offered by favorable legislation and the persuasiveness of the agents of state immigration commissions were important factors in directing the immigrant tide into the Mississippi Valley. . . .

Selling Land to Immigrants

Steamship and railway companies had a special interest in stimulating traffic, for obvious reasons, but the latter had an additional objective in promoting the disposal of their railroad lands to actual settlers. In 1870, Jay Cooke, as the financial promoter of the Northern Pacific Railroad, employed Hans Mattson, who resigned his position as secretary of state of Minnesota to undertake the assignment, to go to Sweden to advertise the resources of the road and to draw up a plan for the disposal of its lands. J.J. Hill may have saved his road from financial disaster by promoting the settlement of Minnesota by Norwegian and Swedish farmers, whose bumper crops quickly tripled the earnings of the railroad.

Hill, in order to make the Red River Valley district more attractive to settlers, described it as an area "where the depth of the humus was equal to the height of a man." The Northern Pacific at St. Paul gave special passes to ministers of the Gospel, so that they might more frequently visit outlying immigrant settlements where no church had as yet been organized. When a trainload of Dunkards [a religious sect] moved from Indiana to North Dakota, they went by special train, with streamers on the railroad cars advertising "the bread basket of America." The Atchison, Topeka, and Santa Fe Railroad, through its foreign immigration department, extended its activities to the Ural Mountains, bringing over 15,000 Russian-German Mennonites to Kansas. By 1883, they had settled along the route of the railroad in Kansas, with branch settlements in Oklahoma and Colorado. The Burlingame and Missouri Railroad also was active in attracting Mennonite settlers to the American West.

The Illinois Central Railroad carried on one of the most vigorous colonization programs of any road in the United States. It sent a Norwegian clergyman to Quebec to work among the immigrants; it made a special effort to attract Germans, enlisting the support of Lieutenant Governor Francis Hoffman of Illinois for this task, who was to receive a commission as land agent for every German he brought in; it maintained an "intelligence office" and immigrant "runners" in New York; and it supported a land department, which issued great quantities of advertising in several languages. After 1870, it employed General John Basil Zurchin, a Russian engineer who had been an officer in the Civil War, to organize the Agencyja Polskiej Kolonizacyi to bring Poles into Illinois. Zurchin was successful to an unexpected degree in developing both Polish agricultural and mining colonies.

A similar intensive program was maintained by the railroads in order to attract immigrants into the Pacific Northwest. The Northern Pacific had a "Land Committee" which published maps and descriptive matter in several languages, and maintained agents in all the leading countries of western and northern Europe. By an arrangement with steamship companies, immigrants could buy through tickets to Duluth or St. Paul. Temporary immigrant houses, with stoves and beds, were prepared to receive the immigrant when he arrived in the West. Farms were sold on easy terms. The advertising program for immigrants was especially extensive after Henry Villard acquired control of the road in the 1880's. It supported two immigration bureaus, one in Boston and one in Portland, Oregon; issued special immigrant half-fare certificates; and waged extensive advertising campaigns in the foreign press. Needless to add, many a customs and immigration officer at Castle Garden, New York [where most immigrants first arrived], was in the pay of some railroad company and was expected to use his persuasive powers, supported by his official status, to direct the immigrant to some particular spot in the Western prairie country.

Europeans Left Home for Many Reasons

Maldwyn Allen Jones

In the 1800s Europe was undergoing major transformations. One was a rapid growth in population. This population explosion was brought about by a more secure food
supply as well as by improved sanitation. Another change
was the transition from societies organized around small
family farms to nations oriented around large-scale production on both larger farms and in industrial factories.
Having lost their traditional livelihoods on small farms,
many Europeans moved to large cities, often as a first step
toward immigration to a new country like the United
States of America.

As Maldwyn Allen Jones points out in the following selection from his history of American immigration, these
factors helped to build "emigration fever" in many European countries. He notes, however, that the desire of Europeans to strike out for a new country was also based on
religious and political discontent as well as on larger social
and economic transformations.

Maldwyn Allen Jones was a professor of American history at University College, London. He was also a visiting
professor at Harvard, Princeton, and Stanford Universities.

The extraordinary increase in immigration to the United
States in the early decades of the nineteenth century was one
of the wonders of the age. The huge scale of the movement
and its seeming inexhaustibility captured the public imagi-
nation on both sides of the Atlantic and inspired a flood of
fascinated comment. The remark of the *Democratic Review* in

Excerpted from Maldwyn Allen Jones, *American Immigration*, The Chicago History
of American Civilization series (Chicago: University of Chicago Press, 1960).
Copyright © 1960 by The University of Chicago. Reprinted with permission of the
publisher and author.

July, 1852, that there had been nothing to compare with the exodus in appearance "since the encampments of the Roman Empire or the tents of the crusaders" was but one expression of a sentiment that pervaded discussion at every level. The same sense of awe was apparent in newspaper accounts of the movement's progress, in the efforts of pamphleteers and publicists to trace its origin, and in the debates of legislative bodies upon its probable outcome.

This did not mean, however, that opinion was unanimous about the new phenomenon. In Europe, some people welcomed the rise of mass emigration as a much needed blood-letting and as a safety valve for discontent, but there were others who deplored a process which seemed to them to be draining the Old World of its most vigorous inhabitants. Similarly, in America opinion ranged from the excited warnings of the nativist against the menace of foreign influence to the enthusiasm of those who, like Ralph Waldo Emerson, welcomed the spectacle of "a heterogeneous population crowding in on ships from all corners of the world to the great gates of North America."

Most of the attention the movement attracted, and not a little of the disagreement it provoked, were due to a recognition of its uniqueness. Though immigration had been a familiar aspect of American development throughout the colonial period, there was no precedent for a movement of such magnitude and persistence as that which began in 1815. In the hundred years between that date and the outbreak of World War I, no fewer than thirty million people, drawn from every corner of Europe, made their way across the Atlantic. They came in a series of gigantic waves, each more powerful than the last and separated one from another only by short periods of time.

Waves of Immigration

The first of these waves began soon after the close of the Napoleonic Wars, and after gathering momentum steadily during the 1830's and 1840's, reached its crest in 1854. Its progress could be followed in the immigration statistics which the federal government began to collect in 1820. In the decade of the 1820's, the number of arrivals was only 151,000; but the 1830's brought a fourfold increase to 599,000. This figure was in turn dwarfed by the 1,713,000 immigrants of the 1840's; even more staggering was an immigration of 2,314,000 in the 1850's. Later on, the figures would climb to still greater heights, but in assessing the impact of this first great wave one should bear in mind the comparative smallness of the American population. The five million immigrants of the period 1815–60 were greater in number than the entire population of the United States at the time of the first census in 1790. Moreover, the three million who arrived in the single decade 1845–54 landed in a country of only about twenty million inhabitants and thus represented, in proportion to the total population, the largest influx the United States has ever known.

Though every country in Europe was represented to some degree in this pre–Civil War movement, the overwhelming majority of immigrants came from areas north of the Alps and west of the Elbe. Over half of the total of five million had been born in the British Isles, two million of them in Ireland and a further three-quarters of a million in England, Wales, and Scotland. Germany was the next largest contributor with a million and a half, though to this total must be added a large proportion of the 200,000 immigrants listed as Frenchmen, most of whom were in fact German-speaking people from Alsace and Lorraine. No other country sent anything like as large a number, the only ones to send sizable contingents being Switzerland with 40,000, Norway and Sweden also with 40,000, and the Netherlands with 20,000.

Comprehension of the causes of this vast movement must begin with a recognition of their complexity. To attempt to explain mass immigration by means of an all-embracing formula, or by a mere listing of European discontents, or again by a graph tracing the fluctuations of the trade cycle would be to miss its deeper significance. One must insist, first, on the infinitely varied motives of the immigrants. The "push" and "pull" of impersonal economic forces must certainly be part of the answer, but no less important were the hopes, fears, and dreams of millions of individual immigrants.

Moreover, it is an error to imagine that emigration conditions were identical in every part of Europe. The situation which resulted in emigration from Ireland, for example, was quite different from that which uprooted people in England, while the German movement owed much to forces which were unknown in the British Isles. Emigration derived some of its sweep from local and temporary influences and consequently changed in character with variations in time and place. Then, too, there is a point beyond which economics and politics can no longer serve as guides to the understanding of mass movements. It was no accident that so many contemporaries spoke of emigration as a kind of fever, as mysterious in its origin as the cholera epidemics which periodically ravaged the land. The movement bore in fact a distinct air of irrationality, even of frenzy, and many of those who took part in it were simply carried along by a force they did not understand.

Population Growth in Europe

Having made these qualifications, one can nevertheless single out a number of social and economic factors which underlay the movement as a whole and which gave it most of its impetus. The first of these was the doubling of the population of Europe in the century after 1750. This unprecedented increase was due in the first instance to a sharp decline in the mortality rate resulting from improved medical and sanitary knowledge and the absence of serious plagues. Other contributory factors were the greatly increased food supply made possible by the introduction of improved farming methods and by the adoption of the potato as the staple diet of the European peasant. With hunger and disease in retreat, population increased by leaps and bounds, though the full extent of the increase could only be guessed at before official censuses were instituted in the early nineteenth century.

Population increase was not in itself a cause of emigration; it served merely to accentuate the effect of other changes which at the same time were transforming the social and economic life of western Europe. The most striking transformation of all resulted from the growth of the factory system. Originating in England in the middle of the eighteenth century and spreading from there to the Continent, the Industrial Revolution destroyed the old system of domestic manufacture and threw countless artisans out of employment. In Great Britain many displaced artisans moved to nearby factory towns to become wage-laborers, but a considerable number preferred emigration to America as a means of "perpetuating a rural existence." From Germany there was an even greater exodus of handicraftsmen, for the factories which had deprived them of work were not near at hand but in England. Indirectly, too, industrialism was to prove a spur to emigration in that it bound the urban worker more closely to the trade cycle and thus subjected him to repeated periods of unemployment. At such times emigration was for many the only alternative, if not to starvation, then at least to a narrowing range of opportunities.

Modern Farming Techniques Pushed Europeans Off Their Lands

An equally important change was the fundamental reorganization of rural economy resulting from the rise of large-scale scientific farming. The expansion of urban markets for foodstuffs called for changes in the system of cultivation and especially for the application of new agricultural techniques to large units of land. These changes appeared in a variety of forms; in England and Scandinavia in the enclosure movement, in Ireland and southwest Germany in the consolidation of estates and the transition from arable to pasture, and in the Scottish Highlands in the conversion of farm land to sheep runs. But the social effects were everywhere the same. The old communal system of agriculture was replaced by modern large-scale production, and a large proportion of the rural population was cut loose from the soil. Nor were these displaced people the only ones affected. Because of the competition of large-scale agriculture the small farmer's difficulties multiplied and his hold on the land weakened. As for his children, only emigration offered an alternative to a reduction in status to the rank of a paid laborer.

Political and Religious Motives

Though economic factors predominated as causes of emigration, the influence of political and religious discontent cannot be entirely ignored. During the first half of the nineteenth century Europe witnessed a succession of political upheavals, each of which produced a wave of exiles. Some of them chose to remain in Europe in order to continue their revolutionary activities from a convenient base, but a considerable proportion made their way to the New World. By far the largest group to do so came with the failure of the revolutions of 1848 in Germany, Italy, and Austria-Hungary and the simultaneous collapse of the Young Ireland movement. Even before this the United States had granted political asylum to a motley group which included German *Burschenschaften* [youth societies] fleeing from the tyranny that followed the liberal demonstrations at Wartburg and Hambach, Polish and French refugees of the 1830 revolutions, and disappointed English and Scottish Chartists. Yet these earlier victims of political unrest came in mere handfuls, and even the Forty-eighters numbered only a few thousand. In short, political exiles accounted for only a tiny proportion of the total immigration of the period.

Many contemporaries in the United States tended nevertheless to attribute immigration largely to the political attraction of their country. But the falsity of this belief was evident even at the time to the more perspicacious observers of the movement. As a Belgian commentator remarked in 1846:

> The influence of American institutions acts in a very indirect way upon European immigration. When the immigrants are established in the United States, they often eagerly take advantage of the privileges that are offered them; but they did not leave their native villages to seek political rights in another hemisphere. The time of the Puritans and of William Penn is past. Theories of social reform have given way to a practical desire for immediate well-being.

While religious factors alone were hardly ever responsible for emigration, they were nonetheless a significant element. They were particularly important in stimulating emigration from regions which had hitherto contributed little to the outgoing stream. Thus emigration from Norway to the United States originated in part in the anxiety of Stavanger Quakers to escape persecution at the hands of the official clergy; that from Holland stemmed in some degree from the discontent of seceders from the Dutch Reformed Church at the numerous petty annoyances to which they were subjected; and the beginning of a movement from Prussia in the 1830's can be partly attributed to the reluctance of the Old Lutherans to conform to the United Evangelical Church. Yet in all these cases religious discontent was blended with economic pressure, and one can safely say that the prospect of earthly ease was a stronger stimulus to emigration than that of heavenly bliss.

Immigrant Destinations

Maxine Seller

The period from 1830 to 1880 was one of rapid expansion in the United States both territorially and economically. Not only were many new territories in the Midwest and the Great Plains opened to settlement, but America also added the Southwest and Pacific Northwest. By 1850 the United States stretched across the North American continent from the Atlantic to the Pacific. In economic terms, America began to industrialize, particularly in East Coast cities such as Boston and New York.

Immigrants were drawn, according to Maxine Seller in the following selection, to areas where they could take advantage of economic opportunity. Many of the better-off and more ambitious immigrants, especially Germans and Scandinavians, headed to farmlands in the Midwest, Great Plains, and Pacific Northwest. Poorer immigrants, such as the Irish who often lacked even the funds to travel west, settled in the East Coast cities where they found work not only in industrial factories but also as domestic servants in the homes of the affluent. As Seller notes, immigrants faced huge challenges wherever they settled.

Maxine Seller is professor of education and history at the State University of New York at Buffalo.

Immigrants went immediately to the areas where opportunities could be found. Welsh miners went to the coal and iron centers of Pennsylvania where their specialized skills were needed. Scottish weavers settled in the textile producing areas of New England. Chinese headed for the farms and mines of California. Successful immigrants of every ethnic group served as a magnet attracting friends and relatives to their area

Excerpted from Maxine Seller, *To Seek America: A History of Ethnic Life in the United States*. Copyright © 1977 by Jerome S. Ozer, Publisher Inc. Reprinted by permission of Jerome S. Ozer, Publisher Inc.

of settlement, thus creating new ethnic communities.

A sprinkling of the Irish went as far west as San Francisco, where they were among the earliest and most prominent English-speaking settlers. Most of the immigrants who joined the westward movement, however, were Scandinavians and Germans. As in the colonial years, immigrants chose frontier areas that resembled as closely as possible the terrain of their native country. Scandinavians settled in the northern part of the Mississippi Valley, from Iowa to Minnesota, where the cold climate, lakes, and forests reminded them of home. Interestingly, they tended to occupy the same latitudinal positions relative to one another in America as they had in Europe, immigrants from Iceland settling furthest north, Danes furthest south, and Swedes and Norwegians in between.

A few Germans went to the edges of the frontier, like John Sutter, on whose land gold was first discovered in California. But most of the Germans who went west settled in Missouri, Wisconsin, Illinois, Indiana, and Texas, where they usually bought improved land, wooded and well watered. Wisconsin was highly favored because the traditional German crops of oats and hops could be grown there and because Milwaukee boasted a Roman Catholic bishop of German origin.

The Dangers of Rural America

Ethnic Americans who settled the interior and western farmlands in the mid nineteenth century shared the hardships of their Anglo-Saxon [British] neighbors, plus a few more distinctly their own. Like other frontier Americans, they suffered from lack of medical care. Because many immigrants were debilitated from the long ocean and overland journey, the bad housing, poor water, and inadequate sanitation of the new settlements were even more devastating to them than to the native born. Cholera, typhoid, pneumonia, and malaria were so common that immigrants declared the American air unwholesome and doubted that American food could nourish them as well as the familiar grains of their homeland.

Like other frontier Americans, ethnic immigrants came into conflict with the Indians in whose territory they took up residence. A German settlement at New Ulm, Minnesota, for example, was wiped out by the Sioux, angry at the broken promises and unfulfilled treaties foisted upon them by the American government. Ethnic Americans, particularly the Irish and the Germans, served in the American army in numbers greater than their proportion in the population and thus played a major role in the bloody Indian wars of the ninteenth century. Immigrants had no particular grudge against Indians. It was simply a job, well-paid and, unlike many other jobs, available to all without discrimination. Moreover, by serving under the Stars and Stripes, the immigrant could assert that he was, after all, a "real" American.

European knowledge and experience were not always relevant to American situations. In Europe farmers tilled small plots using the methods of their ancestors, and looked to the tightly-knit community of relatives and neighbors for assistance in time of need. In America, farms were larger and more isolated, soil and weather conditions were unfamiliar, and the supportive network of friends and relatives was often not available. Individual families were thrown back on their own resources. . . .

Unfamiliar Customs

Immigrants often had to cope with a strange and hostile moral landscape as well as a hostile physical landscape. Customs and values long honored in the old environment seemed out of place, even counterproductive in the new. In the relatively stable society of the European farming village, the family that behaved peaceably, cooperatively, and predictably, fulfilling its traditional obligations to its own members and others, was respected by all. Such a family was likely to be successful in its undertakings.

Not so in the rapidly changing, highly individualistic United States, particularly in the frontier areas in the mid nineteenth century. In the raucous, often violent, "boom or bust" world of the American West, population spread more quickly than legal institutions could follow. Cut loose from the moorings of family, church, and community back east, many of the new westerners felt free to make their way in the world at any cost. Under such conditions, might often meant right. It was the aggressive individual, unhampered by traditional morality, who seized the best mining claim or the well-watered homestead or who succeeded in getting the new railroad, canal, or county seat in the location most favorable to his interests.

Some ethnic Americans accepted, even thrived upon, the pragmatic, rough and ready frontier morality. "Just kick the dog that bites you, that's always the easiest way, and the simplest, too," said Per Hansa, the central character in [Norwegian novelist Ole] Rölvaag's novel, *Giants in the Earth*. Others could not give up the traditional values taught them in an Old World childhood. Appalled by the changes she saw taking place in her husband, Per Hansa's wife worried that the entire family would desert the Christian decencies to become savages in a new and savage land.

If immigrants were more vulnerable than the native-born to the hardships of frontier life, they were also more appreciative of its rewards. Coming from a land of tiny farms that had been cultivated century after century, they rejoiced in the size and virgin fertility of their new American holdings. Their traditionally large families, liabilities in overcrowded Europe, became assets in labor-starved America. Of course, many ethnic homesteads were not successful. Thousands returned to the East, or even to Europe, defeated by loneliness, illness, or natural disasters. Agrarian America prospered, however, in the mid nineteenth century; and as it prospered, becoming the supplier of raw materials to America's growing cities and to the outside world, ethnic farmers prospered too. In time, sod houses and log cabins were replaced by sturdy frame and brick farmhouses, with large and well stocked barns and silos. Many humble families, heir to a few rocky acres in Europe, became the proud owners of the American manors that exceeded their wildest dreams. . . .

Building the Railroads

Nothing changed the face of nineteenth century America as radically as the building of the transportation network. Miles of new turnpikes, canals, and most important of all, the railroads, opened the West to settlement, supplied the growing urban areas, and provided the new industrialists with the largest tariff free market in the world. This revolutionary transportation network was built largely by ethnic Americans. German-trained engineers contributed much of the technology, and foreign capital, raised by the foreign-born, was indispensable. But the greatest contribution of ethnic Americans was, of course, their labor.

The work was backbreaking—too unpleasant and too poorly paid to appeal to any but the most desperate. In the East it was done by Irish, in the South by Irish and blacks, in the Midwest by Irish and Scandinavians, and in the Far West by Chinese. Railroad companies advertised in urban newspapers or sent agents to ports where immigrants landed to recruit gangs of workmen, a system used by mining and logging companies as well. The worker was offered what appeared to be good wages, with an advance for transportation to the work site, often hundreds of miles from his home. Upon arrival he found the work harder, the wages lower, and his supplies (available only at the company commissary) costlier than he had anticipated. Already in debt for his transportation, he had little choice but to stay.

Sometimes entire families followed the progress of the railroad as laborers for—and victims of—the corporations. In 1841 Charles Dickens described the plight of a colony of Irish families building railroads in upstate New York:

> With means at hand of building decent cabins, it was wonderful to see how clumsy, rough, and wretched its hovels were. The best were poor protection from the weather; the worst let in the wind and rain through the wide breaches in the roofs of sodden grass and in the walls of mud; some had neither door nor window; some had nearly fallen down, and were imperfectly propped up by stakes and poles; all were ruinous and filthy. Hideously ugly old women and very buxom young ones, pigs, dogs, men, children, babies, pots, kettles, dunghills, vile refuse, rank straw and standing water, all wallowing together in an inseparatable heap, composed the furniture of every dark and dirty hut.

Conditions were so bad in some of these labor camps that the state governments abandoned their usual hands-off policy to pass laws against the grossest abuses. From the point of view of the Irish, however, conditions in railroad towns were no worse than they had been in the old country—indeed, they were probably better. There was at least one beneficial side effect. The railroad shantytowns helped spread the Irish population out of the overcrowded eastern cities, creating little "Paddy's Quarters" in Indiana, Ohio, Illinois, and even west of the Mississippi. . . .

The Immigrant City

At least half of the new immigrants never got to the rural frontier, either as homesteaders, hired hands, peddlers, or railroad workers. By choice or by necessity they settled in the mushrooming towns and cities instead. San Francisco had its famous Chinatown. Milwaukee, Chicago, St. Paul, Minneapolis, Cleveland, and Cincinnati had large German and Scandinavian colonies. Many Germans settled in the older eastern urban centers of New York, Philadelphia, and Baltimore. The largest ethnic community in the eastern cities, however, was the Irish.

A rural people in the Emerald Isle, ninety per cent of the Irish settled in cities in the United States, concentrating their population in New York, Boston, and Philadelphia. Many of the Irish lacked the skills and the capital to become farmers in America. By mid century the frontier was a thousand miles or more from the port of arrival. Even if land were cheap or altogether free, impoverished immigrants could not afford the cost of transportation, seed, and equipment, nor could they maintain themselves until the first crop was harvested. Moreover for many of the Irish, the isolation of rural life in the United States had no appeal. They preferred the city, where Catholic churches were available and where they could enjoy the sociability of being among their countrymen.

As immigrants poured into an expanding urban America, so too did the native-born. The cities were magnets, luring all kinds of people with their promise of adventure, excitement, and fortunes to be made. As centers of commerce and transportation, the cities were, indeed, filled with opportunities. Moreover, as farms began to mechanize, proportionately fewer people were needed to produce the nation's food. Thus while the western farming frontier has often been seen as a "safety valve" for the excess population of the city, the opposite was closer to the truth. From mid century on, the growing cities provided a safety valve for the excess farm population of both Europe and the United States.

Never before or since has urban growth taken place at such a rapid rate. The old eastern cities got larger, while whole groups of new cities in the Mississippi Valley, along the Great Lakes, and on the west coast made their sudden appearance. New York City grew from 60,489 in 1800 to 202,589 in 1830, to more than a million in 1860. St. Louis doubled its population every nine years; Buffalo, every eight; Cincinnati, every seven. In the two years following the completion of the transcontinental railroad, Los Angeles increased its population five hundred per cent!

Unprecedented growth presented unprecedented problems. How could the cities provide jobs and housing for so many newcomers? What about drinking water, waste disposal, transportation, and fire protection? How could law and order be maintained when neighborhoods changed in a matter of months and when people were strangers to one another? American cities were totally unprepared to solve such problems. Many had corrupt and antiquated forms of government and were unaccustomed to providing any but the most elemental services. At mid century New York City had no public police force or fire department. Such order as there was was kept by private guards, the militia being called out in case of dire emergency. Volunteer fire companies fought with one another while buildings burned. Disease, crime, and vice were rampant in an urban society growing too fast to meet its needs.

Foresight, planning, and the judicious use of regulations and public moneys might have alleviated some of the problems. Such policies were impossible, however, given the climate of opinion in the mid nineteenth century. Political leaders, like most of their constituents, were committed to "privatism," a government hands off policy in the area of social problems. Cities provided poorhouses and public hospitals, dreary institutions shunned by all but the most desperate, and committees of benevolent women dispensed food and fuel to "deserving" widows with small children. Beyond this, little was done. Poverty and other social problems were believed to be the result of vicious and improvident personal habits which the victims could correct if only they would try.

Because so many were concentrated in the poor and working classes, ethnic Americans suffered proportionately more than the native-born from the growing pains of the city. Immigrants were coping with many changes at once. First they were moving from the European or Asian culture of their birthplace to the predominantly English culture of the United States, a change that often involved a totally different language and life style. In addition, most were moving from a rural to an urban environment—a formidable change in itself. And finally, the city to which they were coming was in itself in a state of constant change. Under these conditions, the urban frontier, like the rural frontier, offered problems as well as opportunities.

One of the most immediate and most difficult problems was finding a decent place to live. At no time in American history has the supply of urban housing kept pace with the demand, but in the pre–Civil War years the situation was especially acute. As newcomers poured into the cities, all hoping to live near commercial areas where jobs were available, there was simply no place to house them. Dwellings built for one family were divided and subdivided as the population doubled and doubled again. Sheds, stables, and warehouses were pressed into service, as were windowless garrets and underground cellars. By 1850, 29,000 people in New York City were living underground.

Recognizing the profits to be made from the housing shortage, landlords erected rows of tenements. The tenements often used every available foot of land on the building lot leaving many of the rooms without sunlight or ventilation. Outdoor privies in the alleys overflowed, contaminating the water supply and seeping into the buildings. Still, the hapless tenants rarely complained, fearful of being put upon a "black list" and unable in any case to find other quarters. The prudent set aside the rent money before buying lesser necessities such as food, fuel, and clothing.

The Rise of Anti-Immigrant Sentiment

Roger Daniels

Although the United States had small communities of Germans, Swedes, Dutch, and others ever since the early 1600s, the great majority of the (nonslave) American population had a British background and practiced Protestant Christianity. The immigration wave of the early 1800s brought, for the first time, large numbers of "foreigners" to the country. The Germans and Scandinavians, for instance, spoke unfamiliar languages, though most of the Irish spoke English. Of greater concern to many Americans, however, was the fact that the Irish and many of the Germans were Roman Catholics.

Americans opposed to Roman Catholic immigration, partly on the grounds that they believed Catholics would be loyal to the pope rather than the president, formed into "nativist" mobs as early as the 1840s. Also, as Roger Daniels, a professor of history at the University of Cincinnati, makes clear in the following passage, the nativist movement became formalized in the mid-1850s with the formation of the American, or Know-Nothing, political party. Not all Americans, however, agreed with the Know-Nothings, particularly as the Civil War approached. Constitutional amendments in the 1860s, moreover, guaranteed that all people born on American soil would be U.S. citizens.

When relatively large numbers of Irish and German Catholic immigrants, many of them desperately poor, began to arrive in the late 1820s and early 1830s, what had been a largely rhetorical anti-Catholicism became a major social and political force in American life. Not surprisingly, it was in eastern cities, particularly Boston, where anti-Catholicism turned violent, and much of the violence was directed against convents and churches. Beginning with the burning down of the Ursuline Convent just outside Boston by a mob on August 11, 1834, well into the 1850s violence against Catholic institutions was so prevalent that insurance companies all but refused to insure them. Much of this violence was stirred up by Protestant divines, ranging from eminent church leaders such as Lyman Beecher (1775–1863) to anonymous self-appointed street preachers. [Historian Ray Allen] Billington notes that:

> Frequently crowds of excited Protestants, whipped to angry resentment by the exhortations of some wandering orator, rushed directly to a Catholic church, bent on its destruction. A dozen churches were burned during the middle 1850s; countless more were attacked, their crosses stolen, their alters violated, and their windows broken. At Sidney, Ohio, and at Dorchester, Massachusetts, Catholic houses of worship were blown to pieces with gunpowder. . . . In New York City a mob laid siege to the prominent cathedral of St. Peter and St. Paul, and only the arrival of the police saved the building. In Maine Catholics who had had one church destroyed were prevented from laying the cornerstone of a new one by hostile Protestants, and statues of priests were torn down or desecrated.

Nor were the priests themselves safe from public assault. The abuse in public was all but constant. At least two were badly beaten while on their way to administer last rites. In 1854 one Portland, Maine, priest described his ordeal:

> Since the 4th of July I have not considered myself safe to walk the streets after sunset. Twice within the past month I have been stoned by young men. If I chance to be abroad when the public schools are dismissed, I am hissed and insulted with vile language; and those repeated from children have been encouraged by the smiles and silence of passers by. The windows of the church have frequently been broken— the panels of the church door stove in, and last week a large

rock entered my chamber unceremoniously about 11 o'clock
at night.

If convents, churches, and priests were seen as something
to attack, nuns were seen essentially as victims, first of the
church's authoritarianism, and later as the targets of sexual
abuse and worse by priests and bishops. There was a spate of
"confessions" of former nuns—or in most instances of persons
who claimed, falsely, to have been nuns. The first of these of
any significance, Rebecca T. Reed's *Six Months in a Convent*
(1835), was relatively mild, described nothing either illegal or
immoral, and was concerned mostly with the penances she
was allegedly forced to endure. But it quickly sold hundreds of
thousands of copies and served as an encouragement for further confessions, which were soon numbered in the dozens.
Far and away the most important were Maria Monk's *Awful
Disclosures of the Hotel Dieu Nunnery of Montreal* (1836) and its
inevitable successor, *Further Disclosures . . .* (1837). Although
the first and more influential book was execrably written, it
has been called, with good reason, the *Uncle Tom's Cabin* of
nineteenth-century anti-Catholicism. Maria, or her ghost-
writer, told a lurid and preposterous tale of secret passage-
ways leading from a nearby priests' residence to the convent
so that the fathers could exercise their carnal lust on the
nuns, and of babies born to nuns there being strangled regularly by the mother superior. Maria herself, according to
the tale, was seduced by a priest and made pregnant. Not
wishing to see her child murdered, she fled the convent, was
rescued, and taken to a hospital, and was eventually saved by
a Protestant clergyman who brought her to the United
States, where her story was written and published. That
Maria was unmarried and pregnant was true. All the rest was
fantasy, perhaps psychotic fantasy. Maria had never been a
nun or even been inside the Hotel Dieu convent, and eventually even many of her supporters came to disbelieve her
stories, especially after she again became pregnant. Her
managers took most of the enormous profits from the books;
she spent the rest; and in 1849 poor Maria was arrested for
picking the pocket of a customer in a New York whorehouse
and died in prison shortly thereafter.

A Head Tax on Immigrants

It was against this background of religiously inspired anti-Catholicism, that the political and economic anti-immigrant attitudes of the pre–Civil War decades take on their full meaning. Many of the immigrants, as we have seen, were poor, others utterly destitute. The costs of maintaining the poor were mounting and were borne solely by the port cities and their states. In an effort to regain these costs, some eastern states passed modest head taxes—New York charged $1.50 for cabin passengers, Massachusetts a simple $2.00 a head—to be paid by the owners of the immigrant vessels. Not in themselves a great deterrent to immigration, they led the United States Supreme Court to lay down an important principle. In the *Passenger Cases* (1849) the court declared these state laws unconstitutional, holding that the right to regulate immigration under the commerce clause of the Constitution—Article I, Section 9, gives Congress the power "to regulate Commerce with foreign nations, and among the several states, and with the Indian Tribes"—was prescriptive. Thus even though Congress had passed no legislation concerning immigration, individual states could not tax it for any purpose, since, as John Marshall had put it earlier, the power to tax was the power to destroy. For the time being the court left the police powers of the states unimpaired: A state could, for example, quarantine a ship on which smallpox or cholera was raging.

This ruling only added supporters to an anti-immigrant bloc that was already flourishing in the country. As early as 1837 a nativist-Whig coalition was able to elect a mayor and council in New York City, and in Germantown, Pennsylvania, a Native American Association was formed that opposed foreign-born officeholders and voters. In New Orleans a similarly named organization denounced the immigration to the United States of "the outcast and offal of society, the vagrant and the convict—transported in myriads to our shores, reeking with the accumulated crimes of the whole civilized world." The major strategies of these movements, which coalesced in the 1840s and early 1850s in the American, or Know-Nothing, party, were to call for a change in the naturalization laws. The most common proposal was to require a twenty-one-year period for naturalization and bar the foreign born from holding any but minor local offices. Other measures proposed in Congress included forbidding the immigration into the United States of paupers, criminals, idiots, lunatics, insane persons, and the blind. Although such proposals had much support on both ideological and economic grounds, they never had enough to force a vote on them in either house of Congress. At the same time the new Free-Soil party, which would eventually be absorbed into the Republican Party, was advocating a program of continued immigration and land for the landless. The Republican party platform of 1864 stated well the ideological attitude of most Americans toward immigration. A specific immigration plank of that year—echoed in later years—read:

> Foreign immigration which in the past has added so much to the wealth, resources, and increase of power to this nation—

Abraham Lincoln Speaks Out Against the Know-Nothings

In 1855, when the anti-immigrant Know-Nothing party was at its most powerful, future president Abraham Lincoln wrote that he disliked antiforeigner attitudes as much as pro-slavery ones.

I am not a Know-Nothing. That is certain. How could I be? How can any one who abhors the oppression of negroes, be in favor of degrading classes of white people? Our progress in degeneracy appears to me to be pretty rapid. As a nation, we began by declaring that *"all men are created equal."* We now practically read it "all men are created equal, *except negroes.*" When the Know-Nothings get control, it will read "all men are created equal, except negroes, *and foreigners, and catholics.*" When it comes to this I should prefer emigrating to some country where they make no pretence of loving liberty—to Russia, for instance, where despotism can be taken pure, and without the base alloy of hypocrisy.

Moses Rischin, ed., *Immigration and the American Tradition*, Indianapolis: Bobbs-Merrill, 1976.

the asylum of the oppressed of all nations—should be fostered and encouraged by a liberal and just policy.

Anti-Immigrant Attitudes and the Know-Nothing Party

Nativism grew in the pre–Civil War years for a variety of reasons, including a growing uncertainty about the future of the nation. Much of the direction that future would take was decided by the Civil War. The truly dangerous subversive forces, it suddenly became clear, were not foreigners but Southern white Americans; those with a penchant for seeing a conspiracy in every threat no longer had to worry about the pope, the Jesuits, or the crowned heads of Europe: They had instead a homegrown slave power conspiracy to worry about. In addition, immigrants and foreigners had been of great assistance to the Union forces. Whole ethnic regiments, chiefly Irish and German, sustained the Union cause, and the Civil War draft worked even more against the poor—including immigrants—than have subsequent drafts. A drafted upper-class or middle-class individual could, if he wished, legally hire a substitute to go in his place, usually by providing a cash bounty of three hundred dollars or more. A future president, Grover Cleveland, chose this method of avoiding military service, as did the father of Theodore Roosevelt and thousands of other persons, almost all of them native-born Americans. Immigrants, it should be noted, fought in the Confederate armies as well.

As a result of the Civil War, Congress did change the Constitution and the naturalization statute, but not in the way that Know-Nothings and their allies had imagined. The Fourteenth Amendment, ratified in 1868, for the first time established a uniform national citizenship and provided that "all persons born or naturalized in the United States . . . are citizens of the United States and of the State wherein they reside." Intended to protect the rights of the former slaves, it would serve, in the twentieth century, to protect the rights of second-generation Asians. In addition, the abolition of slavery made the phrase *free white persons* in the naturalization statute redundant, and in 1870 Congress made the first significant change in that law since Jefferson's time. A few Radical Republicans, led by Senator Charles Sumner of Massachusetts, sought to make the statute color-blind and refer simply to "persons." In this Sumner and his allies were almost a century ahead of their time: Congress chose instead to broaden the law to allow the naturalization of "white persons and persons of African descent."

Chapter 2

The Second Great Wave: European Emigration from 1880 to 1924

Turning|Points
IN WORLD HISTORY

Immigrants and Their Accomplishments

John F. Kennedy

John F. Kennedy (JFK), president of the United States from 1961 until 1963, had a great interest in immigration, and he was well aware of the many contributions immigrants had made to America. Kennedy himself was the grandson of a poor Irish immigrant who had come to America during the first great wave of immigration in the 1800s. The Kennedy family achieved great success in America, and, in JFK, produced the first Roman Catholic president.

In this excerpt, Kennedy describes the major groups who made up the second great wave of emigrants from Europe. These new arrivals, who came to America largely between 1880 and 1924, were mostly Italians, southern and eastern Europeans such as Poles and Greeks, and Jews from Poland and Russia. Kennedy notes that these immigrant groups, like their predecessors, came for a variety of reasons, ranging from religious persecution to a search for economic opportunity. Finally, Kennedy shows how, in ways, ranging from home ownership to scientific and cultural leadership, members of these new immigrant groups both succeeded in and contributed to American life.

Toward the end of the nineteenth century, emigration to America underwent a significant change. Large numbers of Italians, Russians, Poles, Czechs, Hungarians, Rumanians, Bulgarians, Austrians and Greeks began to arrive. Their coming created new problems and gave rise to new tensions.

For these people the language barrier was even greater than it had been for earlier groups, and the gap between the

Excerpted from *A Nation of Immigrants*, by John F. Kennedy. Copyright © 1964 by Anti-Defamation League of B'nai B'rith. Reprinted by permission of HarperCollins Publishers, Inc.

world they had left behind and the one to which they came was wider. For the most part, these were people of the land and, for the most part, too, they were forced to settle in the cities when they reached America. Most large cities had well-defined "Little Italys" or "Little Polands" by 1910. In the 1960 census, New York City had more people of Italian birth or parentage than did Rome.

The history of cities shows that when conditions become overcrowded, when people are poor and when living conditions are bad, tensions run high. This is a situation that feeds on itself; poverty and crime in one group breed fear and hostility in others. This, in turn, impedes the acceptance and progress of the first group, thus prolonging its depressed condition. This was the dismal situation that faced many of the Southern and Eastern European immigrants just as it had faced some of the earlier waves of immigrants. One New York newspaper had these intemperate words for the newly arrived Italians: "The flood gates are open. The bars are down. The sally-ports are unguarded. The dam is washed away. The sewer is choked . . . the scum of immigration is viscerating upon our shores. The horde of $9.60 steerage slime is being siphoned upon us from Continental mud tanks."

Immigrants from Italy

Italy has contributed more immigrants to the United States than any country except Germany. Over five million Italians came to this country between 1820 and 1963. Large-scale immigration began in 1880, and almost four million Italian immigrants arrived in the [twentieth] century.

The first Italians were farmers and artisans from northern Italy. Some planted vineyards in Vineland, New Jersey, in the Finger Lakes region of New York State and in California, where they inaugurated our domestic wine industry. Others settled on the periphery of cities, where they started truck gardens.

But most Italians were peasants from the south. They came because of neither religious persecution nor political repression, but simply in search of a brighter future. Population in Italy was straining the limits of the country's resources and more and more people had to eke out a living from small plots of land, held in many instances by oppressive landlords.

In many ways the experience of the later Italian immigrants parallels the story of the Irish. Mostly farmers, their lack of financial resources kept them from reaching the rural areas of the United States. Instead, they crowded into cities along the Eastern seaboard, often segregating themselves by province, even by village, in a density as high as four thousand to the city block.

Untrained in special skills and unfamiliar with the language, they had to rely on unskilled labor jobs to earn a living. Italians thus filled the gap left by earlier immigrant groups who had now moved up the economic ladder. As bricklayers, masons, stonecutters, ditchdiggers and hod carriers, they helped build our cities, subways and skyscrapers. They worked on the railroads and the dams, went into the coal mines, iron mines and factories. Some found a place in urban life as small storekeepers, peddlers, shoemakers, barbers and tailors. Wages were small and families were large. In the old country everyone worked. Here everyone worked too. Wives went into the needle trades. Boys picked up what pennies they could as news vendors, bootblacks and errand-runners. Through these difficult years of poverty, toil and bewilderment, the Italians were bolstered by their adherence to the church, the strength of their family ties, Italian-language newspapers and their fraternal orders. But they overcame obstacles of prejudice and misunderstanding quickly, and they have found places of importance in almost every phase of American life. Citizens of Italian descent are among our leading bankers, contractors, food importers, educators, labor leaders and government officials. Italians have made special contributions to the emergence of American culture, enriching our music, art and architecture.

An Italian, Filippo Traetta, founded the American Conservatory in Boston in 1800, and another in Philadelphia shortly thereafter. Another Italian, Lorenzo da Ponte, brought the first Italian opera troupe to New York in 1832, where it developed into a permanent institution. Italians have founded and supported the opera as an institution in

New York, Chicago, San Francisco and other large cities, providing from their ranks many impresarios and singers. Italian-born music teachers and bandmasters are numerous. Arturo Toscanini, for many years leader of the New York Philharmonic, and our most distinguished conductor of recent years, was Italiain-born.

Italians have also been among our most prominent sculptors, architects and artists. A West Indian and a Frenchman designed our nation's Capitol. An Italian beautified it. Constantino Brumidi painted the historical frieze in the rotunda of the Capitol building. Other Italian painters and sculptors depicted our history in paintings, murals, friezes and statues. Historical monuments and statues up and down the country have been wrought by Italian-American sculptors. On an humbler scale, the taste and skill of Italian-American landscape gardeners and architects have placed our homes and communities in beautiful settings.

The Diversity of Eastern European Immigrants

About the time the Italians began coming, other great tides of immigration from the countries of Eastern and Southeastern Europe also began arriving in the United States. In the years between 1820 and 1963 these areas, Italy included, sent over fifteen million immigrants to our shores.

They came for all manner of reasons: political upheavals, religious persecution, hopes for economic betterment. They comprised a wide ethnic variety, from Lithuanians and Latvians on the Baltic to Greeks, Turks and Armenians on the eastern Mediterranean. They brought with them a bewildering variety of language, dress, custom, ideology and religious belief. To many Americans already here who had grown accustomed to a common way of life, they presented a dismaying bedlam, difficult to understand and more difficult to respond to. Indeed, because of the many changes in national boundaries and prior migrations of races within that area of Europe, there is no way of accurately reporting on them statistically.

The largest number from any of these countries of Eastern Europe were Poles, who for 125 years had been under the domination of Russia, Germany and Austria-Hungary.

Some followed the pattern of the Germans and Scandinavians, settling on individual farms or forming small rural communities which still bear Polish place names. But most gravitated to the cities. Four-fifths were Roman Catholic. Longer than most immigrant groups they kept their language, their customs and their dances. At first, like other immigrants, they lived under substandard conditions. Gradually they, too, improved their status. They aspired to own their own homes and their own plots of land. In Hamtramck, Michigan, an almost wholly Polish community, three-quarters of the residents own their own homes.

By 1963, almost 130,000 Czechs had migrated to this country. They tended to gravitate to the farming communities. It is one of these homesteads that is portrayed by novelist Willa Cather in *My Antonia*. They also formed enclaves in cities, principally in Chicago, Cleveland and New York.

A potent force in the development of Czech life in this country has been the *Sokol*, a traditional cultural, social and gymnastic society. These societies stressed high standards of physical fitness and an interest in singing, music and literature.

The immigrants from Old Russia are estimated at almost three and a half million. Most of this wave of immigration went into the mines and factories. However, there were also many Russian intellectuals, scientists, scholars, musicians, writers and artists, who came here usually during periods of political oppression.

Most students of the history of immigration to America make special mention of the Jews. Although they appeared as part of several of the waves of immigration, they warrant separate discussion because of their religion, culture and historical background.

Jewish Peoples in the United States

In colonial times most Jews in America were of Spanish-Portuguese origin. Throughout the nineteenth century most came from Germany. Beginning at the end of the nineteenth century they began to come in large numbers from Russia, Poland, Austria-Hungary, Rumania and, in smaller numbers, from almost every European nation. The

American Jewish population today [in 1963] numbers approximately six million.

The Jews who came during the early nineteenth century were often peddlers, wandering throughout the land with their packs and their carts or settling down to open small stores. They prospered in this era of opportunity and expansion, for from these humble beginnings have grown many of our large department stores and mercantile establishments.

The exodus from Germany after 1848 brought Jewish intellectuals, philosophers, educators, political leaders and social reformers. These shared much the same experiences as the other immigrants. "Like the Scandinavian Lutherans and the Irish Catholics," says Oscar Handlin, "they appeared merely to maintain their distinctive heritage while sharing the rights and obligations of other Americans within a free society."

At the turn of the century the Jews fleeing persecution in Russia came in such numbers that they could not be so readily absorbed into the mainstream of life as the earlier comers. They clustered in Jewish communities within the large cities, like New York.

Like the Irish and the Italians before them, they had to work at whatever they could find. Most found an outlet for their skills in the needle trades, as garment workers, hatmakers and furriers. Often they worked in sweatshops. In an effort to improve working conditions (which involved child labor and other forms of exploitation), they joined with other immigrant workers to form, in 1900, the International Ladies' Garment Workers Union. In time, they developed the clothing industry as we know it today, centered in New York but reaching into every small town and rural area. The experience and tradition of these pioneers produced many effective leaders in the labor movement, such as Morris Hillquit, Sidney Hillman, Jacob Potofsky and David Dubinsky.

Jewish immigrants have also made immense contributions to thought: as scholars, as educators, as scientists, as judges and lawyers, as journalilsts, as literary figures. Refugee scientists such as Albert Einstein and Edward Teller brought great scientific knowledge to this country.

Ellis Island: The First Stop for Most Immigrants

Georges Perec with Robert Bober

In October 1886 authorities dedicated the Statue of Liberty, a gift to the United States of America from the Republic of France. Inscribed on the base of the statue was an excerpt from a poem by a Jewish American named Emma Lazarus. The poem included the lines "Give me your tired, your poor,/Your huddled masses yearning to breathe free,/The wretched refuse of your teeming shore." Together with the Statue of Liberty, Lazarus's lines appeared to indicate that America would, from that point on, welcome emigrants from Europe's "teeming shore."

Not far from the Statue of Liberty in New York City's harbor stands Ellis Island, the arrival point for most of Europe's emigrant ships from 1892 until 1924. French writer Georges Perec traveled there in 1995 with filmmaker Robert Bober. Together they produced the book from which the following excerpt is taken. The authors note that the tired arrivals came ashore at Ellis Island to face long waits in crowded rooms, medical examinations, and questions about their politics. Sometimes, the authors show, immigrants had their names changed to make them simpler to American ears.

More or less free until about 1875, the admission of foreigners onto American soil was gradually subjected to restrictive measures, initially defined and applied locally (by port or municipal authorities) and later centralized in a bureau of immigration responsible to the federal government. The opening of the Ellis Island reception center in 1892 marked the end of virtually unregulated immigration and the advent of official, institutionalized and, so to speak, industrialized immigration. Between 1892 and 1924, nearly sixteen million people passed through Ellis Island, at a rate of five to ten thousand a day. The majority spent a few hours there; no more than two to three per cent were turned away.

Essentially, Ellis Island was a sort of factory for manufacturing Americans, a factory for transforming emigrants into immigrants; an American-style factory, as quick and efficient as a sausage factory in Chicago. You put an Irishman, a Ukranian Jew, or an Italian from Apulia into one end of the production line and at the other end—after vaccination, disinfection, and examination of his eyes and pockets—an American emerged. But at the same time, as the years passed, admission became more and more strictly controlled. Gradually the Golden Door swung shut on the leg-

Immigrants newly arrived from Europe stand in line at Ellis Island in New York harbor. They endured long waits, medical examinations, and questions about their politics.

endary America where turkeys fell onto your plate fully cooked, where the streets were paved with gold, where the land belonged to everyone. Immigration slowed down, in fact, after 1914, initially because of the war, later because of a series of discriminatory measures both qualitative (the Literacy Act) and quantitative (the quota system) that virtually denied entrance to the "wretched refuse" and "huddled masses" whom, according to Emma Lazarus, the Statue of Liberty was meant to welcome. In 1924 the responsibility for immigration procedures was transferred to the American consulates in Europe; Ellis Island was reduced to the status of detention center for those immigrants whose papers were not in order. . . .

Only Poor Immigrants Passed Through Ellis Island

Not all immigrants were obliged to pass through Ellis Island. Those with enough money to travel first or second class were quickly examined on board ship by a doctor and an immigration officer and could land without further ado. The federal government assumed that these immigrants had the wherewithal to look after themselves and were not likely to become wards of the state. The immigrants who went to Ellis Island were those who traveled third class, that is, in steerage, which in fact meant below the water line in the hold, in vast dormitories not only without windows but practically without ventilation or lighting, where two thousand passengers were crammed together on tiers of straw mattresses. The trip cost ten dollars in the 1880s and thirty-five dollars after World War I. It lasted about three weeks. The food consisted of potatoes and salt herring.

A whole series of official procedures took place during the crossing. These were performed by the shipping companies, who were more or less responsible for the passengers they took aboard—they had to pay for their passengers' living expenses on Ellis Island, and they were obliged to repatriate any emigrants who were turned away. The procedures included a medical examination (usually bungled), disinfections, vaccinations, and the establishment of a personal record for each emigrant that listed his name, country of origin, destination, means, judicial record, sponsor in the United States, and so forth.

On Ellis Island itself the examination procedures lasted at best from three to five hours. The arrivals first underwent a medical examination. Any doubtful case was detained and subjected to a much more thorough medical inspection; a number of contagious diseases, particularly trachoma, favus, and tuberculosis, meant automatic expulsion. Emigrants who emerged from this examination unscathed were then asked, after a waiting period of variable length, to appear at the legal desks. Behind each of these sat an inspector and an interpreter. (For many years Fiorello La Guardia, before becoming mayor of New York, was an interpreter in Yiddish and Italian on Ellis Island.) The inspector had about two minutes in which to decide whether or not the emigrant had a right to enter the United States. He made his decision after asking a series of twenty-nine questions:

What is your name?

Where are you from?

Why have you come to the United States?

How old are you?

How much money do you have?

Where did you get this money?

Show it to me.

Who paid for your crossing?

Did you sign a contract in Europe for a job here?

Do you have any friends here?

Do you have any family here?

Is there anyone who can vouch for you?

What kind of work do you do?

Are you an anarchist?

—and so forth.

If the new arrival answered in a manner that was deemed

satisfactory, the inspector would stamp his papers and let him leave, after wishing him "Welcome to America." If there was any kind of problem, he wrote an "S.I." on the arrival's record. This stood for Special Inquiry, and after another waiting period the arrival would be summoned before a committee made up of three inspectors, who subjected the would-be immigrant to a far more detailed interrogation.

In 1917, overriding President Wilson's veto, Congress passed the Literacy Act, which required immigrants to be able to read and write in their native language and also obliged them to take various intelligence tests. The system was already unfavorable to the new emigrants from eastern Europe, Russia, and Italy. (Those who arrived during the first three-quarters of the nineteenth century had come from the Scandinavian countries, Germany, Holland, England, and Ireland). These new measures made the admission procedure even longer and, from one year to the next, much more difficult.

New Names for New Americans

The majority of the inspectors did their work conscientiously and, with the help of their interpreters, did their best to obtain exact information from the new arrivals. A great many of them were of Irish origin and had little familiarity with the spelling and pronunciation of the names of central Europe, Russia, Greece, or Turkey. Furthermore, many emigrants hoped to acquire names that sounded American. Hence the innumerable incidents of name changes that occurred on Ellis Island. A man from Berlin became Berliner; another whose first name was Vladimir received Walter as his given name; a man whose first name was Adam became Mr. Adams; a Skyzertski was transformed into Sanders, a Goldenburg into Goldberg, and a Gold became Goldstein.

One old Russian Jew was advised to pick a truly American name, one that the immigration authorities would have no difficulty in transcribing. He asked the advice of an employee in the baggage room who suggested Rockefeller. The old Jew kept repeating "Rockefeller, Rockefeller" to be sure he'd remember. But several hours later, when the immigration officer asked him his name, he had forgotten it and answered in Yiddish, "Schon vergessen"—"I've already forgotten." And so he was registered with the truly American name of John Ferguson.

The story is perhaps too good to be true, but ultimately it hardly matters whether it's true or false. To emigrants yearning for America, a new name might seem a blessing. For their grandchildren today, things are different. It is remarkable that in 1976, the Bicentennial year, several dozen Smiths whose families had come from Poland asked to be renamed Kowalski (both names mean blacksmith).

No more than two per cent of all emigrants were turned away from Ellis Island. That still amounts to two hundred and fifty thousand people. And between 1892 and 1924, there were three thousand suicides on Ellis Island.

Settlement and Work for the New Immigrants

Sean Dennis Cashman

By the 1890s, when the second great wave of European emigrants was well underway, the United States had completed most of its territorial expansion. In addition, the nation was heavily industrialized. Consequently, the United States had much less need for agricultural immigrants and a greater need for industrial workers. As Sean Dennis Cashman points out in the following passage, industrial jobs, indeed, were the main draw for many of the new immigrants in the first place. For America, of course, the new immigrants provided cheap labor, thus allowing industrialism to expand even more rapidly.

Cashman shows that most immigrants settled in cities rather than in the countryside. In fact, many cities, such as New York, Chicago, and Cleveland, seemed to be mostly inhabited by immigrants and their children. As with other waves of immigration, Cashman goes on to point out, immigrants were concentrated in particular regions, although small groups were scattered throughout most of the rest of the country.

Not all urban immigrants, however, took up industrial work or stayed with it for very long. The most successful immigrants were those who brought skills with them from home. They could then prosper by practicing their trade, or use it as a springboard to starting their own businesses.

Sean Dennis Cashman has been professor of American studies at both the University of Manchester, England, and New York University.

Excerpted from Sean Dennis Cashman, *America in the Age of the Titans*. Copyright © 1988 by New York University. Reprinted by permission of New York University Press.

While the proportion of immigrants in 1910 was only 14.5 percent of the total population (much as it had been in 1860 when it stood at 13.2 percent), the immigrants were increasingly concentrated in the industrial Northeast. Indeed, four states contained almost half the foreign-born population: New York, Massachusetts, Pennsylvania, and Illinois.

Although the new immigration had now exceeded the old, we should note that even in 1910 Germany still accounted for the largest number of first-generation immigrants, over 2.5 million. However, Russia and Austria-Hungary came next, each with over 1.5 million. Then came Ireland and Italy with over 1.3 million while Scandinavia, Britain, and Canada had about 1.25 million. The largest German contingents had settled in the Midwest, notably Illinois, Wisconsin, Ohio, and Minnesota, with lesser (but still large) numbers in New York, Pennsylvania, and New Jersey. Scandinavians were concentrated in Minnesota, Illinois, Wisconsin, North and South Dakota, and Washington State. Finns settled in Massachusetts, Michigan, and Minnesota. Almost half the Canadians settled in New England, and most of the rest in New York, Michigan, and the states round the Great Lakes. The Irish settled in New England and the mid-Atlantic states as well as California and Illinois, states that received the greatest numbers of Italians. Immigrants from Russia and Austria-Hungary settled in New York, Pennsylvania, New Jersey, Massachusetts, and Illinois.

Polish immigrants settled in thousands of communities in at least thirty-six states, but primarily in the industrial cities of the Northeast from Illinois to New York. They became miners in Scranton, Pennsylvania, meat packers in Chicago, and steelworkers in Buffalo. Although most Greeks settled in the industrial cities of the Northeast and worked as artisans or in menial service jobs, others ventured west. By 1907 between 30,000 and 40,000 Greeks had settled west of the Mississippi. In Colorado and Utah they worked as miners and smelters; in California as construction workers for railroads. Few moved to the South, although John Cocoris and his family established a sponge business in Tarpon Springs, Florida, in which they employed 500 Greek immigrants to dive for, clean, and pack sponges.

Crowded Immigrant Cities

Observers of early twentieth-century America remarked how immigrants seemed far more in evidence in the largest cities than ever before. It seemed there were masses of newcomers in unusual costumes speaking foreign languages and following strange customs. When novelist Henry James returned to the United States in 1907 after being away for twenty-five years, he experienced a profound "sense of dispossession." Whatever their numbers, immigrants never threatened to overwhelm the native-born population. Although there were times when the foreign-born comprised a fifth of the population of Canada and a third of the population of Argentina, they never exceeded more than a seventh of the population of the United States, although sometimes in such midwestern states as Wisconsin the fraction rose to a quarter. . . .

The South tried to attract immigrants, especially to man its expanding railroad systems or work the land. In 1903 the Southern Railway settled 2,000 families on 2.27 million acres. The Southern Pacific sold 3 million acres in the ten years from 1894; the Mobile and Ohio sold off 600,000 acres and the Illinois Central sold off almost as much in Alabama, Kentucky, Louisiana, and Mississippi. The Louisville and Nashville sold 105,143 acres of farm land and 255,540 acres of timber and mineral lands along its lines in 1903. Twice a month the main southern railroads ran special homesellers' trains charging prospective settlers half fare. Yet these efforts resulted in only small colonies of Danes, Germans, Hungarians, Italians, and Swedes settled along the southern railroads, as were some migrants from the Midwest. Dunkers and other religious sects settled in Alabama and Georgia. Nevertheless, as southern historian C. Vann Woodward concludes, "The flood tide of European immigration, in 1899–1910, swept past the South leaving it almost untouched and further isolating it in its peculiarities from the rest of the country." Thus the small northern state of Connecticut received more immigrants than the entire South and New Jersey received twice as many.

It is, however, true that most immigrants preferred cities to the countryside. Attempts to induce old immigrants with neither aptitude nor experience to take up farming fell by the wayside. Thus organizations like the Irish Catholic Benevolent Union could not turn Irish laborers into independent farmers in Virginia, Kansas, and Minnesota. Potato farming back home was simple. It involved planting, trenching, and digging potatoes. This was no preparation for running a farm of 160 acres in the Golden West. Among the new immigrants only Czechs and Germans from Russia took readily to agriculture. They had the advantage of arriving early enough to find land still available on the prairies. Moreover, it was similar terrain to that of their native steppes. Pioneer farmers cleared the trees or prairie grasses and exploited the land. They grew the same crop again and again until the soil was too impoverished for them to continue. In Marcus Lee Hansen's striking phrase, "The land was mined, not farmed.". . .

Better the Factory than the Farm

Many new immigrants concluded from their harsh experience in the Old World that farming was physically and psychically draining. Thus Joseph Lopreato studies Italian patterns of settlement in his *Italian Americans* (1970) and concludes how Italian immigrants considered farming a punishment for both stomach and soul. The contadini's reliance on agriculture had "reduced him nearly to the status of the donkey and goat." Hence, for such people immigration was a liberation from the arduous work and penury of agricultural labor and they did not want to return to it.

Moreover, it was primarily the industrial revolution with its splendid promise of opportunity that had attracted immigrants, old and new. Indeed, without massive immigration the United States could not have developed industrially at anything like the rate it did. More significantly, the new immigrants' willingness to take on menial work enabled earlier groups to assume more skilled work or to enter the professions. The Dillingham Commission of 1907–10 disclosed that immigrants accounted for 57.9 percent of employees in twenty-one industries and, on average, some two-thirds of them came from southern and eastern Europe. The fraction

was higher in certain industries: clothing, textiles, coal mining, and meat packing.

   In any ethnic group the first group of immigrants were
young men in their late teens or twenties. Thus up to the
turn of the century 78 percent of Italian and 95 percent of
Greek immigrants were men. Twenty years later the emphasis had shifted in some ethnic groups. In 1920 the proportion of men and women among Polish immigrants was
about even, whereas among Slovaks 65 percent were female
and among Italians 48 percent were female. However, almost 80 percent of Greek immigrants were male. Some
male migrants were known as "birds of passage" because
they moved across the Atlantic in either direction, according to seasonal employment prospects. Thus in the period
1908–14, 6,709,357 immigrants arrived in, and 2,063,767
people departed from the United States, either temporarily
or permanently. In this same period over half the Hungarians, Italians, Croatians, and Slovaks went home. After all
their original intention was to earn money for their families
at home and return with it. Between 1908 and 1916
1,215,598 Italians left America. In the end, only 67 percent
of all immigrants settled permanently in the United States.
However, many immigrants who had originally planned to
return home once they had made some money kept post-
poning the journey and, in the end, settled as naturalized citizens of their new country. . . .

   However, who worked where and when depended on all
sorts of social and economic factors. Italians preferred to
work outdoors, rather than in factories. It was largely Italian labor that built the New York subways and some major
bridges. In Florida they rolled cigars; in California they
cultivated vines; on the prairies they helped lay tracks for
the transcontinental railroads. French-Canadians worked
in the textile factories of New England because their immigration coincided with increased demand for labor in
the cotton mills of states close to Quebec. Moreover, the
mills of Maine, Massachusetts, and Rhode Island took on
women and children as well as men. Thus whole families
could be employed together.

Only 11 percent of Jewish immigrants had worked as tailors in Europe but they now turned to the rag trade, despite its exploitation, for a mix of cultural, social, and career reasons. In New York the rag trade employed about 50 percent of Jewish men and boys living in the city and two-thirds of the city's Jewish wage earners. Journalist Hutchins Hapgood described in his *Spirit of the Ghetto* (1902) how homes became work rooms. "During the day the front room, bedroom, and kitchen became a whirling, churning factory, where men, women and children worked at the sewing and pressing machines." The clothing industry was not attractive to Russian Jews because it offered work to women and children. Their women usually stayed at home after marriage. Their children stayed at school until they were in their teens. The principal attraction of the rag trade was as an avenue to commerce. Pay was by piecework. Thus earnings were related to individual effort. Workers could therefore amass capital and invest in their own businesses. Jewish workers also found employment in cigar factories, printing works, and book binderies. It has been thought the sweatshops offered the opportunity to discuss Zionism. Yet the World Zionist Organization, founded in Basle in 1897, was slow to attract Jewish Americans and had no more than 20,000 active supporters in the United States by 1914. It ran counter to the philosophy of the Reform tradition that had no interest in the idea of a restored Jewish state. Socialists such as Morris Hillquit considered the Jewish state an irrelevance.

Skilled Immigrants Adapted Best

Moreover, the major cities were centers of commerce and provided extra opportunities for skilled work in handicrafts and such household manufacture as shoes, clothes, tableware, and toys. In his study of Italians, Rumanians, and Slovaks in Cleveland, *Peasants and Strangers* (1975), Josef Barton finds that it was those immigrants who had developed skills as merchants or artisans in Europe who adapted themselves most easily to American towns. About half the subjects he studied entered skilled work in the United States and another 40 percent immediately took white-collar jobs.

Within twenty years such immigrants had settled comfortably in the middle class. Sixty-six percent of all Jewish men and boys who immigrated to the United States in the period 1899–1914 were classified as skilled, compared with an average of only 20 percent for all male immigrants in the same period. Their adjustment to life in American towns was made easier because they had valuable skills. Sicilian fishermen also adjusted quite easily. They immigrated with their families and were thus better able to cope with social dislocation. Moreover, they were used to business, originally fishing and selling their catch. In comparison, peasants, laborers, and their sons found it far more difficult to rise socially in the United States. Yet Andrew F. Rolle observes in *The Immigrant Upraised* (1968) how some Italians went west and prospered. In fact, the few who moved to the country succeeded better and became more quickly assimilated than those who remained in urban ghettos. However, for the majority, such a move was out of the question, especially if they ever intended to return to Europe.

Many immigrants became entrepreneurs, first on a small scale, as peddlers. According to contemporary observer Charles Bernheimer, in 1905 New York had almost 1,000 Jewish "peddlers and keepers of stands, the number varying according to the season of the year." In Sholom Aleichem's stories, the young men are willing to try any jobs. Eli works as a tailor, as a waiter in a delicatessen, and is ready to shovel snow—but not on the street. "Do you want your portion of snow brought to you in the house?" asks Pinney. When the family of seven decide to sell candy and cigarettes, they scare away prospective customers because there are so many of them behind the counter.

Greek entrepreneurs moved into confectionery as described by Theodore Saloutos in his *The Greeks in the United States* (1963). It has been estimated that 70 percent of Greek makers of candy in the United States were in Chicago, "the Acropolis of the Greek-American candy business," according to Saloutos. The Greek newspaper, *Hellinikos Astir* reported in 1904 how "practically every busy corner in Chicago is occupied by a Greek candy store." It was their strict dietary laws that led many Jews into the meat and poultry trade. In 1900 80 percent of the wholesale meat trade in New York and 50 percent of the retail trade was run by Jews. There were about 500 Jewish bakers in New York at this time. As immigrants prospered, ethnic restaurants opened to cater to their special tastes and some, such as *Mama Leone's* (1906) which specialized in Italian dishes, quickly gained a reputation nationwide.

Assimilating the New Immigrants

Richard Krickus

Many of the immigrants of the second great wave were even more "foreign" to native-born Americans than the earlier (and, in fact, still arriving) emigrants from Ireland, Germany, and Scandinavia. Few spoke English, for instance, and they wore unfamiliar clothes and practiced what seemed to be strange customs. Moreover, many of the newcomers practiced religions that were still strange to many Americans: Judaism, Eastern Orthodox Christianity, and Roman Catholic Christianity. The era, in addition, was one of the growing nationalist sensitivities; Americans feared that these new immigrants might remain loyal to their home governments or practice extreme left-wing politics.

As Richard Krickus points out in the following selection, major efforts were made to quickly "Americanize" these newcomers. Some Americans took a fairly benign approach and held classes to simply teach immigrants English and help them find their way in their new home. Others were more aggressive, as Krickus demonstrates, seeking to turn immigrants into not only English-speakers but also peaceful, hard-working, loyal Americans.

Richard Krickus is a freelance writer and consultant who helped found the National Center for Urban Ethnic Affairs.

The authorities in Russia and Austria-Hungary sought to impose cultural uniformity among minority peoples by prohibiting the use of "foreign" languages, cultural practices, and religious rituals which sustained cultural autonomy. In contrast the American authorities paid little attention to the growing number of "minority persons" in the United States until the late nineteenth century. The native Americans were confident that they could absorb the foreigners who settled in the vast reaches of America. With the exception of the abrasive Germans who were convinced they gave more than they got, the peasants from Eastern and Southern Europe clung to their culture more out of habit than conviction—at least this was the conclusion many American observers of the New Immigrants had favored. Teach them English and the natal cord which nourished their foreign ways in the United States would be severed.

By the 1890s it was apparent that by virtue of the number of newcomers and their propensity to settle in compact ethnic enclaves, the problem of assimilating them no longer was to be taken lightly. Two different approaches to the disruptive presence of the New Immigrants developed. On the one hand, [social reformer] Jane Addams, who directed the activities of Hull House in Chicago, developed programs to treat culture shock, to integrate immigrants into the neighborhood, to provide them with instruction in English, thus enabling them to communicate with the "strangers around them." She cautioned workers in the settlement house movement to be careful, in the process of lending a helping hand, not to denigrate the immigrants' cultural legacy, for it was a source of comfort to them. She noted that great damage was wrought where the immigrants were taught that their values, ideals, and beliefs were worthless baggage from a bygone era, useful perhaps in the Old World but certainly not in the new one. Indeed, she attempted to demonstrate to immigrant youngsters that their parents possessed artistic talents and vocational skills which were useful and creative; they were to be admired for such talents, not to be objects of ridicule. Many settlement house workers concluded that the immigrant children who engaged in various forms of antisocial behavior were defenseless because they had forsaken the old ways before they learned how to cope with the New World which mesmerized so many of them.

Fear of Foreign Influence

As the steamers discharged their human cargo from Europe, persons motivated out of fear and not humanitarianism began to take note of the New Immigrants' presence. The Daughters of the American Revolution (DAR), the Sons of the Revolution, the Colonial Dames, and various and sundry other "patriotic" organizations feared that the newcomers represented a threat to the American way of life. And they lobbied energetically to press educators, editors, and the public to pay proper attention to the problem. They sponsored lectures and disseminated literature to immigrant neighborhoods laced with patriotic messages. The good ladies in the DAR were guided in their work by the thought that "obedience" was "the groundwork of true citizenship." Industrialists who had little patience with do-gooders like Jane Addams—"who pamper the alien scum"—responded more positively to hardheaded "Americanizers" who warned that the immigrants were largely responsible for the rising incidence of social and labor unrest in the country. The immigrants were harbingers of alien doctrine which was poisoning the minds of native Americans. Labor unrest and the "unending demands" which the workers were making were all traced to the odious presence of the New Immigrants. The quest to Americanize them was essential to secure labor peace and it was in this vein that industrialists and business organizations sponsored adult education courses for their immigrant workers. The first English words immigrant auto workers at Henry Ford's night school learned were "I'm a good American."

The First World War [1914–1918] gave a new sense of urgency to the campaign to Americanize the immigrants, who represented a virtual "fifth column." Thus Frances Kellor, a Cornell-educated lawyer who had written with feeling about the exploitation of the immigrant worker and had masterminded legislation to fight it, drifted toward the hucksters of hundred per cent Americanism on the eve of the war. She was instrumental in replacing the slogan which government propagandists had favored early in the war, "Many People, But One Nation," with the new one which stated cryptically, "America First." In a speech before the National Security League she spoke about the immigrants as an internal peril and left her listeners with the thought that Americanization was the civilian side of national security. Henceforth, Protestant fundamentalists, racist bigots, and political reactionaries began to play a dominant role in the crusade to Americanize the immigrants. "To a nation charged with evangelical impulses, Americanization was a mission of redemption; to a country of salesmen, it offered an adventure in high pressure salesmanship."

English Only

During World War I (1914–1918), Iowa governor William L. Harding declared publicly that speaking any language other than English was a threat to the nation's war effort.

The official language of the United States and the State of Iowa is the English language. Freedom of speech is guaranteed by federal and State Constitutions, but this is not a guaranty of the right to use a language other than the language of this country—the English language. Both federal and State Constitutions also provide that "no laws shall be made respecting an establishment of religion or prohibiting the free exercise thereof." Each person is guaranteed freedom to worship God according to the dictates of his own conscience, but this guaranty does not protect him in the use of a foreign language when he can as well express his thought in English, nor entitle the person who cannot speak or understand the English language to employ a foreign language, when to do so tends in time of national peril, to create discord among neighbors and citizens, or to disturb the peace and quiet of the community.

Moses Rischin, ed., *Immigration and the American Tradition*, Indianapolis: Bobbs-Merrill, 1976.

Nativist bigots had reached the conclusion that there was no room for cultural pluralism in twentieth-century America, that dissent, whether it took the form of "alien doctrine" or "resident foreigners" who refused to conform to the American way of life, could not be tolerated. People like John Dewey, who wrote that each race could make a contribution to a cosmopolitan society in which many cultures thrived, drifted away from the Americanization movement with the termination of the war. The problem would take care of itself as the immigrants, through educational and job mobility, overcame their social and economic problems and blended in with everybody else.

As long as liberal-minded Americans participated, they served as a countervailing force to the yahoos, racists, and reactionaries in the campaign, but with the postwar red scare, the hundred percenters pressed state authorities to take action against the new peril—alien radicals. In 1919, fifteen states passed laws which legislated that English must be used in all public and private schools; in Iowa the governor proclaimed only English could be used in public gatherings, including telephone conversations. California passed a new tax law which punished alien residents; it was declared unconstitutional. The Americanization drive gave new purpose to the teachings of civics in the school system and special attention was paid to the instruction of immigrant students. As the red scare faded from the people's consciousness with the bright prospect of prosperity in the mid-1920s, the steam which had driven the engine of the crusade for Americanization evaporated. Nonetheless, the campaign had left its mark upon the immigrant and second-generation youngsters who sought to take their place in American society.

The Challenges of Fitting In

Philip Taylor

The Europeans who left home to go to America were often peasants who had left their ancestral lands—villages inhabited by their ancestors for decades if not centuries—only recently. The European population explosion of the 1800s reached southern and eastern Europe by the end of the century. Unable to secure a living in their traditional villages, many people left for crowded European cities before finally embarking for the United States. Indeed, not only did the second great wave of immigrants transform America, but it also transformed the immigrants themselves.

According to Philip Taylor, immigrants were forced to juggle a number of different worlds. First, they might live in a community dominated by people from their same country or even region. At the same time, however, they might attend church with people from other backgrounds; for example, Italian Catholics might congregate with Polish Catholics. All the while, immigrants had to adapt to a new language, a new country, and often new ways of making a living. Finally, Taylor suggests, immigrant families faced generational conflicts as immigrant children became "Americanized" and turned away from old-country traditions.

Philip Taylor was professor of American studies at the University of Hull in the United Kingdom.

On their arrival, immigrants inhabited, not merely the United States, but several worlds at the same time. They lived in a district of homesteads, or in a city ward, surrounded, most probably, by fellow-members of their own ethnic group. North-eastern Iowa was Norwegian, the

Lower East Side of Manhattan was Jewish, South Boston was Irish and Boston's North End Italian. Yet they had the recent memory of an equally real and local community somewhere in the old country. Relations and friends were still there, and they followed its news as closely as they could. If these were worlds of direct personal association, the world of German or Irish or Italian nationality was not much more remote. Whether marching in a St Patrick's Day parade, secretly drilling with Fenian forces, flocking to hear Michael Davitt expound the Land League, or reading in the *Irish World* of the advancement to public office of their compatriots in other states, Irish immigrants felt themselves part of the history of Ireland, and part of an Irish-America in the New World. Similarly, Germans were aware of having founded in America a special community, a special culture, while at the same time they celebrated the 1848 revolutions or [chancellor Otto von] Bismarck's triumph of 1870-71. For Croats and Slovaks and Finns, too, a sense of national identity in the United States preceded national status in Europe, and indeed helped to achieve it. Immigrants inhabited at the same time a city, a state, a country, whose history and institutions affected their lives, and some of them had already judged these with approval before leaving home. Many immigrants, however, lived also in one more world, that of the Roman Catholic Church. While growing rapidly in America, that Church was at the same time suffering territorial loss in Italy, defining its doctrines and practice, defending its position against nineteenth-century ideologies. German or Irish or Italian Catholics in America were necessarily involved, whether they were paying from meagre earnings to put up a handsome new church, listening to their priest's command to send their children to parochial schools, sending a contribution from Boston to aid [Pope] Pius IX in 1849, or testifying sympathy and admiration for the same pontiff in 1871 and 1873.

At varying speeds, each of these worlds changed. Italy and Germany became politically united. Much later, Poland and Czechoslovakia and most of Ireland became independent nations. To that extent historical agitations were brought to an end and one of the immigrants' worlds ceased to exist. The city in which they lived was transformed: Boston's Back Bay and more and more of the South End and South Boston were reclaimed from water, more streets and railways were constructed, old buildings were torn down and new ones put up. New occupations, new demands for skill and education, exercised their influence. With rising income and savings, immigrants might begin the move to new and less purely ethnic districts, or see their children do so, while their original American home became flooded with newcomers from other parts of Europe. In not much more than half a century, parts of Boston changed from Yankee to Irish, and from Irish to Jewish or Italian. Similarly, the Catholic Church multiplied its churches and elaborated its parochial life, and instead of searching western Europe for trained priests, or sending its few American-born youths with a vocation to Montreal or Paris or Rome to be trained, it built colleges and seminaries, produced more and more of its own clergy at home, and by the end of the nineteenth century could support missions overseas. Not every change, of course, was forward and upward. The lives of millions of rather recent Americans were affected by the disaster, in the 1940s, to central Europe's Jewish communities.

Assimilation Was a Slow Process

The immigrants' place in their surviving worlds changed too. They came to understand more about America, advanced themselves at work, became more accepted by neighbours outside their own group, made more and more successful political claims. Inevitably, therefore, their perception of the relationship between their worlds, of their relative significance, also changed.

Even more was this true of later generations—but as soon as the words are used, qualifications have to be brought in. Generations were not simple blocks, placed edge to edge in time. In each immigrant group, for half a century or more, original immigrants grew a little more American, their children became assimilated much faster, but, simultaneously, newcomers continued to arrive. Moreover, in any state or

city, each ethnic group displayed a somewhat different balance between its generations, The 1890 census showed
Massachusetts to possess 657,000 foreign-born inhabitants:
it had half a million others, born in the United States but
with one or both of their parents born abroad. The oldest
group, the Irish, already had slightly more members of the
second generation than survivors of the first. By 1910, the
census showed more inhabitants of Massachusetts with foreign parentage than had been born abroad. The Irish had a
ratio of almost two to one, the Canadians had a small preponderance of the second generation, the British generations were approaching equality. New York State's Germans,
like its Irish, had a larger second generation, while, as might
be expected, Italians, and peoples from Austria-Hungary and
Russia, were dominated by recent arrivals. The overall
foreign-ness of certain states and cities was therefore great,
enough to impress all observers and horrify some old-stock
Americans: as early as 1890, only 300,000 of New York
City's one-and-a-half million inhabitants had both parents
born in America. But it is the variety of stages of development, as between one group and another, that impresses the
modern scholar even more. Variety, of course, was further
extended by differences in personal attitudes as between
members of any group. American Yiddish developed several
words to denote such shades of difference: *deitschuks* (assimilated like German Jews), *machers* (men of affairs), *alrightniks*
(smart climbers), *lodgeniks* (joiners), *radikalke* (emancipated
women), and *ototots* (half-assimilated men who compromised
by wearing only a very small beard). Only when reinforce-
ments from the old country ceased, and the immigrants died
in large numbers, was assimilation likely to accelerate
markedly and the group's institutional life fall into decline.
Even then, the second generation was likely to have mixed
attitudes, and the third, unrecognized in the censuses and
swallowed up in the category "native," might still display
traces of its ethnic heritage in the way members chose their
marriage partners or cast their votes.

Ethnic groups were not all the same, even though it is
easy to identify many common needs. An Englishman's situ-

ation, on arrival at Fall River from a Lancashire mill town to do an identical job, was very different from that of a French-Canadian farm worker arrived in the same town, and from that of a Slovak peasant just arrived in the steel mills of Homestead, Pennsylvania. A Russian Jew, who despaired of prosperity, dignity, and even safety in the Pale [of settlement, or Jewish sector], and who in crossing the Atlantic knew that he was making an irrevocable fresh start, was very

---

Immigrant Children Were Caught Between Two Worlds

Italian American Richard Gambino remembered that the children of emigrants from southern Italy were encouraged to follow "the true way" ("la via vecchia") by their parents, but they faced other messages at school.

It was a rending confrontation. The parents of the typical second-generation child ridiculed American institutions and sought to nurture in him *la via vecchia.* The father nurtured in his children (sons especially) a sense of mistrust and cynicism regarding the outside world. And the mother bound her children (not only daughters) to the home by making any aspirations to go beyond it seem somehow disloyal and shameful. Thus, outward mobility was impeded. Boys were pulled out of school and sent to work at the minimum legal age, or lower, and girls were virtually imprisoned in the house. Education, the means of social and economic mobility in the United States, was largely blocked to the second generation, because schools were regarded not only as alien but as immoral by the immigrant parents. When members of this generation did go to school the intrinsic differences between American and Southern-Italian ways were sharpened even further for them. The school, the employer and the media taught them, implicitly and often perhaps inadvertently, that Italian ways were inferior, while the immigrant community constantly sought to reinforce them.

Richard Gambino, "Twenty Million Italian-Americans Can't Be Wrong," *New York Times Magazine,* April 30, 1972.

different from a Sicilian labourer who hoped in a few years to save enough from his American wages to buy land back home. Skills, ambitions, attitudes to education and to success, all differed greatly from group to group; and immigrants' opportunities and problems also varied according to the American environment in which they lived, and the stage at which they arrived in America's rapid growth.

Conflicts Between Immigrant Parents and Americanized Children

For all these reasons there could be nothing simple about assimilation. It should not be viewed as a steady fading of memories, as a smooth transition from one set of relationships, one dominant immigrant world, to another. Rather, against a background of most complex change, it was a series of conflicts between competing influences, one environment pressing upon another, influences from the wider American society battling with the entrenched leadership of heads of families or of ethnic institutions. Some parents deplored the loss of their authority over their children's behaviour and over their earnings, and bitterly contrasted the American situation with that of the stable world of the old village. Although Poles and other Slav peoples felt this very acutely, Jews too were sometimes aware of it. "Once you used to get respect and honour at least," one of them complained. "Here they throw you away. You become a back number." Jewish parents, however, might react very differently. Mary Antin put it thus: "They had no standards to go by, seeing America was not Polotzk." Handing over his children, as did Mary's father, to the public school "as if it were an act of consecration," a parent might defer excessively to his children's ways, or he might expect too much success to follow from their new advantages. For their part, children might dislike their parents' language, resent their religious orthodoxy, rebel against the attempt to limit their dating and arrange their marriages. Yet they could not wholly break away: they felt the pull of affection, and they knew that their acceptance by older Americans was far from complete. The change that occurred, whatever might be individual attitudes, can be seen in two Polish examples. Quite early in the Polish migration, a Pole in America accepted a bride from the old country, sight unseen, on the basis of a recommendation from a family whose reputation in his home village was beyond question. Half a century later, a third-generation Polish woman explained that she could speak English but scarcely write it, so completely had her parochial school been run in the old language. Yet she could point to the contrast between her own generation and her mother's, which wore shawls over their heads as in Poland, and knew no English at all. Even more significant, "the boys and girls marry for love. The parents don't select the persons they are to marry."

Ways of life outside the family were equally in dispute. After the Great War, French-Canadian organizations in New England were issuing statements defending the old language. In the 1930s, two generations of Jews in a small Massachusetts town were disputing bitterly the seating arrangements in their synagogue, and the style of its service. Roman Catholic parochial schools were being used, not only to inculcate religious and ethnic values in children, but, through those children, to influence parents. Rural Lutherans in the Middle West in the 1940s were arguing furiously about the character of social activities to be permitted in their high school. Ethnic institutions, however, might themselves help prepare their members for assimilation. Some were designed, from the start, to encourage people to take out first papers for citizenship. Others, social in their emphasis, gave symbolic expression to their respect for the United States by putting up, as in the Slovenes' hall at Waukegan, Illinois, a portrait of [President Abraham] Lincoln, and by planning to add similar pictures of [President George] Washington and [Woodrow] Wilson.

Chapter 3

Emigration from Asia

America Wanted Asian Laborers

Ronald Takaki

The United States of America expanded greatly in the nineteenth century. Territorial expansion not only stretched America to the Pacific Ocean, but it was also reflected in the emergence of American economic interests in such faraway areas as the Hawaiian Islands. Agricultural and industrial expansion allowed Americans to make these new territories productive. A major feature of this expansion was the construction of a network of railroads to transport people and goods.

All of this activity required laborers. As historian Ronald Takaki points out in the following selection, American agriculturalists, factory owners, and railroad builders saw Asia as a potential source of labor. At various points between the 1850s and 1920s, Chinese, Japanese, Korean, East Indian, and Filipino laborers all made their way to Hawaii or the American mainland to help build America. However, as Takaki asserts, employers used Asian workers to keep wages down or to control other groups of laborers.

Ronald Takaki is professor of history at the University of California at Berkeley. There, he designed and heads the university's renowned ethnic studies program.

"Get labor first," sugar planters in Hawaii calculated, "and capital will follow." During the second half of the nineteenth century, they ushered in a modern economy and made sugar "King." Mostly American businessmen and sons of American missionaries, the planters transformed this archipelago into a virtual economic colony of the United States. They were instrumental in arranging the 1875 Reciprocity Treaty between the governments of Hawaii and the United States, which permitted the island kingdom to export sugar to America duty free. Investments in cane growing became a "mania," and the production of sugar jumped from 9,392 tons in 1870 to 31,792 tons ten years later to nearly 300,000 tons in 1900. Between 1875 and 1910, cultivated plantation lands multiplied nearly eighteen times, or from 12,000 to 214,000 acres. Sugar was Hawaii's most important export: in 1897, a year before the United States annexed the islands, sugar exports accounted for $15.4 million out of an export total of $16.2 million.

Before this tremendous growth of the sugar industry could occur, planters had to find labor. They were reluctant to invest capital in sugar production as long as they had to depend on Hawaiian labor. Native workers were not abundantly available because their population had been declining precipitously for several decades. Moreover, Hawaiian workers generally were not easily disciplined; farming and fishing offered them alternative means of survival. In 1850 planters founded the Royal Hawaiian Agricultural Society to introduce workers from China. Two years later, after the arrival of the first Chinese contract laborers, the president of the society predicted: "We shall find Coolie labor to be far more certain, systematic, and economic than that of the native. They are prompt at the call of the bell, steady in their work, quick to learn, and will accomplish more [than Hawaiian laborers]." To satisfy their demand for labor, planters scoured the world—mainly Asia, but also Europe—in search of workers. . . .

Working the Hawaiian Sugar Fields

In their orders for laborers, planters systematically developed an ethnically diverse work force as a mechanism of control. During the 1850s, they used Chinese laborers to set an "example" for the Hawaiian workers. Managers hoped the Hawaiians would be "naturally jealous" of the foreigners and "ambitious" to outdo them. They encouraged the Chinese to call the native workers "wahine! wahine!" [Hawaiian for "women! women!"]

Three decades later, realizing they had become too dependent on Chinese laborers, planters turned to Portuguese workers. "We need them," they explained, "especially as an offset to the Chinese. . . . We lay great stress on the necessity of having our labor mixed. By employing different nationalities, there is less danger of collusion among laborers, and the employers [are able to] secure better discipline." Meanwhile, planters initiated the importation of Japanese laborers as "the principle check upon the Chinese, in keeping down the price of labor." During the 1890s, planters recruited laborers from both China and Japan, thinking "discipline would be easier and labor more tractable if Chinese were present or obtainable in sufficient numbers to play off against the Japanese in case of disputes.". . .

[By 1900], however, planters could no longer import Chinese laborers, for Hawaii had been annexed to the United States and federal laws prohibiting Chinese immigration had been extended to the new territory. Worried the "Japs" were "getting too numerous," planters scrambled for new sources of labor. "There is a movement on foot [sic]," wrote the director of H. Hackfield and Company to planter [George] Wilcox on December 22, 1900, "to introduce Puerto Rican laborers, and also some Italians, Portuguese, and Negroes from the South. . . . We would ask you to let us know at your earliest convenience how many laborers of each nationality you need." A year later, planters transported two hundred blacks from Tennessee to Hawaii.

But planters preferred to "mix the labor races" by dividing the work force "about equally between two Oriental nationalities." Consequently, they turned to Korea as a new source of Asian labor, and they developed a plan to import Koreans and "pit" them against the "excess of Japanese." In 1903, they introduced Korean workers on the plantations, certain the Koreans were "not likely to combine with the Japanese at any attempt at strikes." An official of William G. Irwin and Company, a labor supplier, predicted: "The Korean immigration scheme which has been inaugurated will in due course give us an element which will go far towards not only assisting labor requirements but will be of great service in countering the evil effects in the labor market caused by too great a preponderance of Japanese." A planter, angry at Japanese workers for demanding higher wages, asked William G. Irwin and Company to send him a shipment of Korean laborers soon: "In our opinion, it would be advisable, as soon as circumstances permit, to get a large number of Koreans in the country . . . and drive the Japs out."

But the Korean labor supply was cut off when the Korean government prohibited emigration to Hawaii in 1905. A year later, the planters began bringing laborers from the Philippines, a U.S. territory acquired from Spain after the 1898 war. Labor recruiter Albert F. Judd, displaying the first group of Filipino laborers on the dock in Honolulu, promised that if the Filipino were treated right, he would be a "first-class laborer," "possibly not as good as the Chinaman or the Jap, but steady, faithful and willing to do his best for any boss for whom he has a liking." Shortly afterward planters imported massive numbers of Filipino workers. The 1908 Gentlemen's Agreement restricted the emigration of Japanese laborers and the 1909 Japanese strike threatened planter control of the work force. During the strike, on July 28, 1909, the labor committee of the Hawaiian Sugar Planters' Association reported that several hundred Filipino laborers were en route to Hawaii: "It may be too soon to say that the Jap is to be supplanted, but it is certainly in order to take steps to clip his wings [and to give] encouragement to a new class [Filipinos] . . . to keep the more belligerent element in its proper place." Again, like the Chinese and Koreans, the Filipinos were used to control and discipline Japanese workers. One planter, for example, complained to C. Brewer and Company about the high wages demanded by the Japanese laborers on his plantation. On August 7, he wrote to the company: "If possible for you to arrange it I should very much like to get say 25 new Filipinos to put into our day gang. . . . In this way perhaps we can stir the Japs a bit." Twenty days later, he wrote again, stating that he was very pleased to receive the shipment of thirty Filipinos and that he hoped he could use them to bring the Japanese workers to "their senses."

From Hawaii to the Mainland

Like the planters in Hawaii, businessmen on the U.S. mainland were aware of the need to "get labor first." Many of them saw that advances in technology had transformed Asia into a new source of labor for American capitalism. Steam transportation had brought Asia to America's "door" and given American industries access to the "surplus" labor of "unnumbered millions" in Asia. "Cheap" Chinese labor was now "available." In an article entitled, "Our Manufacturing Era," published in the *Overland Monthly* in 1869, Henry Robinson described California's enormous economic potential: it had every variety of climate and soil for the production of raw material, a nearly completed railroad, an abundance of fuel and water power, markets in Asia and the Pacific, and an unlimited supply of low-wage labor from China. "If society must have 'mudsills,' it is certainly better to take them from a race which would be benefitted by even that position in a civilized community, than subject a portion of our own race to a position which they have outgrown." Robinson concluded: "If Chinese labor could be used to develop the industries of California, it would be the height of folly to forbid its entrance to the Golden Gate." A California farmer stated frankly that he could not get white labor to do stoop labor in the fields: "I must employ Chinamen or give up." Noting the need for Chinese workers for the railroads, agriculture, and manufacturing, San Francisco minister Otis Gibson reported in 1877 that there was a constant demand for Chinese labor all over the Pacific Coast because reliable white labor was not available at wages capital could afford to pay. . . .

But the Chinese could also be pitted against and used to discipline white workers. E.L. Godkin of *The Nation* predicted that the importation of Chinese labor would become a favorite method of resisting white workers' strikes now that American capital had within its reach millions of Chinese "ready to work for small wages." In California, a traveler reported in 1870: "In the factories of San Francisco they had none but Irish, paying them three dollars a day in gold. They struck, and demanded four dollars. Immediately their

Japanese farm workers pick fruit in California. Demand for labor resulted in farmers employing Japanese to meet labor needs.

places, numbering three hundred, were supplied by Chinamen at one dollar a day." Capital used Chinese laborers as a transnational industrial reserve army to weigh down white workers during periods of economic expansion and to hold white labor in check during periods of overproduction. Labor was a major cost of production, and employers saw how the importation of Chinese workers could boost the supply of labor and drive down the wages of both Chinese and white workers. The resulting racial antagonism generated between the two groups helped to ensure a divided working class and a dominant employer class.

Six years after the Chinese Exclusion Act of 1882, Japanese labor was introduced: sixty Japanese were brought to Vacaville [California] to pick fruit. During the 1890s, the demand for farm labor rose sharply with the development of sugar-beet agriculture. By the turn of the century, farmers in California were complaining about tons of fruit and vegetables rotting in the fields as a result of the labor shortage, and increasingly they were employing Japanese to meet their labor needs. Testifying before a congressional committee in 1907, sugar-beet king John Spreckels said: "If we do not have the Japs to do the field labor, we would be in a bad fix, because you know American labor will not go into the fields." Farmers saw another advantage in the use of Japanese labor. "The Japs just drift—we don't have to look out for them," explained an official of the California Fruit Growers' Exchange. "White laborers with families, if we could get them, would be liabilities."

Demanding Higher Pay

By then, however, farmers were facing demands for higher wages from Japanese workers. In 1907, the *California Fruit Grower* complained that "the labor problem" had become "extremely troublesome." Labor was in shortage and employers had been forced to increase wages. What was needed, the journal recommended, was the introduction of Asian-Indian laborers. "Not long ago a small colony of full-blooded Sikhs arrived from India, some of whom are now working in Fresno vineyards. . . . A report is current that a scheme is on foot [sic] to railroad these people into the United States by hordes. . . ." A year later California farmers employed Asian Indians as "a check on the Japanese," paying them twenty-five cents less per day. Shortly after the introduction of Sikh laborers in 1908, John Spreckels told a congressional committee that "if it had not been for the large number of these East Indians coming in there . . . we would have had to take all Japs."

During the 1920s, farmers turned to Mexico as their main source of labor: at least 150,000 of California's 200,000 farm laborers were Mexican. An official for the California Fruit Growers' Association praised the Mexican workers. Unlike the Chinese and Japanese, they were "not aggressive." Instead they were "amenable to suggestions" and did their work obediently. Fearful Mexicans would be placed on a quota basis under the Immigration Act of 1924, growers began to import Filipino laborers, for the Philippines was a territory of the United States and represented an unimpeded supply of labor. "The Filipinos," reported the *Pacific Rural Press*, "are being rushed in as the Mexicans are being rushed out." In 1929 the Commonwealth Club of California stated that the "threat of Mexican exclusion" had created an "artificial demand for Filipino laborers," the "only remaining substitute in the cheap labor field." A representative of the Watsonville Chamber of Commerce told an interviewer in 1930: "We don't want the Filipino and Mexican excluded. Raising the crops that we do it is necessary to have a supply of this labor."

Nor did California farmers want other groups of workers excluded, for a racially diverse labor force enabled them to exercise greater control over their workers. Frank Waterman of the state employment agency told an interviewer in 1930 how farmers could get a maximum amount of work out of Japanese and Chinese workers: "Put a gang of Chinese in one field and a gang of Japanese in the next, and each one works like hell to keep up with or keep ahead of the other." Noting the presence of Mexican, Chinese, Japanese, Asian Indian, Portuguese, Korean, Puerto Rican, and Filipino farm workers, the California Department of Industrial Relations reported that growers preferred to employ "a mixture of laborers of various races, speaking diverse languages, and not accustomed to mingling with each other. The practice [was] intended to avoid labor trouble which might result from having a homogeneous group of laborers of the same race or nationality. Laborers speaking different languages [were] not as likely to arrive at a mutual understanding which would lead to strikes."

Chinese and Japanese Emigrants Find Their Way

Robert A. Wilson and Bill Hosokawa

The first major groups of Asian emigrants were those from China and Japan. Many Chinese came to the United States in the 1840s and 1850s, seeking to take advantage of the development and settlement of California in the Gold Rush era. After anti-Chinese agitation resulted in the so-called Chinese Exclusion Act of 1882, which largely ended Chinese emigration for many years, Japanese laborers were sought in their stead.

In the following selection, Robert A. Wilson and Bill Hosokawa examine the ways in which Chinese and Japanese emigrants established themselves in the United States. Often, for instance, they settled in familiar communities; the Japanese, in fact, gravitated toward the established Chinatowns in West Coast cities. In addition, the authors demonstrate that both Chinese and Japanese emigrants developed their own support societies, cultural associations, and groups of community leaders. Such efforts helped immigrants to, among other things, keep alive ties to their homelands as well as prosper in their new country.

Robert A. Wilson was professor of Japanese history at the University of California at Los Angeles. Bill Hosokawa is the author of many books on Japanese American life, including *Nisei* and *The Two Worlds of Jim Yoshida*.

To most white Americans, Japanese and Chinese looked and acted very much alike. This is understandable in that they had certain characteristics in common. Many Caucasians professed to be unable to distinguish one Oriental from an-

From pages 102–108 of *East to America*, by Robert A. Wilson and Bill Hosokawa. Copyright © 1980 by Robert A. Wilson and Bill Hosokawa. Reprinted by permission of HarperCollins Publishers, Inc.

other. But anyone making the effort to look beneath surface similarities would have perceived significant differences. The story of how each group became established in the United States, and how they reacted to the American challenge, is also quite different.

Both the push and the pull played a part in the earliest Chinese immigration. The push was economic depression that hit Kwangtung [Guangdong] Province in South China after its chief city, Canton, lost its monopoly of trade with the Western World in the 1840's. The economic difficulties were compounded by flood and famine, creating a definite push to leave the area in search of something more promising. Thus it was that the earliest Chinese immigrants came to the United States from Canton Province, five districts in particular.

The pull was the developing need for contract laborers in California, men to undertake the hard and menial work of a frontier region. In much the pattern that the Japanese were to follow a half century later, enterprising Chinese established urban footholds after periods of labor on farms and forests. By the 1850's, Chinese businesses of various kinds were to be found in several sections of San Francisco. The ghetto character of the San Francisco Chinatown developed later, partly as lonely immigrants were drawn together by common language and cultural heritage, and partly as a defensive reaction to white hostility.

The term "Chinatown" was in popular usage long before the Japanese appeared in significant numbers. Indeed, some of the earliest Japanese arrivals found the Chinatown atmosphere reassuring and worked and lived there until their own ethnic communities came into being.

Chinese, like many other immigrants, were generally of the lower socio-economic class. As a rule they came under indenture or the credit-ticket system, and were burdened with substantial debts which amounted to more than just the cost of passage from China. Out of this status developed a system of control which cost the individual much of his freedom until the debt was repaid.

The China that the immigrants left was more a culture

than a nation-state. South China had never become fully reconciled to the Manchu dynasty in Peking and the imperial government exercised little influence over the Chinese in America. Thus, the attachment of the Chinese to their homeland was more in terms of cultural traditions than politics. They had come from a civilization that regarded outsiders as *fan kuei* (foreign devils) and it is understandable that they should respond in kind to the prejudices they encountered. It is also understandable that they should regard their Old World institutions as superior to that of the West. Thus, many preferred life in the ghetto, where they could retain their traditions. Though they worked "out," they liked to live "in." In Chinatown they reproduced Chinese institutions, continued to wear the queue [a long, braided pigtail] until the overthrow of the Manchus who had imposed it on them as a sign of submission, continued to wear Chinese clothing, and made few compromises toward acculturation and integration.

Aid Societies for Chinese Immigrants

Among the immigrants were a few members of revolutionary, anti-Manchu secret societies. Not surprisingly, secret societies became a feature of Chinese life in America. In time they dominated the Chinatown underworld and lost their revolutionary character. They were conservative in the sense that, having won a measure of power, they became status quo oriented. Their activities centered largely around control of gambling and prostitution, charitable activities among members, or conflict with rival secret societies. (In this sense they were not unlike the gambling clubs that became a part of early Japanese American communities. In fact the Japanese justified their clubs as providing outlets so gamblers would not take their money to the Chinese.) Only occasionally did the secret societies show any interest in China's political problems, and never did they concern themselves with American politics aside from petty bribes to local police.

The Chinese in America also developed clan associations made up of persons bearing the same surname. They functioned as a kind of immigrant aid society as well as an instrument of discipline. Marriage was not permitted between persons of the same surname. The clan association was likely to be the immigrant's first contact after arrival. It helped him find food and shelter and often, employment. The association also never permitted the immigrant to lose sight of his obligations to family and village in China. Associations of all who spoke a common dialect also came into being. . . .

Associations of district, clan, language, and secret societies all were the support structure which maintained the overall authority of an umbrella organization popularly known as the Chinese Six Companies . . . , but officially titled Chinese Consolidated Benevolent Association. The extent of "benevolence" is difficult to determine; those in need were taken care of, those who died were given the traditional amenities. When in trouble the immigrant looked to the association, or one of its subsidiary groups, for help, protection, and guidance. But at least in the earlier years of his life as an immigrant, his debt was the overwhelming factor in his life. Collection of this debt was certain until 1880 since it was necessary for anyone returning to China to secure clearance from the Six Companies before steamship companies would sell him passage. (The United States enforces a somewhat similar regulation today: Resident aliens leaving the country must present an Internal Revenue document certifying they have paid income taxes due.) The Six Companies maintained order and discipline within the community and also dealt with the white man's world outside. And as the years passed, that became an increasingly hostile world.

A Mostly Male Community

The early Chinatowns were overcrowded, disease- and poverty-ridden slums marked by a terrible sexual imbalance. It was common practice for village elders to insist on the marriage of a young man about to go abroad. Since he lacked the means to take his bride with him, the husband went alone while his wife stayed with his parents, in many cases as a virtual servant. The presence of a wife in China tied the young man to his homeland and provided a lien on his earnings. The remitting of earnings to his family was often delayed until the immigrant had met his other obligations. Thus, few but merchants and the wealthy were able to bring their wives with them. The more successful immigrants could send for their wives or, as often happened, they returned home for periodic visits during which they sired a succession of children. The Chinese Exclusion Act of 1882 barred not only laborers but the wives of laborers already in this country, effectively sealing off even the small influx of women that existed. Thus, custom and law dictated that a sexual imbalance be perpetuated until contemporary times.

The United States had virtually no immigration policy when the Chinese initially came to the California gold fields. They were a largely helpless minority quickly brutalized in the raw frontier atmosphere of the American West. "John Chinaman" got the hardest, most menial, most undesirable jobs at the lowest pay. He was discriminated against legally; he was not permitted to testify on his own behalf in some courts when be stepped forward to accuse a white man of theft, fraud, or a physical beating. The harassment escalated to new heights after the transcontinental railroad was completed in 1869. Thousands of Chinese who had been employed by the Central Pacific were thrown on the labor market to compete with white men for jobs. Attempts to use the Chinese as strikebreakers in Massachusetts, New Jersey, and Pennsylvania, and on Southern plantations as a club to discipline recently freed blacks were unsuccessful. These attempts served only to stir up anti-Chinese feeling. Organized movements against them were spawned, and in 1877, . . . an Irish immigrant, Dennis Kearney, founded the Workingmen's Party in California to agitate for exclusion of all Chinese.

Kearney and his associates soon found the Burlingame Treaty of 1868 made provisions for Chinese immigration. To stop immigration it was necessary to change the treaty. A diplomatic offensive would be required with the help of a rapidly forming anti-Chinese political coalition in Congress.

Excluding Chinese but Accepting Japanese Immigrants

China would not agree to total exclusion, but in 1880 the imperial government accepted the right of the United States to suspend immigration of laborers. Congress quickly followed up with the Chinese Exclusion Act of 1882 which barred all immigration for ten years. The act was renewed in 1892 and 1902, and after that it was kept in effect until 1943 when Congress was made aware of the injustice of excluding as undesirable the citizens of an ally in the war against the Axis powers. It was the exclusion of Chinese laborers after 1882 that opened the doors of opportunity for the first Japanese immigrants. . . .

The first Japanese community of substance, not surprisingly, also developed in San Francisco. They came from a nation in the throes of vast change caused by the impact of the West. They represented a culture which was in large part borrowed from China. Perhaps conscious of their cultural debt to the Asian Continent, the Japanese brought with them a resiliency and adaptability that was to serve them well in America. Yet they were keenly conscious of their identity as Japanese and possessed a pride which sustained them in times of trial.

The first Japanese usually settled close to Chinatowns. Separation into distinct communities seems to have been in part a consequence of developments in Asia. Japan's victory over China in their war of 1894–95 led to some hostility in San Francisco and Honolulu, particularly when the Japanese celebrated. The Chinese now had to accept the military superiority of a people they had long regarded as inferior.

Census takers in 1890 found enough Japanese to comprise an ethnic community only in San Francisco. In the next decade Japan towns developed in Sacramento, Fresno, Portland, Seattle, Tacoma, and Salt Lake City.

In contrast to Japanese in labor gangs, who were largely insulated from American society, the urban dwellers early came to grips with it. Many attended language schools, usually operated by Christian churches. Some established restaurants catering to Western or Japanese tastes or both. Inexpensive hotels and boardinghouses came under Japanese management, as did laundries, bathhouses, barbershops, and stores specializing in Japanese goods. The businesses that prospered were those that catered to the needs of other Japanese, services that were unobtainable for various reasons in the larger community. Just as Chinatown had been a service center for Chinese laborers entering the country or returning from seasonal employment, so Japan towns were sanctuaries for Japanese "birds of passage."

Established Japanese American Families and Communities

As women arrived in increasing numbers during the first two decades of [the twentieth] century the original pattern of these urban Japanese communities changed. And with their coming, Japanese families were established and Nisei children became a growing and progressively more important part of the scene.

Governance in these communities within cities is not easy to discern. Unlike Chinatown, where power was exercised by the Six Companies, power within Japan town was diffuse. Priests and ministers, newspaper publishers, leaders of the local Japanese associations . . . , heads of local prefectural associations . . . , bankers and business leaders, and at least in the early period, Japanese consular officials—all these and perhaps others participated in determining proper Japanese behavior.

Out of this welter of forces emerged certain men who, as elder statesmen, became the accepted community leaders. Although they often quarreled among themselves, they nevertheless dominated the community and were responsible for policy and tactics in maintaining order within and dealing with the white community without. They prevailed, not through wealth or power or violence, but through general acquiescence by a people accustomed to status and order. They were the American counterpart of those who dominated comparable communities in Japan.

Unlike the Chinese, who paid little or no attention to Chinese government officials, the immigrant Japanese acknowledged the authority of Japanese consular representatives. So long as the immigrants lived in expectation of returning in time to Japan, they regarded consular officials as a tie to the homeland. This also was understandable in that the immigrants, being denied American citizenship, had to retain their Japanese nationality or become stateless.

The rise of hostility toward the Japanese caused them to organize against it. The triggering event was a bubonic plague scare in 1900 when, following the annexation of Hawaii to the United States, thousands of Japanese contract laborers left the sugar plantations to seek a better life on the mainland. The sudden influx, which alarmed the West, coincided with the reported discovery of one case of plague in San Francisco's Chinatown. Mayor James D. Phelan ordered the Chinese and Japanese sections of the city quarantined. This was a totally uncalled-for medical precaution which the Japanese correctly read as anti-Oriental discrimination. To coordinate their efforts to combat it, the Japanese organized the *Zaibei Nihonjin Kyogikai* which was reorganized in 1905 as the Japanese Association of America. . . . It became a loose federation of regional organizations with relatively little actual power.

By 1924, approximately 12 percent of the immigrant Japanese were members. This was not a large membership, but it included the most influential segment of the population. In that year the Southern California region headquartered in Los Angeles had some twenty affiliates. The Northern California unit included thirty-eight locals in northern and central portions of the state. An office in Seattle was headquarters for units in Washington and Montana. Another office in Portland had affiliates in Oregon and Idaho. Affiliates also were organized in Colorado, Arizona, Utah, Texas, Illinois, and New York City. As the organization purporting to represent all Japanese, it tried to be a unifying force, but it had to contend with a certain amount of provincialism. The Japanese Association of America has been characterized as a coordinating rather than controlling group. It had five departments of concern—finance, social welfare, commerce, education, and young people's welfare. With none of the support structure such as underpinned the Six Companies, the Japanese associations exercised little social influence and none of the economic power that made the Chinese organization such a dominant force.

Chinese Emigrants Adapted Well

Jack Chen

Chinese emigrants, usually from the Guangdong Province in southern China, began to come to the United States in the 1840s and 1850s. Not only did these immigrants seek to escape instability and poverty at home, but they also believed they could prosper in the United States and, perhaps, return to Guangdong rich. For most Chinese, their destination was California, referred to by some as Gold Mountain. The Chinese, indeed, were part of the life of California from the time it first became part of the union.

As Jack Chen points out in the following selection, Chinese workers sometimes worked in the gold fields, but more frequently they were either contract laborers for railroad builders or started support businesses in the booming Gold Rush city of San Francisco. Chen writes that Chinese workers prospered in a variety of San Francisco businesses and contributed a great deal to the city's early cultural life. Moreover, Chen asserts, the Chinese had little trouble adapting themselves to the needs of their new home as well as assimilating into American society.

Jack Chen, a historian, worked for the journal *Peking Review* in China for many years before immigrating to the United States and working as a university lecturer and writer.

The early Chinese immigrants . . . faced the choice between working in the mines and catering to the mines and miners by working in the towns, serving the Gold Rush and the cities' populations. Of the 30,000 or so Chinese in California in the 1850s—and that means in the United States—over

50 percent chose to work and live in San Francisco. The rest were in the Mother Lode on the flanks of the Sierra.

The few Chinese who lived in the small settlement of San Francisco in 1848 were scattered over its area. The liberal atmosphere of the new land allowed them to live more or less where they pleased. In 1850, there was a camp for fishermen, for instance, out at Rincon or China Point. With twenty-five boats, in 1852, they were bringing 3,000 pounds of fish to market every day.

Chinese merchants were established at several locations in the town. Later, in 1850, when some 700 Chinese were in the city, economics dictated that their restaurants, laundries, and shops should cluster around the hotels that had grown up in the then center of the city, Portsmouth Square. The St. Francis Hotel, Brown's City Hotel, the Parker House Hotel, the Opera House, and some Chinese restaurants were on the square or within a block of it. Business was good, and so was the service. There was also a cluster of Chinese businesses and houses on Clay Street between Stockton and Kearny. As their numbers grew, they branched out into neighboring streets, to present-day Grant, to the north, and along Kearny. Called "Little Canton" in 1850, this area had thirty-three retail stores, some fifteen pharmacies (Chinese herbal cures were much appreciated in a city with few doctors), and five restaurants serving both Chinese and non-Chinese. This was the beginning of San Francisco's "Chinatown," the oldest and largest in the United States. Chinatown was so christened by the press in 1853.

Restaurants

Chinese restaurants marked themselves with triangular flags of yellow silk. They early earned a name for themselves in a city famous for its varied and excellent cuisines—French, Italian, Spanish, and Anglo-American. Connoisseurs were probably the more delighted with them because at that time there was no attempt to conciliate Western tastes. The gold miner William Shaw, writing in *Golden Dreams and Walking Realities* (1851), declared that

the best eating houses in San Francisco are those kept by Celestials and conducted Chinese fashion. The dishes are mostly curries, hashes and fricasee served up in small dishes and as they are exceedingly palatable, I was not curious enough to enquire as to the ingredients.

It was a custom in this easygoing city to offer patrons of saloons and restaurants meals of as much as one could eat for a set price. Chinese restaurants followed this trend. Bayard Taylor, the roving reporter of the *New York Tribune* at that time, wrote that "Chinese meals cost $1 to eat as much as you like at Kong-Sung's near the water, Whang Tong's on Sacramento Street, and Tong Ling's on Jackson Street."

From the very start, as the Chinese population in California grew, merchants began to import Chinese foodstuffs. Chinese farmers were soon growing the fresh vegetables and herbs that a Chinese cook must have, and fishermen in the Bay were bringing in the seafood delicacies the southern Chinese love: shrimp, seaweed, abalone, squid, and fresh fish in great variety. The result is that, from then until now, the food cooked in most Chinese houses and the best restaurants is the same as that cooked in the mother country. Quite a number of Chinese eating places, however, served Western fare.

The flourishing of Chinese restaurants to this day is proof enough of their excellence and the demand for them in San Francisco, which still has the habit of "dining out," part of the tradition of the early days of a pioneer, bachelor society in which most men had no real home. Like Chinatown itself, restaurants are an essential ingredient of the tourist lure that now brings the city over three million tourists and one billion tourist dollars a year. . . .

Shops and Home Deliveries

Merchandising was another field in which the Chinese made their contribution to the California style of living, not only through their shops but also through their services as distributors and peddlers of goods. In the early days, housewives looked forward to the fresh vegetables, fruits, and flowers the Chinese brought from house to house. It was the Chinese peddlers who introduced pampas grass to the home market, and this feathery decoration became a "must" in every Victorian household. The visit of a cloth trader was always a delightful event. The peddler did not use the hard-sell, aggressive techniques one usually associates today with house-to-house sales. He brought his goods neatly wrapped in a square of blue cotton cloth and transformed a living room into a private store of exotic wares from which the housewife could choose at her leisure.

Leaving Home

The words of this folk song reflect some of the doubts and concerns of Chinese emigrants seeking to make money in America.
In the second reign year of Haamfung [1852], a trip to Gold Mountain was made.

> With a pillow on my shoulder, I began my perilous journey:
> Sailing a boat with bamboo poles across the sea,
> Leaving behind wife and sisters in search of money,
> No longer lingering with the woman in the bedroom,
> No longer paying respect to parents at home.

Ronald Takaki, *A Different Mirror: A History of Multicultural America.* Boston: Little, Brown, 1993.

At many towns such as Bodie on the California-Nevada border, right up into the 1880s, when Chinese still formed a part of the town, they were the main providers of firewood to keep the communities warm. Vegetable, fruit, and flower peddlers carrying fresh produce in from the countryside were eagerly welcomed in towns where the horse and cart was still a luxury.

Domestics

The excellence of the Chinese as domestic workers was proverbial. They were widely regarded as splendid cooks, quick to learn Western ways of cooking and scrupulously clean when conditions allowed. They commanded good wages for those days, from $40 to $50 a month, as much as white servants or cooks. To this day on Nob Hill, the elite residential district of the city, you can still see the "Chinaman's room" in old houses, the dark basement room that a Victorian society considered suitable for domestic help to live in. Due to the absence of their own families, the Chinese usually lavished their affection on the children of their employers. This is attested to by innumerable testimonials and memoir after memoir. On Nob Hill, few homes did not boast of a Chinese domestic. In the rural areas, as J.H. Russell writes in *Cattle on the Conejo*, Chinese were almost always the ranch cooks up to about 1919.

The following exchange took place at the congressional hearing held on Chinese immigration in California in 1876:

> *Q:* "Why are [Chinese] employed as domestics?"
> *A:* (By Mr. Francis Avery, a longtime California resident) "Because they make better servants. . . . The wages paid them are the same as the wages paid by persons employing white servants."

In the City's Service

It was soon clear, once the gold mines had been exhausted, that San Francisco's destiny and lasting prosperity would be in trade. Trade needed plenty of land for warehouses, roads, and offices. Yerba Buena Cove was rapidly filled in and turned into dry land. Chinese were widely employed in this work in landfill operations and in manning the scows that brought sand to the landfill sites. They leveled and graded many San Francisco streets from 1855 to about 1870, under the contractor David Hewes. The first street graded was Bush, from Kearny to Mason Streets. Their last job was to level the old Yerba Buena cemetery for the building of a new city hall. In the early stages of his operations, Hewes used Chinese labor exclusively.

Before this work was done, the city had been notorious for its mud and potholes. In 1859, three bodies were found mired in the mud of Montgomery Street. On one occasion, a mule and wagon were lost in quicksand inside the city limits.

Building the City

The rapid population increase set off a building boom. Because of lack of local timber and skilled labor, it was profitable to import ready-made houses from many places, China among them. On one trip, the British ship *Kelso* brought in Chinese-made houses, together with the carpenters to put them up. Some of these houses used mortise joints that needed no nails, a decided savings in those days when all such things had to be imported into California, a developing country. Although men of many kinds hurried to California at the start of the Gold Rush, not many were skilled artisans. Whole stone buildings with their stones cut, shaped, and numbered were imported from China, together with the masons to put them up. The Parrott Building, the first stone building in San Francisco, was thus imported. It was the first commercial building of any importance in California. Its Chinese builders worked from sunrise to sundown according to a contract that paid them a dollar a day, a quarter-pound of fish, and a half-pound of rice.

The Parrott Building was due to be erected at the corner of Montgomery and California Streets, but the Chinese workmen protested that the *feng shui* (wind and water) orientation of the site was not propitious, and they refused to build it on the corner selected, preferring a site on the opposite corner. Despite their prognosis, it was built anyway in 1853 while Wells Fargo's new office was built at the propitious opposite corner. When the panic of 1855 occurred, there was a disastrous run on the two banks housed in the Parrott Building, and they went bankrupt. The Chinese who banked with Wells Fargo, however, were unperturbed. They disdained to withdraw their accounts from this good-luck bank, known to Chinese miners from one end of the Mother Lode to the other, and Wells Fargo weathered the financial storm to go on to become one of the largest financial institutions in the West with a capital today of $17 billion.

Entertainment

San Francisco was a rest and recreation center for the mining population, and the place where men came with their savings to take ship back home. Entertainment and the pleasures of the day—good food and song, dance and music, drink and less innocent vices—were part of San Francisco's reason for being. All tastes were catered to. One of the first Chinese theatrical performances in America was a puppet show staged in the back of a Chinese grocery store in Sacramento. Such shows became a regular feature of San Francisco entertainment and prepared the way for the Hook Took Tong, a Chinese theatrical troupe with 123 performers that opened with a program of Cantonese opera at the American Theater (October 18, 1852). This was so successful that the troupe imported its own theater building from China and erected it in Chinatown by the end of the year.

We also hear of a Chinese "Punch and Judy" show (probably a puppet show) on Portsmouth Plaza in the summer of 1853, of a "Chinese dancing salon where exhibitions were given of dancing by elaborately costumed performers" in 1854, and of jugglers and acrobats that astonished audiences.

In 1860, a Chinese play, *The Return of Sit Pin Quai*, a comedy, was performed at the Union Theater. The Chinese Theater, with its performances of Cantonese opera, quickly became one of the attractions of the city and Charles Nordhoff, writing in 1872, made it clear that a visit to the Chinese opera was a must for every tourist to San Francisco.

Gambling

The spirit of gambling was in the very air of California in Gold Rush days. Gold was at first easily obtained, and it was much a matter of chance. "Easy come, easy go" was a prevalent philosophy. And this was the spirit around the gambling tables. American and English gamblers preferred faro; Spanish and Italian liked monte. Stakes were often high. On one occasion, $200,000 was at stake on a monte table. The Chinese games were fantan and paijiu (lotteries). Everyone played dice. And when the Mining Stock Exchange opened in 1864 it had a ready made clientele of eager speculators.

A Home Away from Home

Far from being unassimilable, as the leaders of anti-Chinese campaigns later claimed, Chinese adapted their traditional skills to the service of the new land and integrated themselves into the society of pioneering California. The men who

worked in the mines and later on the railways were not essentially different from those who were so eagerly welcomed
into the intimacy of households as cooks and domestics.

Those who came as "sojourners," like those from Italy
and other lands, did not, of course, usually try to learn more
of the language than was needed to do their work; they simply did not try to make the great adjustments needed to become permanent residents because when they returned
home they would be like fish out of water.

The record shows that the relatively small number who
planned to make the United States their permanent home
were no less adaptable than other immigrants when convinced that adjustments in their way of work or life had to be
made as a condition of enjoying a prosperous and creative
life here. They quickly became part of the California scene.
They took part in its community parades and activities. In
1888 a champion Chinese hose company of firefighters in
Deadwood, South Dakota was generously eulogized. Many
photographs exist of Chinese participants in anniversary parades in San Francisco, Calistoga, and other towns. Their
contingents in the San Francisco ceremonies to pay tribute
to the memory of President Taylor and the admission of
California to statehood moved the daily *Alta California* to
eulogize them as "among the most industrious, quiet, patient
people among us. . . . They seem to live under our laws as if
born and bred under them."

Special mention must be made of the Chinese merchants.
Their scrupulous business dealings with their American
counterparts, the accepted understanding that their word
was their bond, had a great deal to do with creating a positive image of Chinese in America.

Tales of life in America were taken back to China, and despite reports of difficulties and worse, there were always
those who thought the chances of betterment made the risks
acceptable. The attraction of a voyage to California was
enormous. In the 1850s a laborer might earn $3 to $5 a
month in South China while a wage of $1 a day was common
in California. In the gold fields, a man might strike it lucky
in a single day and retire to his Guangdong village a rich

man. Working on the railway in the 1860s, he could earn $30–$35 a month and live on $15–$18 a month. With savings of $300–$400, he could return in triumph to his family. At the very least, he could send home $30 a year.

And these were not just stories. Returning immigrants and the hard cash they sent ahead of them were proof positive that an enterprising, hardworking man could succeed in the Golden Mountains of the United States. By the 1850s, it became a regular thing for any young man of spirit and filial piety to make the voyage. Emigration fever was endemic in the twenty-seven Guangdong areas that provided the bulk of Chinese immigrants to America.

The Japanese Were Unique Among Immigrant Groups

Thomas Sowell

According to Thomas Sowell, Japanese emigrants were different in many ways from other newcomers. They tended to be well educated, or at the very least literate. In addition, they were often selected by the Japanese government, which sought both effective representatives of Japan abroad and hoped that hardworking immigrants would be able to send remittances home. They also were those who, authorities believed, would be able to pay back their travel expenses.

Moreover, Sowell gives historical background on Japan. A new regime, the Meiji, took over Japan in 1868 and sought to modernize the country rapidly. This transformation, as elsewhere, inspired villagers to move first to cities and then, sometimes, to immigrate to new countries. The first Japanese emigrants left for Hawaii as agricultural laborers. They did this, however, long before Hawaii became an American possession in 1898. In the 1880s, due to bad economic conditions, the Japanese government authorized immigration to the mainland United States.

Thomas Sowell is currently a senior fellow at the Hoover Institution in Stanford, California. He has taught at Cornell and the University of California at Los Angeles and has been a columnist in a number of newspapers and magazines.

Meiji Japan was a country in which people could no longer simply follow ready-made patterns of work and life, as in feudal times, but now had to look for work and seek to make

From *Ethnic America*, by Thomas Sowell. Copyright © 1981 by BasicBooks, Inc. Reprinted by permission of BasicBooks, a member of Perseus Books, L.L.C.

a place for themselves in the world. Many sought opportunities overseas, where standards of living were much higher than in Japan. Contemporary American workers were earning five to ten times what Japanese workers were receiving in Japan. Although the Japanese had long been a village-bound people, the new economic conditions of the Meiji Era had made internal migration a familiar pattern, both to those who relocated to the city and those who became migratory workers moving from one end of the country to the other. The tension between village-consciousness and migratory work patterns was resolved by leaving and returning. Many traveled to seek economic benefits, within Japan and beyond, and yet came back to live among family and neighborhoods and to be buried with their ancestors. Leaving for a foreign land was not seen as emigration but as a sojourn, as in the manner of the Italians or the Chinese. But while many Japanese carried out their plans for return migration, many others did not—also like the Italians and the Chinese.

The decision to migrate, even temporarily, was not a random individual decision. Neither was the destination chosen. In Japan, as in other countries, the particular destinations and experiences of the initial emigrants strongly affected the later migration patterns of those from their respective localities in Japan. This continued to be true even in post–World-War II Japan. For example, 90 percent of those who emigrated from Miho Village in postwar Japan settled in one specific area of Canada. More than 90 percent of Okinawan immigrants to the United States went to Hawaii, while 8 percent reached the continental United States. In an earlier era, over half of all Okinawans from one district went to the Philippines. Ironically, one of the Japanese prefectures that sent a concentration of people to the United States during the initial immigration period and in the twentieth century was Hiroshima.

Part of the reason for such patterns were human ties based on family, friends, or local acquaintances. Partly it was the result of the activities of commercial recruitment organizations that found it economical to concentrate in a limited area in soliciting people to work overseas.

Japanese Laborers Go to Hawaii

Emigration began in the first year of the Meiji Era, 1868, when 148 contract laborers sailed from Japan to Hawaii. Mutual dissatisfaction of Hawaiians and Japanese led the Japanese government to intervene, repatriating some workers immediately and allowing no others to go to Hawaii for many years. Japan's interest in Japanese overseas, and its possession of the national power and prestige to intervene in their behalf, were factors distinguishing Japan from contemporary China, which was too weak to prevent itself from being dismembered, much less effectively act on behalf of overseas Chinese. The general effectiveness of Japan's control of working conditions abroad need not be exaggerated, however, but it was there and was an influence to be reckoned with.

Dire economic conditions in Japan in 1885 forced the Japanese government to reconsider its ban on immigration to Hawaii. In 1886, an informal agreement between Hawaii and Japan permitted the resumption of Japanese migration, which supplied the growing sugar plantations with much-needed workers. Japan controlled the selection of these temporary emigrants. Whereas the first Japanese emigrants had been urbanized workers from the prefectures of Hiroshima and Yamaguchi, the later contract laborers were from a farming and fishing community in the latter prefecture, avoiding the mismatching of workers and work that had contributed to the early mutual disappointments of the Japanese and the Hawaiians. Almost all the Japanese who went to Hawaii in this era became plantation workers in the sugarcane fields. They were overwhelmingly young males.

Japanese migration to the United States began in the same era as their movement to Hawaii, which did not become an American possession until 1898. Japanese migration to the mainland of the United States was just over 200 in the decade of the 1860s, less than 200 in the decade of the 1870s, but rose rapidly thereafter. More than 2,000 Japanese moved to the mainland of the United States during the 1880s, then tripled this during the 1890s and reached a peak of more than 100,000 in the first decade of the twentieth century. After the restrictive American immigration laws of the 1920s, very few Japanese entered the United States. The Japanese migration was predominantly male—seven times as many males as females in 1890 and twenty-four times as many in 1900—and involved much return migration.

Many stayed, however. Less than half the passports issued by Japan for travel to the United States in the 1880s and 1890s were ever returned, whereas most Japanese who went to Russia or China did return their passports. The sex imbalance among Japanese in Hawaii was less, although still substantial. There were three and a half males to every female among the Japanese in Hawaii in 1900, about two to one in 1910, and only 16 percent more males than females by 1930. The migration of Japanese to the United States thus had the classic characteristics of a temporary or tentative migration. The Japanese government in fact designated the emigrants as temporary, and American laws growing out of anti-Chinese feelings made Asians ineligible for American citizenship. Nevertheless, many who came chose to stay.

Describing the "Yellow Peril"

On the Irish holiday of St. Patrick's Day in 1900, a San Francisco newspaper published an article claiming that both Chinese and Japanese workers were a threat to society.

Chinatown with its reeking filth and dirt, its gambling dens and obscene slave pens, its coolie labor and blood-thirsty tongs, is a menace to the community; but the snivelling Japanese, who swarms along the streets and cringingly offers his paltry service for a suit of clothes and a front seat in our public schools, is a far greater danger to the laboring portion of society than all the opium-soaked pigtails who have ever blotted the fair name of this beautiful city.

Allen R. Bosworth, *America's Concentration Camps*. New York: Bantam Books, 1967.

The people who left Japan were usually neither the lowest nor the highest classes. Although the Japanese are justly known for their hard work and careful saving, such traits were by no means universal across the class structure. In

Meiji Japan, there were lower classes in which "the money earned by the right hand is quickly spent by the left hand" and in which absenteeism from work was common right after payday. Such people did not go to America. Neither did the nobility. The Japanese who migrated to Hawaii or to the United States were the ambitious young men of limited means, from farming backgrounds, who could get family and village notables to vouch for them and to agree to be responsible for their passage expenses.

Sending Money Home

They more than repaid their debts. The average amount of money sent back annually by migrants from the Hiroshima prefecture in the early twentieth century was more than two years' average earnings in Japan. Similar patterns were found in other prefectures. The average savings brought back to Japan by migrants from one district of Hiroshima were greater than the average annual income of the top one percent of the Japanese population. Such results reflected the great differences in economic conditions between Japan and the United States, as well as the frugality of Japanese migrants.

Many of those who returned to Japan could not only pay off obligations incurred for passage money but had enough left to buy substantial amounts of farmland or to go into business. Japanese villages that had many emigrants in the United States or migrants returning from the United States tended to be visibly more prosperous—even if they had been poverty-stricken before. Homes were more expensive and often of Western design. Nationally, the sums of money were significant alongside Japan's international balance of payments. Locally, as in Hiroshima prefecture; the remittances and sums brought back amounted to more than half as much as the whole prefecture government spent. In short, the importance of Japanese migrants in America was substantial in Japan. It may even be that the money earned in America helped build Hiroshima into such an industrial center that it became a prime military target in World War II. . . .

Unlike other nations, Japan did not send America its tired,

its poor, its huddled masses. The Japanese were perhaps unique among immigrants to America in the extent to which they were a highly selected sample of their homeland population. They were not usually from wealthy or affluent families, however. The average sum of money brought by Japanese immigrants to America ranged from about eleven dollars in 1896 to a high of twenty-six dollars in 1904—more like the poverty-stricken eastern and southern European immigrants than like the emigrants from northern and western Europe. Their selectivity was not financial but in terms of human potential.

The Hardworking First Generation

The male *Issei* [first-generation Japanese] were a group preselected in Japan by the government for their health, character, and willingness to work. They also grew up in an era when the people of Japan were predisposed to accept and emulate the American way of life. The women who sailed across the Pacific to join them in America were sufficiently traditional and dutiful to go halfway around the world to marry men selected for them, sight unseen, by their parents in Japan. Both the males and the females were an uncommon generation, in terms of their values and self-discipline. The rising role of Japan on the world scene made it easy for them to maintain their pride in being Japanese, while following American ideals that were already part of the culture in Meiji Japan.

The *Issei* were an educated people who valued reading, although their occupations were overwhelmingly manual (in either agriculture or industry). Almost all could read and write Japanese, and numerous Japanese-language newspapers flourished among them. While literacy in Japanese was of no immediate economic value to American employers, it was indicative of their cultural level—and literacy even in a foreign language has long been associated with economic progress in America for many races and nationalities. In short, education is generally a symptom of other social characteristics, such as local, class or family aspirations and the inculcation of individual values and traits likely to help realize such aspirations. Among Japanese males born in Japan, the general level of education in the prefecture from which they originated was more highly correlated with their later success in America than was their own individual education. The ambitions and character traits of their locality may have been more fundamental factors in their level of success.

Quantitatively, the Japanese immigration to the United States was quite small, despite widespread cries of "yellow hordes" or a "yellow peril" in California in the early twentieth century. The largest immigration recorded for any year was about 30,000 Japanese in 1907 and 40,000 Chinese in 1882. Even if unrecorded illegal immigration was enough to double these figures, they would still amount to a tiny fraction of the immigration from Europe. At its peak in 1907, Japanese immigration was less than 3 percent of the total immigration to the United States. Moreover, the return migration to Japan was high. From the time of the Gentlemen's Agreement of 1908 to the complete cutoff of immigration from Japan (and other countries) in 1924, about 160,000 Japanese arrived and about 70,000 departed. Their concentration in parts of California created an impression of a much larger Japanese "invasion" than in fact existed, and even in California, the Japanese were never more than 3 percent of the total population. As a noted economic historian observed: "Seldom have so few innocuous people inspired so much irrational hatred and apprehension."

In Hawaii, where the Japanese were a larger proportion—more than 20 percent—of the population, the alarm was not nearly so great. However, even in Hawaii, there was pay discrimination against the Japanese and efforts to block their rise into skilled occupations. A strike of Japanese agricultural laborers in 1909 exacerbated relations between the whites and the Japanese, although it produced some benefits to the Japanese fieldhands.

Americans from Asia: The Filipinos

H. Brett Melendy

In 1898 the United States successfully defeated Spain in the Spanish-American War. One result was that the United States gained control over portions of Spain's long-standing empire. Among the new American possessions was the Southeast Asian island group known as the Philippines, which had been colonized by Spain in the sixteenth century.

The Filipinos soon joined the waves of other Asian emigrants to the United States, according to history professor H. Brett Melendy of the University of Hawaii. Many went as agricultural laborers to Hawaii. Later, Filipinos went to the American mainland to work on both farms and in factories. Others, most famously a group of young men known as *pensionados* because they were supported by wealthy Filipinos back home, went to the United States to get university educations.

These Filipino migrants possessed an uncertain legal status and, like other Asian emigrants, faced discrimination. As residents of America's colonial empire, they were indeed U.S. nationals. On the other hand, no Filipino born in the Philippines was eligible for American citizenship. Moreover, Melendy notes, large numbers of Filipinos arrived on the American mainland only in the 1920s, when America was turning hostile toward immigration, especially the immigration of Asians.

The actual impulse for migration varied. Some sought, in the view of [author] Manuel Roxas in 1930, adventure in a land described in Philippine schools as the place of opportunity; education merely increased these aspirations. Roxas claimed that the Filippino "To satisfy his wants, seeks a white collar job. He fails to get it because of the limited opportunities at home. To him, America is the land of promise." Additionally, steamship companies, such as the Dollar Line, sent agents into provinces to advertise the ease of transportation westward across the Pacific. Letters from those in the United States about the good life, the enclosure of money orders, and the presence of returned *Hawaiianos* all stirred young men to want to escape from economic difficulties and seek success in the United States.

The Journey Across the Pacific

Whatever the motivation for emigration, the gathering place was Manila. Most of those who were going to Hawaii checked into the HSPA [Hawaiian Sugar Planters' Association] Manila office where they received physical examinations and were issued bedding and clothing for the trip. As the emigrants awaited their sailing, doubts sometimes began to enter their minds and rumors about the Hawaiian Islands grew. One such traveler recounted:

> At four o'clock the boat sailed from Manila Harbor carrying about two hundred or perhaps more Filipino emigrants to a new land which would mould and determine the lives of so many people. We were all ushered to the very bottom of the boat where several families slept on the floor on their mats in one big room. The smell of freight and oil together with Japanese food filled the air as we sat together like a pack of sardines in our room. Different tales concerning Hawaii were the main topics of conversation among the passengers. Some said that Hawaii had great big eagles which swept away children from the very cradles of their homes whenever they were hungry. . . . Some said that women and maidens were often seized from their homes to be mates of bachelors who captured them. Others said that some men were going to be forced to join the army. . . .

> The boat journey was very trying. The smell of machines and

food was enough to make everyone sick. One by one became seasick for lack of pure air. No one was allowed to go upstairs on deck. Food was placed and served in a great bucket and the taste was very oriental. Everyone ate bread instead of the usual rice for breakfast, food which every hardworking Filipino cannot do without, especially in the morning.

As the immigrant ships approached Honolulu, people forgot their sicknesses as they anticipated with some apprehension this new venture. Upon disembarking, the immigrants were segregated by assignment to the plantations and then transported to their final destination. . . .

In the face of growing West Coast animosity against the Filipinos during the 1930's, the Hawaii Sugar Planters' Association grew uneasy about the permanence of its source of manpower. Even with mounting unemployment in the Hawaiian Islands, the association sought an exemption from any federal legislation which might cut off the supply from the Philippines. The planters lobbied successfully during the 1934 hearings on the Tydings-McDuffie bill. Section 8 of the bill permitted unlimited Filipino immigration to the islands whenever the need could be demonstrated. The determination of any labor shortage and the approval to import workers were vested in the Department of Interior. While this represented a major victory for the Hawaiian planters, they only asked once—in 1945—for the utilization of that section.

As World War II ended, the HSPA and the Pineapple Growers' Association sought permission to bring six thousand male laborers and their families, if any, to Hawaii. On August 11, 1945, Territorial Governor Ingram M. Stainback authorized the importation. During the war, laborers, regulated under martial law, were frozen in their pre-war occupations. Even so, thousands of Filipinos received permission to work at one of the major military installations on Oahu. Few intended to return to the plantations. . . .

Large-scale emigration of Filipino agricultural workers to the mainland coincided with the influx to Hawaii. The mainland movement, started early in 1920, continued until the depression and the Tydings-McDuffie Act which stopped any significant traffic after 1934.

The first migration of any consequence . . . was the arrival of the *Pensionados*, though there were others. In 1903, the first Filipinos coming to the United States encountered discrimination when a group of island carpenters on their way to St. Louis to build a Philippine village at the Exposition was detained on the West Coast by immigration agents. Since workers did not have funds to pay the required head tax, the agents felt they were likely to become public charges. The United States War Department secured their release and the Commissioner General of Immigration ruled that people migrating from the Philippine Islands did not have to pay the head tax. It was as a consequence of the St. Louis Exposition of 1904, where Igorots and other tribes demonstrated village living, that some Americans gained the impression that all inhabitants of the archipelago were not too far removed from a primitive tribal stage. Hostile and prejudicial attitudes against all Filipinos resulted subsequently.

In 1910, 2,767 Filipino immigrants resided in the United States, but only 406 lived outside Hawaii. The state of Washington had seventeen while California had only five. The largest mainland group of 109 was centered around New Orleans. By 1920, 5,603 Filipinos lived either in Alaska or on the mainland as young Filipinos and West Coast agriculture and the northern fisheries discovered each other. Just under four thousand resided on the Pacific Coast—of these, 2,674 lived in California; 958 in Washington. The second largest regional grouping was in the northeastern states where there were 1,844 Filipinos.

An Expanding Population

The decade of the 1920's was a period of dramatic increase—at a time when exclusionists were working to eliminate unassimilable alien elements. During these years, some 45,000 Filipinos arrived on the Pacific coast; about 16,000 of these came from the Hawaiian Islands. While most immigrants remained on the West Coast, many moved to Chicago, Detroit, New York, and Philadelphia.

California's Filipino population increased about 91 percent in the 1920's. In 1930, the California Department of Indus-

trial Relations, in response to racist pressure, released its find-
ings on this most recent influx of Asians. For the ten-year period, 1920–29, just over 31,000 disembarked at the ports of
San Francisco and Los Angeles. In 1923, 2,426 were admitted;
one-third of these came from Hawaii, where a major sugar
strike was in progress. The failure of the strike and subsequent
blacklisting of strikers accounted for large numbers from
Hawaii the next year as well. The high point was reached in
1929 with 5,795 arrivals. The California study estimated that
35 percent of the total number of immigrants arrived directly
from Manila, 56 percent moved from the Hawaiian Islands,
and the remaining 9 percent came from Asian seaports such as
Hong Kong, Shanghai, Kobe, and Yokahama.

Most of those Filipinos who came during the 1920s were
single young males. One-third were between sixteen and
twenty-one years of age while another 48 percent were in
the 22–29 year range. In 1930, by comparison, only 23 percent of California's total population was less than thirty years
old. State compilers also saw the unbalanced sex ratio as a
danger—a view endorsed by white exclusionists. For persons
of Filipino descent, the ratio was fourteen males to one female while for the total population it was 1.1 male to one female. While about 22 percent of those Filipino men migrating to California were married, only 12 percent brought
their wives. The Department of Industrial Relations observed with some alarm that Filipino and Mexican immigrants had more single persons in their groups than did any
other contingent of aliens being admitted to the United
States. The department had forgotten earlier charges of a
similar nature made against the Chinese and Japanese.

Most of the 1920 immigrants had little formal education
and spoke neither English nor Spanish. Upon arrival, these
newcomers sought jobs—both in urban and rural areas.
They were immediately herded, or manipulated, by others
into a variety of occupations. Carey McWilliams estimated
that in 1930 about twenty thousand Filipinos worked in
West Coast agriculture; some eleven thousand were employed as servants or in hotels and restaurants; and another
4,200 labored in Alaska salmon canneries.

As racial fervor climaxed in the 1930's, Filipino unemployment and the inability of these American nationals to secure federal relief in Pacific Coast states relayed the message to other young men of the Philippines not to come. And many in the United States returned home. By 1940 the Filipino population on the mainland and in Alaska hardly increased over the 1930 census count while in California the number increased by 928, a major slowdown when compared to the 1920's. Hawaii's Filipino population declined significantly—9,725 less than in 1930; most of these returned home at the completion of their labor contracts.

The Tydings-McDuffie Act of 1934 brought immigration to a virtual halt. During the spring of 1934, Filipinos who still hoped to migrate to the mainland bought steerage tickets in the face of the uncertainty of immigration limitation to be imposed by the act. In early April, 160 Filipinos sailed on the S.S. *President Hoover* in an attempt to reach San Francisco and clear immigration before the 50-per-year quota went into effect. On April 26, 1934, the *San Francisco Chronicle* reported the S.S. *President Grant* left Manila without a single Filipino passenger; the newspaper stated that the Dollar Line was not accepting any reservations until the exact status of immigration was solved. One of the exclusionists' goals was being realized.

Chapter 4

Emigration from Mexico

Turning|Points
IN WORLD HISTORY

Moving from Mexican to American Control

James Diego Vigil

In 1846 the Mexican-American War ended with an American victory. The Treaty of Guadalupe Hidalgo, the postwar agreement between Mexico and the United States, ceded a huge amount of Mexican territory to the Americans. The Gadsden Purchase of 1853 added still more territory. These areas became the states of Texas, New Mexico, Arizona, Utah, Nevada, and California. Furthermore, the residents of these territories changed, at a stroke, from Mexican to American residents.

In the following selection, James Diego Vigil writes that Americans quickly forgot their postwar promises to respect Mexican claims to landownership as well as Mexican culture and the Spanish language. Mexicans, like the immigrant groups of the mid-1800s, were expected to assimilate into American culture. Vigil claims that it was very difficult for these former Mexican citizens to assimilate. Many of them were as much Native American as Mexican, and Americans saw them as "Indians." In addition, language, culture, and racist attitudes on the part of "Anglos," or white Americans, encouraged Mexican Americans to live in separate communities.

James Diego Vigil is professor of anthropology at the University of California at Los Angeles and director of the Center of the Study of Urban Poverty.

Mexicans and Indians are the only minority groups in the United States who were conquered and whose rights were protected by treaty provisions. The Treaty of Guadalupe

Reprinted by permission of Waveland Press, Inc., from James Diego Vigil, *From Indians to Chicanos: The Dynamics of Mexican-American Culture* (Prospect Heights, IL: Waveland Press, 1998). All rights reserved.

Hidalgo (1848) resolved several issues and established a political boundary. Through it, a huge region that was formerly the northern-most province of Mexico became the Southwestern province of the United States. The most noteworthy articles concerned the protection of land grants and cultural rights, especially the protocol added later, which referred to the Louisiana Purchase stipulation of 1803. According to this treaty, some Mexican practices would be protected. Land grants and tenure rights established during the Mexican period would be respected on the basis of international law. On paper, the treaty serves as a guarantee for legitimate land grants in Texas, New Mexico, Arizona, and California, but it never was seriously embraced by the United States government. "It joined the ranks of hundreds of other treaties that the United States made with Native American tribes in the nineteenth century that have been almost totally ignored since then."

Furthermore, Mexican cultural customs and patterns were to be given equal consideration with Anglo culture; this meant recognition and accommodation of the Spanish language and Catholic religion. For example, in California the first state constitution was written in Spanish and English. In other regions there was a definite trend, at least initially, toward respect for the Spanish language. This policy came to an end somewhat abruptly when a backlash occurred on several fronts. In addition to the conflict conditions already noted, the Mexican-Americans began to be subjected to prejudice and discrimination on the basis of their cultural customs and language.

Ethnic Rivalry and Hostility

It was not mere coincidence that land rights and cultural accommodation declined sharply at the same time. There is clear evidence of Anglo encroachments and eventual absorption of both small and large parcels of Mexican property. One observer of Texas says: "But it is certain that the traditional belief in unfair deprivation of private property in land remains an element in the background of Mexican emotional hostility to Americans. Both Mexicans and Americans told me their versions of what happened, the Americans often corroborating the Mexicans."

After the Mexican-American War of 1846, a dual economy with a dual wage system evolved. "Chicanos were excluded from education, or their education was inferior. Political participation was impossible, and they lost the land (the basis of their wealth). Chicanos suffered religious discrimination, shootings, hangings, and general violence. Many women were raped and otherwise violated. . . . Women, men, and children resisted the hated and feared Texas Rangers."

All in all, after the Mexican-American war and up to 1880, U.S. citizens of Mexican descent lost some 20 million acres.

Moreover, the dominant Anglos became increasingly convinced that socioeconomic and cultural privileges should not belong to a "culturally and racially inferior" people; they were a "mongel race that not only incorporated the genes of the 'redskin' but also those of the 'nigger.'" For example, Anglos complained that the large ranchos were poorly developed by the Mexicans. They also believed that Mexican customs retarded the full use of land and natural resources; that is, too many fiestas hindered large-scale development. The new leaders maintained that the cause of civilization would advance with land control in Anglo-American hands, and that "if Mexicans could not keep pace with Yankee progress, or improve their standard of living, it was their own fault."

In this era of Anglo-Mexican relations, Manifest Destiny provided a cultural reason to expropriate land and continue the growth and development of the United States, as "territory lost by Mexico to superior arms was used by the United States to launch its own industrial revolution." During the war, hostile attitudes were sown and nurtured by each ethnic group. When competition over land intensified, there was an increase in invective on both sides. During the war, Anglo soldiers, many of them rowdy backwoodsmen, took special joy in killing "greasers," desecrating Mexican churches, and raping the women; Mexican women were also stereotyped as sluts who would willingly sleep with any man. The word "greaser" became a commonly used derogatory term for Mexicans. According to one writer, it referred to their greasy food. To Jeremiah Clemens, an 1840s observer, the ethnic label described the whole Mexican group: "The people look greasy, their clothes are greasy, their dogs are greasy, their houses are greasy—everywhere grease and filth hold divided dominion." Not to be outmatched, Mexicans referred to Anglos as gringos, a corruption of the Spanish word *griego*, meaning one who speaks Greek (gibberish). Thus attitudes were set, epithets were invented, and the behavior that followed was a vicious demonstration of how territorial conflict can set human against human.

The first target was land, which was gradually taken over by the Anglos. Soon after, Mexican labor was sought, secured, and exploited. With land and labor under Anglo control, it obviously followed that wealth (capital) would also fall into their hands. As a result, the Mexican people were left largely without resources, almost destitute. It is now fairly clear that these initial changes paved the way for a more capitalistic system where the cattle and agriculture industries became commercialized for export, with Mexican labor dominated by entrepreneurs. "This transition took longer in New Mexico than in California or Texas, but the result was the same."

As noted previously, the friction between the two groups, which revolved around racial and cultural issues, obscured the real problem source—economic competition. Racial and cultural practices that establish a dominant/subordinate relationship are often obvious, but there is a reason why one group discriminates against another racially or culturally. The Anglo discrimination only added to the previous burden of racial and cultural oppression experienced by the Mexican people. . . .

Variance in Treatment of Mexicans

A complex situation arose. Those Mexicans who could not look and act the part of Europeans were accorded a subordinate status. Generally speaking, some gente de razon [educated people] had a somewhat easier time because of their

Latin background; but in Texas the distinction between Castilian and Mexican soon lost its usefulness. It was the poor, darker individuals unassimilated to the European model who suffered more abuse. In the words of a modern writer: "One cannot understand the discrimination that has been visited upon Mexican-Americans without taking into account the color of their skin and the fact that they look like Native Americans or part Native Americans." The treatment received by the socially immobile, dark, and Indian-acting Mexicans further emphasized the Anglo attitude that "the only good Indian is a dead Indian." Many of the lighter-hued, Spanish types felt superior to the other Mexicans. The descendants of gente de razon still, to this day, deny their Mestizo heritage and the fact that their ancestors acquired Mexican, rather than Spanish, land grants.

A Mexican intragroup split resulted. Because the more oppressed elements suffered considerably, they tended to group together against those who were above them on the social scale. To protect their interests, many gente de razon joined Anglos in opposing the resistance acts of the Mexican masses. Despite this uneasy alliance, they, too, lost out in the end, becoming bankrupt and poverty-stricken in some instances. They continued to be viewed by Anglo-Americans as being Mexicans, except in ceremonial occasions when certain traits become "Spanish."

The Mexicans' racial makeup was the primary obstacle placed in the path of socioeconomic mobility. If that barrier was not enough, then cultural criteria were used to undermine their advancement. For many, it was truly a perplexing situation, since they were only beginning to master the Spanish language when a new dominant one was substituted for it. However, the new social structure was not so new after all, since it generally resembled the old colonial one in at least one respect: Native Mexicans were on the bottom. Where it differed is in the nature of the macrostructural revampments. How they were situated on the bottom was new, especially in the ways they were being stripped of their traditional lifeways piecemeal and relegated to a different role in an industrial economy.

Basis of New Cultural Blending

The native cultural style was being replaced by a new one. There was some trepidation among natives concerning this "time is money" and "cold materialism" ethic. Although some features of the Anglo social structure contrasted sharply with earlier systems, enough remained to remind natives of past experiences and adjustments. For example, natives were introduced to a new language, customs, beliefs, and values. Regional subcultures within Mexico now formed part of the United States, especially in the border area where there were constant interactions and exchanges. Many Mexican traditions, such as Catholicism, were altered, and this further added to the confusion and growing sense of powerlessness. The Anglo-Americans took over all the administrative, trade, and cultural activities. This meant that the newly conquered Mexicans in the area had little say in government policy. Obviously, certain beliefs concerning the family, work, child-rearing, and the nature of individual and group life had to change if the Mexicans were to survive. . . . The changes from an indigenous to peasant way of life were beginning to take root and become routinized as traditional culture. This syncretic process covering several hundred years was now subjected to another interruption and alteration. It both complicated and aggravated cultural evolution for the Chicano people.

An example of this mixed, uneven change is how Spanish and Mexican society underwent transformations in the area of patriarchy and command and control of the household, especially the subordination of women as an ideal. Spanish customs under the Catholic church definitely granted power and authority to the patriarch, but interestingly, the legal system gave women a number of rights and privileges, such as the ability to inherit property and titles, sign contracts, and so on. With the settlement of northern Mexico, where a harsh environment required new roles and responsibilities for everyone, women found themselves doing things that heretofore were the prerogative of men. Farming, ranching, and household chores were arranged quite differently as the circumstances of everyday life dictated. These adaptations became particularly acute during the 1821–1848 period, in part because of the trade and relations between Mexico and the United States and in larger order because of the egalitarian currents of the time. Matriarchal households and an increase in female employment were a sign of the times. In short, "family life increasingly became a mixture of the old and the new values regarding paternal authority and the proper sphere for women." Late in the century, women also played a role in some of the progressive and radical politics of the labor movement.

Unfortunately, aside from concessions made to the "Spanish" elite, some of whom had participated in the development of the new society, and these only of short duration, most of the natives fared poorly because the Anglos made few efforts at cultural accommodation. Mexican culture in the Southwest was crushed by the American socioeconomic belief system. Mexicans felt morally defeated during these early years of subordination. Over time, positive cultural reintegration finally took place. As noted before, many Anglo-Americans were Hispanicized . . . , thus taking the lead in cultural integration.

Cultural Accommodation or Disintegration

For most natives, a successful life was based on their adoption of new norms; refusal to do so often meant failure. In some respects, the earlier Spanish experience had prepared them for such choices. Perhaps it is universally true that subjugated native peoples must shift and readjust to changing sociocultural conditions. In this prevailing Anglo world, numerous types of native reactions were possible, and most occurred. It must also not be forgotten that "All minorities must cope with the fact of Anglo domination; that is what being a minority in the United States means." Notwithstanding this truism, . . . ". . . the people's sense of identity led them to consider themselves as Mexicans regardless of citizenship or of the boundary line between countries."

More and more Anglo-Americans and European immigrants poured into the Southwest, especially California. This was particularly true after the gold rush (1850s) in the north and the completion of the railroads (1870s and after) in the south. Almost immediately the Mexicans, finding themselves in the way, began to establish their own communities. Since they played such an important role in the growing economy, they remained close to fertile land, jobs, and the homes of the wealthy. This choice was made in order to survive. But also, "Throughout this period, Mexicans north of the imposed border continued to maintain their ties, contacts, and mutual influences in many aspects of socioeconomic life with Mexicans south of the border."

It was necessary for Mexicans to integrate themselves somehow into United States society, even if only partially. All-out resistance was futile. Some reasoned that if this route were selected and held to, they would surely suffer the fate of the American Indians. One avenue eventually taken, the era of social bandit activity notwithstanding, was for Mexicans to group together for defense. Many Mexicans were still being abused without provocation. Suspicion and distrust characterized the Anglo attitude, for Mexicans were perceived as deceitful, treacherous people. Therefore, staying within their own spatial and social boundaries, both groups became isolated from each other.

Many Mexicans Were Only Temporary Residents

Lawrence H. Fuchs

The United States shares a border with Mexico that is approximately two-thousand-miles long. Mexican migrants, therefore, find it easy to travel back and forth between their homes in Mexico and jobs north of the border. While many emigrants from Europe and Asia returned home after some years in America, Mexicans could cross the border regularly.

In the following selection, Lawrence H. Fuchs refers to Mexican emigrants, as well as smaller groups of French Canadian and Puerto Rican emigrants, as sojourners. He notes that, after 1900, many more Mexicans were spending periods of time working in the United States. American employers desired their labor since it was flexible and cheap. In addition, political instability in Mexico encouraged many people to seek a livelihood in Texas, Arizona, or California. Fuchs goes on to suggest that the fact that most Mexicans saw their stays in America as temporary made it easier for them to be exploited or attacked.

Lawrence H. Fuchs is the Meyer and Walter Jaffee Professor of American Civilization and Politics at Brandeis University. He has often served as an adviser on immigration policy to the U.S. government.

Filipinos were easily replaced by Mexicans in California, and for the other border states, Mexico was the obvious source for a steady supply of inexpensive and exploitable labor. An informal system of Mexican sojourner pluralism emerged in the 1890s after U.S. immigration laws excluded Chinese la-

Reprinted by permission of the University Press of New England, from *The American Kaleidoscope: Race, Ethnicity, and the Civic Culture*, by Lawrence H. Fuchs. Copyright © 1990 by Lawrence H. Fuchs. Published by Wesleyan University Press.

borers. For several decades before the beginning of large-scale migrations from Mexico in 1897, exploitation had driven farm laborers deep into poverty. The displacement of small farmers by the expansion of large ranches increased the number seeking work as laborers. Railroad development in northern Mexico, where peons could earn three times as much as in the south, brought many closer to the U.S. Soon, knowledge that American wages could be anywhere from four to fifteen times as high as in rural Mexico enticed increasing numbers to cross the border. Under 1902 congressional legislation, construction of large federally funded reservoirs encouraged labor-intensive irrigated farming, especially in Texas and California. After the Mexican Revolution of 1910, hundreds of thousands fled north. Between 1910 and 1930, 10 percent of the population of Mexico had emigrated to the U.S.; about 685,000 were legal immigrants, an unknown but possibly a larger number illegal immigrants. There were no numerical restrictions on immigration within the western hemisphere, but many Mexicans avoided immigration fees, visas, and various exclusionary tests, including the requirement that they not become public charges, and, after 1917, the literacy test, and hence were in the U.S. illegally. How many illegal aliens came to the U.S. for any one period is impossible to say, but the commissioner general for immigration estimated in 1911 that from 1900 to 1910 ten to twenty times as many "unofficial immigrants" came north from Mexico than entered legally. Although there was no way of knowing how many entered illegally, the number, while no doubt exaggerated, was probably substantial.

Mexican Sojourners Provided Cheap Labor

From an employer point of view, the system was almost flawless. The large number of illegal aliens who came to work provided a strong supply of vulnerable workers who would accept depressed wages and labor standards, thereby keeping employer costs down and preventing formation of any effective labor organization. The growers of perishable fruits and vegetables particularly appreciated a loose labor market since they never knew how many workers they would need, depending upon the vagaries of weather. Nor were they pushed to invest in labor-saving equipment or to spend more for domestic labor. Those Americans who used low-cost, foreign unskilled help for menial tasks, such as hospital orderlies, dishwashers, and housemaids, directly benefited from their presence, and American consumers paid less for their produce. Only American farm workers, an especially weak group politically, suffered directly from the competition. Hence, growers could rely on the flow of undocumented labor and also on the cooperation of government in managing that flow as their needs required.

Migrants from Canada and Puerto Rico

French Canadian workers who came to New England throughout the late nineteenth and early twentieth centuries were most like the Mexicans in the ease with which they moved back and forth across the border, in their reluctance to put down roots in American life, in their strong sense of cultural identity with their homeland, and in their difficulty in acquiring English literacy and fluency. But there were also differences between the two groups. French Canadians were lighter in skin color, and they came to an area where labor unions were relatively strong and where there were large numbers of immigrants from other countries who had already become active participants in American life.

Sojourners from Puerto Rico, like Mexicans in the Southwest, moved frequently back and forth from the mainland. They also had difficulty in acquiring effective use of English. And they, too, suffered from racial prejudice. Large growers' associations often negotiated contracts for Puerto Rican farm workers, after 1948 with the migration division of the Puerto Rican government's Department of Labor. But compared to Mexicans, the scale of migration was small, and Puerto Ricans working in the post–Second World War era were American citizens with recourse to protection from the Constitution and laws of the U.S., especially in the civil rights era.

Puerto Ricans, French Canadians, and Mexicans shared a sojourner mentality. Armando B. Rendon, a Chicano activist of the 1960s, explained that few Mexicans would buy a house, even when it was to their economic advantage, because most believed they would return soon to Mexico. Others shied away from adult education courses. What sense did it make to learn English if they were returning home? Politics was for those who had a future and a stake in the country. Even lawful resident aliens saw little point in being naturalized. Families as far away as Chicago and New York visited their Mexican home towns at least once and sometimes twice a year for a few weeks on vacation.

By the 1980s, research on the effects of the sojourner mentality of illegal aliens had become more sophisticated, confirming Rendon's impressionistic interpretation. The sojourner mentality was well suited to the needs of growers, ranchers, and other employers of unskilled labor in the Southwest and elsewhere; it made it easier for whites generally to think of Mexicans as stoop labor or "wetbacks" or in racist terms as "greasers," and not as persons. Anglo-Europeans could accept the need for sudden roundups, deportations, and contract labor programs and ignore the miserable conditions under which Mexicans and Mexican-Americans often lived and worked.

The circular pattern of Mexican migration, driven in large measure by employer demand with the cooperation of the government, was entrenched early in the century. When workers reached a certain savings goal or when they could not adapt or were terribly lonely for relatives or friends, or a combination of these, they often returned home on their own. The system of sojourner pluralism was distinctive in the Southwest to the extent of government cooperation in amending and administering the immigration law for the benefit of employers without regard to the immigration statutes. For example, the Immigration Acts of 1903 and 1907 imposed head taxes of two dollars and four dollars on immigrants, except for Mexicans, ensuring the Southern Pacific Railroad and others a steady supply of Mexican workers. Laws forbidding entry of contract laborers, the diseased, the insane, and certain classes of criminals were enforced weakly in order to cater to western employers' need for labor; and until 1908, the U.S. Bureau of Immigration did not even bother to count incoming Mexicans except for the few who said they intended to remain permanently. When workers were no longer needed, they would be repatriated, as in the recession of 1907, when several thousand railroad track laborers in California lost their jobs. Mexican officials cooperated with the railroad, which gave workers free transportation to the border city of Juárez, where they received food and free rail passes back to their homes.

Mexicans Were Exempt from Immigration Restrictions

By 1917, when the U.S. enacted the most restrictive (so far) immigration statute in its history, including a literacy test, the law made a special exception for employers in the West. It authorized the secretary of labor to permit otherwise inadmissible persons to enter the country as temporary workers, and in May 1917 the first *bracero* program for Mexican workers was created (later expanded to allow some to be employed in nonfarm work). Regulations called for the *braceros* to return home after their work was done, but the rules were incompletely enforced; of the 76,862 Mexican workers admitted under the program, only 34,922 returned home.

Labor recruiting agencies, deprived of European workers after the restrictive immigration legislation of 1921 and 1924, sought Mexicans for outside the West as well. Because of its central position in the midwestern railroad system, in the 1920s Chicago became a central point for Mexican labor. In 1927, sixteen labor contractors reported that they had placed 75,400 Mexicans in jobs in the Chicago area alone for a fee the employers paid them. A less expensive way for employers to obtain labor was to use smugglers, "coyotes," who, operating along the border, put the workers on a train for Chicago, after which the employer sent the coyote a check for each worker who arrived.

Once in Chicago and other cities, Mexicans were outside the system of sojourner pluralism enforced in behalf of growers and ranchers in the Southwest and California. In the East and Midwest, there was the possibility of joining strong labor unions, and the situation of Mexicans in

Chicago or Detroit resembled that of other sojourners in the North and Midwest, as, for example, dark-skinned West Indians who came to the mainland, many illegally.

The system was particularly brutal in Texas, where around the turn of the century vigilante bands attacked Mexicans and Mexican-Americans. By the early twentieth century, Texas Rangers had replaced the local police as principal enforcers of the system of sojourner pluralism, and later, the Border Patrol of the U.S. Immigration and Naturalization Service (INS) and local police forces took over from the Rangers. Although the Border Patrol itself was not brutal, it developed informal arrangements of cooperation with agricultural employers from the 1920s on through the 1950s. The INS would go easy on enforcement until picking time was over, making only a few raids to indicate that they were doing their job in order to justify federal appropriations. Sympathetic to the needs of the local economy and amenable to political pressures, the INS stepped up enforcement as in its crackdown after the "wetback strikes" of 1951 and 1952.

Turning the spigot that controlled the labor supply on and off with the cooperation of the authorities was a well-established pattern of labor control by the 1920s. At crop-picking time, workers would go north from Mexico. At slack periods and especially at Christmas, they would go home. When employer desires for Mexican labor waned in 1928, U.S. authorities cooperated in keeping Mexicans out by applying the literacy test enacted by Congress in 1917, previously ignored for Mexicans for years. With the onset of the Depression, between 1929 and 1934 more than 400,000 Mexicans were sent home without formal deportation proceedings, including thousands of U.S. citizens of Mexican descent who were deported illegally.

Easily Controlled Workers

The vulnerability of the sojourner Mexican workers was not diminished by the fact that many labor contractors themselves were Mexicans. Italian, Greek, Filipino, and labor contractors of other nationalities also held enormous power in the system of sojourner labor recruitment. But in the

Southwest, where so many workers were smuggled in illegally, the possibilities for corruption and abuse by contractors probably were greater than in other parts of the country. In his autobiography, *Barrio Boy*, Ernesto Galarza, a leader of the Chicano movement in the 1960s, told of going to work for a rancher near Sacramento after being hired by a contractor who never discussed working conditions or wages or even how much Galarza would be charged for his meals. The contractor "could fire a man and his family on the spot and make them wait days for their wages. . . . The worst thing one could do was to ask for fresh water on the job, regardless of the heat of the day; instead of ice water, given freely, the crews were expected to buy sodas at twice the price in town, sold by the contractor himself."

The political control of Mexicans was easiest at the border, where the movement back and forth was constant. Even Mexican-American citizens who lived near the border seldom felt enfranchised. In Hidalgo, Starr, Cameron, and Duvall counties, local Anglo political machines that developed in the late nineteenth century effectively controlled the votes of Mexican-Americans. Although political boss rule of European immigrants was developing in the big cities of the Northeast and Midwest, too, with machines usually run not by Anglos but by ethnics themselves who asserted group interests in the name of American rights, Mexican-American politicians on the Texas border tended to follow an older Mexican pattern of exchanging their votes for favors, this time from Anglos.

The most influential of all Anglo-American bosses in south Texas, James Wells, explained that Mexican-Americans asked ranch managers who they should vote for because they were totally dependent on them; ranchers protected their servants and workers with jobs, help with the law, loans, and other favors, and, therefore, expected the *peons* to vote at their direction as a form of compensation. Since most of the Mexican-Americans worked as ranch hands, farm laborers or sharecroppers or small farmers with little expectation of advancement, and most expected to go home someday, it is not surprising that they did not develop an independent ethnic-American political stance.

Mexican Emigrants Could Only Partially Assimilate

Richard Griswold del Castillo and Arnoldo De León

In the first decades of the twentieth century, huge numbers of Europeans immigrated to the United States, usually arriving at East Coast cities. During the same era, substantial numbers of Mexicans crossed the border into the American Southwest. Scholars estimate that as many as 1.5 million people, perhaps 10 percent of Mexico's population, took the journey north. Like many of their European counterparts, Mexicans sought to escape political instability and repression. These took the forms of the dictatorial regime of Porfirio Díaz, which lasted from 1876 until 1911, and then the revolution that ousted Díaz. In the Southwest, just as in the East Coast cities, employers were happy to use the cheap labor the new arrivals provided.

In the following selection, Richard Griswold del Castillo and Arnoldo De León relate how a unique set of circumstances affected the ways by which Mexican migrants adjusted to American life. On the one hand, the authors suggest, many Mexicans adopted American popular culture and supported the American effort in World War I. On the other hand, the constant arrival of newcomers from Mexico as well as the proximity of Mexico itself served to reinforce Mexican culture.

Richard Griswold del Castillo is the author of many books on Mexican American history and life and is a professor of Mexican American studies at San Diego State University. Arnoldo De León is professor of history at Angelo State University in Angelo, Texas.

From *North to Aztlán: A History of Mexican Americans in the United States*, by Richard Griswold del Castillo and Arnoldo De León (New York: Twayne, 1996).

By the 1910s a fully matured market economy existed throughout the old Mexican settlements in the Southwest, as it did across the United States. So did the new inventions: electricity, telephones, automobiles, movies, trolley cars, paved roads, and other modern accoutrements that accompanied the new urbanization. Politics, meanwhile, still emphasized white supremacy and control. Though reformers, the Progressives of the early twentieth century were too much driven by the moral principles of Anglo-Americans, while Republican party supremacy in the 1920s thrived on a conservative political mood. Society became increasingly nativist, racist, and intolerant. During this epoch the country experienced race riots and the "Red Scare," and saw the rising influence of eugenicists, the Ku Klux Klan, and anti-union ideas.

At the same time, people from Mexico in unprecedented numbers trekked across the international boundary, giving old ethnic communities in the United States fresh injections of immigrant culture. Simultaneously, industrial and agricultural firms in the Midwest, as well as almost all states in the trans-Mississippi, solicited Mexican workers (both foreign- and native-born). Permanent and stable settlements far north of the borderlands resulted.

The repercussions of the new immigration meant far more than increased numbers. The new arrivals suspended, at least momentarily, the direction of ethnic adjustment and evolution that had been under way since 1848. Americanization persisted, naturally, but only within a lean segment of the population, for the newcomers outnumbered native-born Mexican Americans and rejected the legitimacy of American institutions (many of them waited for trouble to subside in Mexico so they could return). Ideological cleavages between the native- and foreign-born thus arose over such issues as politics, patriotism, and citizenship. Ethnic and nationalist differences became a standard characteristic of Hispanic communities. An understanding of their "Mexican" identity, a faith in certain tenets of Mexico's culture, and a common group experience with Anglo discrimination, however, welded the community in solidarity.

Historical processes unfurled in the nation's economy during the early twentieth century. The switch to dry-farming techniques and the federal subsidization of new reclamation projects during the era turned previously unproductive lands into fertile fields. Throughout the country by the 1920s, the farms of the modern age became agribusiness estates resembling rural factories that required huge numbers of mobile, cheap, and not necessarily skilled workers to pick an assortment of crops, including cotton, beets, and a variety of vegetables. Railroads expanded also, reaching their apogee into the trans-Mississippi during the late 1910s. The growing popularity of the motor vehicle caused a decline of railroad construction by the 1920s, but the automobile industry created newer types of work in the country's infrastructure. The exploitation of minerals also saw intensification, though this was localized to regions such as southeastern Arizona and the Central Plains states. The most dramatic transformation in the U.S. economy during the era occurred in industry, with states in the Great Lakes region, among others in the North, seeing expansion in firms manufacturing steel, rubber, automobiles, and electrical products.

Instability in Mexico, Promise in America

The immigration trends of the late nineteenth century peaked during the first three decades of the 1900s, owing in part to revolutionary troubles in Mexico, labor shortages created by World War I, and continued demand for Mexican workers by a flourishing U.S. economy. In the case of pushing factors, the movement to oust the dictator Porfirio Díaz in 1910 initiated bloody strife that destabilized the political order in Mexico until the 1920s. As people of Mexico endured revolution and reconstruction, the United States economy issued enticing offers for an improved life. Since the late nineteenth century, immigration statutes had attempted to keep out foreigners. During the 1880s a series of laws imposed a head tax on people wanting to come to America, prohibited the immigration of anyone who might become a burden on society, and barred the contracting of foreign laborers. Another piece of legislation passed in 1917 restricted illiterates from entering the United States. Starting in 1918 and continuing until the late 1920s, however, federal agencies cooperated with businessmen and agribusiness interests to make special exemption of laborers from Mexico. In 1918 the commissioner general of immigration lifted almost all restrictions imposed since 1882, including the prohibition placed on contract labor. The 1924 National Origins Act, which established quotas for European countries, excluded Mexico.

Between 1900 and 1930, some historians estimate, about 10 percent of Mexico's population moved into the United States, a fraction that adds up to some 1.5 million people. For the most part, the large percentage of immigrants who came north during the early twentieth century descended from the ranks of the lower class. Some 80 percent to 90 percent of them had experience in nothing other than agricultural work or unskilled occupations. The rest were clerks, craftsmen, and other types of skilled laborers. The latter groups encompassed elites escaping the wrath of *campesinos* or revolutionary armies bent on retaliation for past injustices and oppression. Their ranks included political refugees with ties to the Díaz regime, as well as a middle class of *hacendados* [rich landowners], businessmen, and professionals such as lawyers, physicians, journalists, and educators.

The immigrants' destination within the United States, regardless of social standing, varied. Those from northern Mexico streamed into the border states owing to their proximity and the abundance of available jobs therein. Residents from Tamaulipas, Nuevo León, and Coahuila ordinarily gravitated toward Texas. Those from Guanajuato, Michoacán, Jalisco, and San Luis Potosí headed for California, though the same states fed laborers to the U.S. Midwest (immigrants from the Central Plateau of Mexico bypassed the U.S. Southwest because the earlier immigrants from northern states had already claimed jobs throughout the borderlands).

A small element within the immigrant community brought a political agenda with it. Even in the Midwest, for instance, diverse elements could be found wanting to support the old regime (Díaz) while in exile or to oppose the Revolution itself. At another level were immigrants who worked toward relieving the misery of the lower classes in Mexico. The PLM [Partido Liberal Mexicano, or Mexican Liberal Party] led by . . . Ricardo Flores Magón, sought such an end. After being released from prison in 1910 following his conviction for violating the neutrality laws in 1907, Magón regrouped and reinstated *Regeneración* in Los Angeles. Through the pages of this newspaper, Magón and the PLM advocated revolution against Díaz and argued for labor reforms and other radical measures. When the Revolution broke out, the PLM even launched an armed invasion of Baja California. But the campaign went awry and it led to Magón's temporary imprisonment in 1912 on charges of conspiracy to invade a friendly country from U.S. soil. When released in 1914, Magón (in Los Angeles) resumed the cause for Mexico's liberation, but his PLM now lacked effectiveness. Nonetheless, it inspired the Plan de San Diego [a plot hatched by Mexican revolutionaries to foment an uprising among Mexican Americans in the Southwest, particularly in Texas] in 1915, carried on propaganda activities against Mexico's governments, and condemned U.S. exploitation of Mexicans and Mexican Americans. In 1918 the U.S. government charged Flores Magón with espionage and sent him to prison, where he died in 1922.

The majority of the immigrants had little interest in such kinds of politics; they sought to flee conditions in the homeland and find opportunity in the United States. In the new land poor folks tried reconstructing their lives, joining the swelling numbers of refugees in transplanted communities. Elites, for their part, assisted in sustaining Mexico in the United States by their efforts to resurrect a semblance of their former aristocratic lives: they formed societies, social clubs, and theaters and promoted their *mexicanidad* [Mexicanism] by publishing or selling Mexican books, Spanish music, and newspapers. Both groups relied on the Mexican consul when problems with discrimination, unemployment, repatriation, or trouble with the law came up.

Partial Americanization

The course of events during this age touched the new arrivals and modified their sentiments. These developments involved aspects of material culture such as clothing, new durable goods being invented during the age, and modern housing techniques. Other influences included sports (basketball and baseball) and moving pictures in Mexican American–owned theaters that featured the most prominent stars of the day such as Charlie Chaplin and Mary Pickford. The fashions of the 1920s, including bobbed hair and short skirts converted many young women to new lifestyles. The "sheik" look (well-groomed pomaded hair, pointed sideburns, and expensive-looking attire) made fashionable by Rudolph Valentino similarly affected impressionable adolescent males. American values had their own impact, often to the dismay of the older folks who identified American life with independence, defiance of parental authority, and violation of the customs of the motherland. The English language also produced slang expression such as *sitijol* (city hall), *troque* (truck), *tichar* (teach), *esplear* (spell), or *tochar* (touch).

Of major significance in Americanizing communities was World War I. In an effort to integrate all groups into war-mobilization efforts, the government sought at every level the help of the Mexican-descent community, both at the civilian and military front. Anglo-Americans appealed to Mexican Americans and the immigrants to buy liberty bonds, organized "Loyalty Leaguers" in the colonias, and sponsored mass meetings in Mexican communities to explain the war effort. The stridency of these undertakings gave Mexican-descent people a feeling of belonging to the country of residence—the United States—as for the first time the government treated them as citizens instead of stepchildren of the nation. For soldiers, many of whom distinguished themselves in the battlefield, it produced a certain esprit de corps and satisfaction in having contributed to the defeat of the Germans.

Simultaneously, as part of the Americanization drive that developed in the early twentieth century, Anglo-American reformers, charity and religious groups, social workers, and educators launched a crusade to convert the Mexicans, both native- and foreign-born. In California some of the Americanizing programs directed themselves at immigrant women, on the premise that Mexican mothers assumed primary responsibility for instructing the children on cultural values; Americanized mothers would raise American children. In the end such Americanizing efforts yielded only minimal success. None of the reform movements advocated full equality even after acculturation. Consequently, many Mexicans remained distrustful of white society and unwilling to surrender their cultural identity. Until the depression decade, therefore, the Mexican-descent population in the United States lacked command of the English language and still harbored doubts about accepting the credibility of the American way of life.

But the preceding developments planted the seeds of what historians refer to as the "Mexican-American Generation," a cohort that between 1930 and 1960 gave direction to Mexican-American communities as "Americans." During the early period of the twentieth century, however, Mexican enclaves embraced diverse ideological strains; some native- and foreign-born Mexicans still adhered to the traditions of Old Mexico, while others practiced bilingualism and biculturalism. Dilemmas over identity thus surfaced frequently, for there existed among these disparate elements differences in patriotic passion for the United States and Mexico. Problems were posed whenever the American press attacked Mexico, or when during the years of the Revolution the United States invaded Mexican territory and Pancho Villa attacked New Mexico in 1916, or when Anglo-Americans associated, stereotyped, and classified all Mexicans as one regardless of nativity. The latter situation, especially, placed great stress on those who considered themselves Americans and different from the foreign-born; they inclined to disassociate themselves from the newcomers. As had been the case in the nineteenth century, old citizens in New Mexico and California used such terms as *Spanish Americans* and *Hispanos* as self-referents to distinguish themselves from the newcomers (the immigrants reciprocated with the word "*pocho*," meaning that the Mexican-American personality had become a corruption of Mexican and American cultures). In New Mexico, one sociologist has recently proposed, the label also acted as a valid term invoked regularly by Hispano leaders to rally *nuevomexicanos* ["new" Mexicans] behind ethnic platforms.

Despite all this, a common Mexicanist identity solidified communities. Notwithstanding social divergence, variation in degree of acculturation, and philosophical disagreements, most people abided by certain nationalistic principles, emphasized by a common experience of poverty, discrimination, and exploitation that unified them as La Raza or as Mexicanos.

Chapter 5

The Open Door Closes

Emigration from China Is Restricted First

Ellis Cose

Before 1882 the United States welcomed emigrants from anywhere in the world. While a few states had enacted immigration limits, the federal government had no legislation in place that restricted immigration. Although some Americans argued that foreigners such as the Roman Catholic Irish and the Chinese threatened America's peace and stability, the nation's need for settlers and laborers proved a stronger argument, and the borders were left open.

The tide began to turn in the late 1800s, however. In the following passage, Ellis Cose describes the context in which the Chinese Exclusion Act of 1882, the first true limitation on immigration to America, was passed. As Cose notes, Chinese immigrants came to California in large numbers even after the Gold Rush. They helped build railroads but soon proved valuable in other industries as well. By the 1870s, other Californians, often Irish-Americans, claimed that Chinese workers were a threat to their livelihoods because they kept wages low and Irish emigrants out of work. According to Cose, the Irish and others were able to build up anti-Chinese sentiment, often based on the alien culture of the Chinese, and the federal government responded with the 1882 Chinese Exclusion Act.

Ellis Cose, a contributing editor to *Newsweek* magazine, is the author of many books, including *The Rage of a Privileged Class* and *Color Blind: Seeing Beyond Race in a Race Obsessed World*.

"The pressing want of our country is men," proclaimed Pennsylvania congressman William Kelley in the wake of the Civil War. The battle-ravaged South needed rebuilding, the thinly populated West needed settling, and the country's great mineral wealth needed to be mined. Hundreds of thousands arrived from Germany, Ireland, and England and, for the most part, were warmly received, but as increasing numbers of Chinese came to toil in America's mines and on the transcontinental railroad, anti-Chinese sentiment again began to rise.

Abraham Lincoln had signed legislation authorizing the necessary land grants and government bonds for the railroad in 1862, but plans had been largely on hold during the war, due as much to manpower, financial, and organizational problems as to the North-South conflict. Three years after congressional approval, less than fifty miles of the track between Sacramento and Omaha were completed. Unless progress picked up dramatically, the Central Pacific Railroad faced a financial fiasco. For in approving the project, Congress had, in effect, set up a race, issuing government bonds and granting land along the right-of-way in pace with the rate of work. The Central Pacific was building from the West (through the Sierra Nevadas), and the Union Pacific was building from the East; the two companies would meet somewhere in the middle—with the exact point determined by the speed of their respective workers. With the Union Pacific laying track eight times as fast as its Western rival, it stood to accrue substantially more bonds and land.

Workers to Build Railroads

Charles Crocker, the Central Pacific director responsible for construction, was desperate for workers. In the final months of the war, he had even flirted with the idea of hiring Confederate prisoners or black Civil War veterans at military pay. In early 1865, he advertised for five thousand men to supplement his work crews of six hundred. Few appeared. To make matters worse, some of those already on board were talking about striking. Some fifty thousand Chinese were then in California—virtually all of whom were young males eager for work. When Crocker hit on the idea of using Chinese labor, his foreman, James Harvey Strobridge, resisted, but finally agreed to try out fifty Chinese for a month under white supervision. They did well. By the end of the year, an estimated seven thousand Chinese (and less than two thousand whites) were laying track for the Central Pacific. Additional workers were brought in direct from China.

The Chinese were cheaper than whites because they paid for their own food and housing while whites were cared for by the company. They were also considered more expendable, and would routinely be lowered from ropes into the rocks to drill holes for explosives and then race to get to safety before the charges went off. Sometimes they would not succeed. Scores of men of both races lost their lives in the tunnels and snow slides of the Sierra Nevada.

The new surge of Chinese immigrants soon drew fire from politicians and the press. When the Fourteenth Amendment was proposed in 1866—making citizens of all persons born in the United States and guaranteeing equal protection under the law regardless of race—Indiana congressman William Niblack reminded his peers that courts repeatedly had found blacks unacceptable as citizens and that California had found the same to be true of "Chinamen." "Let the white people . . . retain the power of the government in their own good hands and wield it for the good of all," he implored. With California preparing for statewide elections, the *San Francisco Examiner* urged support for the Democratic slate, portraying the opposition as a pro-Chinese, pro-Negro-suffrage "plunder league." "If . . . you are in favor of continuing this as a white man's government such as our fathers made it, and wish to reduce its expenses and taxation to such an extent that white men can live in it, then vote the ticket headed by H.H. Haight for Governor," advised the *Examiner* in 1867.

Henry Haight was elected governor, along with two congressmen and several members of the state assembly who had all run anti-Chinese campaigns. In a victory address repeatedly interrupted with applause, Governor-elect Haight called his election a "protest against corruption and extravagance in our State affairs, against populating this fair state with a race of Asiatics, against sharing with inferior races the government of the country, against the military despotism which now exists at the South under the last acts of Congress."

The following year, the United States negotiated the Burlingame Treaty, recognizing Chinese citizens' right to immigrate to America and conferring most-favored-nation status on China. Nonetheless, anti-Chinese agitation increased, due in part to the completion of the Pacific railway—which brought in settlers from the East. Many Chinese, because of their work with explosives on the railroad, were better qualified for quartz mining than the newly arriving whites, who, for the most part, were not at all eager to compete with Chinese; and politicians pandered to their fears. A California Democratic party platform statement suggested that giving Chinese the vote would not only "degrade the right of suffrage" but "ruin" the white laborer "by bringing untold hordes of pagan slaves . . . into direct competition with his efforts to earn a livelihood." . . .

Attacks on Chinese Workers

As politicians whipped up animosity toward the Chinese, incidents of anti-Chinese violence cropped up. In 1867, a mob drove Chinese workers away from the Potrero Street railway in San Francisco and burned their barracks near the job site. In 1871, after a white man trying to stop a shooting duel between two Chinese in Los Angeles was accidentally killed, a mob of several hundred attacked Chinese bystanders, killing nineteen before running out of steam. West Coast legislators pointed to such incidents as evidence of the need to banish Chinese from America. . . .

Meanwhile, Chinese settlers tried—through letters, newspaper articles, meetings with lawmakers, and countless lawsuits—to allay whites' fears and protect themselves from whites' resentment, but the anti-coolie campaign had achieved such momentum and the political benefit (for white politicians) had become so clear that there was little relief to be had. All problems—including falling wages—in the then-sluggish California economy were laid at the feet of the Chinese; and the result was an upsurge in anti-Chinese violence—much of it organized by militant labor organizations. In Chico, a small town north of San Francisco, several invaders stormed into a home occupied by six Chinese men in March 1877 and held the men at gunpoint before killing two of them and wounding two others. As the assailants fled, they set the home afire. Later in the week, more men raided Chinatown, setting fires to a washhouse and soap factory. Eleven Californians subsequently were arrested for murder and arson. Some two hundred outraged Chinese came out to watch the men marched to jail, and many subsequently contributed funds to aid the prosecution. During the trial, the men revealed that they had been acting on instructions from a secret labor society called the Council of Nine that supposedly ordered killing and intimidation as a method of protesting against and frightening the Chinese. Five were found guilty.

The Chico murders stirred the indignation of the *San Francisco Examiner*, which covered the events with relative compassion. That compassion, however, only went so far. A few weeks following the Chico incidents, the *Examiner* noted that the drought sweeping the region had put white men out of work and urged all employers to fire their Chinese help. "There is now no good reason why they should not do so and hire white men in their place."

That summer the anti-Chinese movement reached a new peak. The evening of July 23, a crowd assembled in a sand-lot near San Francisco's city hall to hear pro-labor orators. Much of the crowd was already in a foul mood because of an aborted attempt by the Central Pacific to cut wages. One speaker fanned the anger by claiming that a steamship company had contracted to deliver twenty-five thousand Chinese to the state by October. Either the whites or the Chinese would have to leave, he said. Other equally incendiary remarks were made, igniting an eruption of violence that went on for three days. Chinese homes and businesses were burned in various parts of town. The wharf and a lumberyard known to hire Chinese were torched, and numerous Chinese were killed.

Irish vs. Chinese Laborers

The rampage led the Committee of Vigilance, comprised of San Francisco's business elite, to call for federal measures to halt Chinese immigration. The Workingmen's Trade and Labor Union of San Francisco headed by Dennis Kearney was also agitating against the Chinese. The organization, also known as the Workingmen's party of California, was dominated by Irish immigrants, like Kearney, who saw Chinese workers as the enemy. The party's manifesto was unmistakably clear: "Before you and the world we declare that the Chinaman must leave our shores. We declare that white men, and women, and boys, and girls, cannot live as the people of this great republic should and compete with the single Chinese coolie on the labor market. . . . To an American, death is preferable to life on a par with the Chinaman."

A Kearney-led Thanksgiving Day parade drew an estimated seven thousand marchers. His candidate, Isaac Kalloch, became mayor of San Francisco, and his associates swept elections to the constituent assembly charged with rewriting the state constitution. That constitution, adopted in 1879, explicitly denied the vote to the criminal, the insane, and those born in China. It also denied Chinese aliens the right to own property, to testify against whites, to bear arms, to engage in mercantile businesses, or to be employed in California public works. While ratifying the new constitution, California's voters also approved—by a vote of 154,638 to 883—a referendum endorsing Chinese exclusion. The ballot had been designed in such a way that in order to reject the measure a voter had to scratch out the word "against" and write in "for." In touting the results of the referendum, California politicians conveniently left out the details of the ballot's design, but pointed to the vote as evidence that—in the words of Senator George Perkins—"Men of all parties and creeds . . . agree that they [Chinese immigrants] are a blight upon our industries and citizenship, and an injury to our people." . . .

[In 1880] the Burlingame Treaty was renegotiated. The Chinese government agreed to provisions barring criminals, contract laborers, prostitutes, and the diseased from migrating to the United States. The most significant Chinese concession, however, was language that gave America the right to suspend but not "absolutely prohibit" immigration, for a limited period, of skilled or unskilled laborers who "endanger the good order of the said country [meaning the United States] or of any locality within the territory."

Fully aware of Congress's escalating anti-Chinese crusade, the Chinese negotiators apparently thought the careful wording would protect Chinese nationals from capricious and unwarranted debarment. They underestimated both the depth of U.S. Sinophobia and the lengths to which politicians, particularly in an election year, would go to cater to it.

Chinese Immigration Stopped

In the months following ratification of the treaty, a blizzard of Chinese restriction resolutions and bills rained down on both houses of Congress—among them one from California senator John Miller that would exclude Chinese laborers for twenty years. He noted that both 1880 party platforms had called for stronger controls on Chinese immigration, and he rehearsed what had by then become standard charges against the Chinese. They were a "servile people," he railed, in eternal bondage to the Six Companies who had imported them; and they lived so cheaply—"like swine in the sty"—that whites could not compete with them. In an unmistakable allusion to the Civil War, he asserted: "An 'irrepressible conflict' is upon us in full force, and those who do not see it in progress are not so wise as the men who saw the approach of the other 'irrepressible conflict' which shook the very foundation of the American empire upon this continent."

After prolonged debate, the bill passed the Senate by a two-to-one margin in March 1882. The House passed it two weeks later by an even larger margin, but President Chester Arthur vetoed it because it violated the recently renegotiated treaty. Almost immediately, several new bills were proposed that got around Arthur's primary objection by shortening the exclusion period. By the end of April both houses had passed a measure providing for a ten-year period of exclusion of all Chinese laborers (including miners) and that commanded, "hereafter no state court or court of the United States shall admit Chinese to citizenship; and all laws in conflict with this act are hereby repealed." Those Chinese nationals who were not laborers thenceforth would need a special certificate from the Chinese government to enter the United States. Those already present could remain; but those who wished to leave and return would be required to present a certificate proving they had originally come to the United States before November 1880. Ship captains who transported Chinese in violation of the law were subject to a five-hundred-dollar fine or a one-year prison sentence for each person landed and the possible loss of their vessel. President Arthur signed the bill in May. That same year Congress passed a general immigration act barring paupers, criminals, the insane, and others likely to become public charges.

The general act was merely the next natural step in the ongoing transfer of responsibility for immigration from the states to the federal government. The anti-Chinese legislation, however, was a direct repudiation of what formerly had been a hallowed U.S. tradition deeming that all nationalities could enter—even if all could not be citizens. It was also the first law to specifically deny naturalization to an ethnic group as opposed to designating those—whites and persons of African ancestry—who could be naturalized.

The Rising Anti-Immigrant Tide

David M. Reimers

According to history professor David M. Reimers of New York University, Americans found many reasons to oppose immigration in the fifty years before wide-ranging immigration restrictions were enacted in the 1920s. Many objections were based on race. Examples of these include the Chinese Exclusion Act of 1882 and the so-called Gentleman's Agreement of 1907, which mostly ended Japanese emigration. Other Americans argued that even the "races" of southern and eastern Europe represented a threat to American culture, and Jewish immigrants faced growing anti-Semitism. Still others claimed that immigrants were often criminals or potentially disloyal political radicals.

During and after American participation in World War I in 1917 and 1918, the call to protect Nordic or Anglo-Saxon America grew even louder, as Reimers notes. Many believed that Asian, southern or eastern European, or Jewish immigrants were in fact racially inferior. Members of Congress responded by enacting legislation in the 1920s that, they believed, would protect America from dangerous foreign influences. On the one hand, immigration was simply restricted across the board. On the other, new laws established a quota system that favored emigrants from northern and western Europe.

In 1875 the Supreme Court held state rules about immigration unconstitutional. As a result the federal government entered the field of immigration regulation. For the next twenty-five years, Congress barred certain classes of immigrants, such as paupers, criminals and the insane, and in the 1890s established Ellis Island as the main receiving station for the millions pouring into America in those years. These laws passed in the late nineteenth century kept out few immigrants.

The Chinese Exclusion Act

Having a greater impact was the first major restriction aimed at a nationality group, the Chinese. Racism prompted this action. In 1875 Congress forbade the admission of prostitutes, a law in part aimed at Chinese women. Then came the 1882 ban on most Chinese immigration. Welcomed at first as desirable workers by the railroad builders and promoters, Chinese immigrants soon found themselves facing discrimination and a rising chorus demanding their exclusion. The depression of the 1870s, especially acute in California, gave birth to a Workingmen's Party, whose platform included halting Chinese immigration. The officers of the Workingmen's Party were blunt: "We have made no secret of our intentions. . . . Before you and the world, we declare that the Chinamen must leave our shores. We declare that white men, and women, and boys, and girls, cannot live as the people of a great republic should and compete with the single Chinese coolies in the labor market."

The emergence of labor unions as a force in the anti-alien movement dates from the conflict in California. Even labor groups in the eastern states, where few Chinese lived, sponsored anti-Chinese rallies. Anti-Chinese leaders also argued that these immigrants were socially and morally inferior to whites and that as a separate race they could never be assimilated into American society. Congress agreed, and barred most Chinese for ten years and periodically extended the ban until it was repealed in 1943.

A new phobia emerged in the 1880s about immigrants: fear of the alien radical, which was fed by violence. When a bomb exploded during a labor rally in Chicago in 1886 it triggered anxiety about the danger of radicalism to America. Although Chicago authorities had no solid evidence on the identity of the bomb-thrower, they nonetheless arrested six immigrants and one American-born anarchist.

Immigrants are depicted seeking directions from a passerby. Assistance from strangers could not be counted on as anti-immigrant sentiment grew during the late 1800s.

They were convicted and sentenced to die.

Anti-Catholicism and antisemitism by no means disappeared after the Civil War. Old stock Americans feared that too many Jews and Catholics were entering. In the 1880s and early 1890s the Iowa-based American Protective Association (APA), with its message of anti-Catholicism, gained strength, especially in the Midwest. The APA was not strictly anti-immigrant. Its members, for example, took an oath never to vote for a Catholic whether American-or-foreign born, never to hire one, and to promote the "American" language in the schools. As it became more anti-foreign it lost some of its support among Protestant immigrants. Moreover, its message of blaming all economic woes on Catholics and warning of a Catholic seizure of power appeared too absurd to many Americans. Consequently it lost strength and collapsed in the 1890s.

Jews were smaller in numbers than Catholics, but they too became the target of nativists. Populist agitators blamed Jewish bankers for their economic troubles, prominent Gentile clubs banned Jewish members, and fashionable resorts turned away Jewish guests.

Beginning in the 1880s greater numbers of Jews and Catholics began to arrive from the southern and eastern regions of Europe, and by 1896, immigrants from those areas surpassed the numbers from northern and western Europe. This shifting pattern made critics of immigration search for a scheme to stem the flow. The Immigration Restriction League, founded in the 1890s by elite Bostonians, proposed a literacy test for incoming immigrants. Such a test would bar adults (those age 16 or older) from entering if they were unable to read and write in some language. Its proponents knew that potential immigrants from southern and eastern Europe were more apt to be illiterate than those from northern and western Europe; hence this was a way to keep out the former. As Senator Henry Cabot Lodge, a member of the League, said, "the literacy test will bear most heavily upon the Italians, Russians, Poles, Hungarians, Greeks, and Asiatics, and very light, or not at all upon English-speaking emigrants or Germans, Scandinavians, and French." During the economically depressed 1890s Congress listened to Lodge and passed the test, but it was vetoed by President Grover Cleveland, and the legislators did not have enough votes to override it.

Ending Japanese Immigration

With the return of good times after 1900 xenophobia temporarily lessened but by no means disappeared. Racism directed at Asians was particularly strong. Japanese immigrants began to arrive in the 1880s, just as the Chinese were being excluded. Historian Roger Daniels points out that it did not take long for West Coast anti-Japanese sentiment to develop. With labor leaders; James D. Phelan, mayor of San Francisco;

and the San Francisco *Chronicle* leading the way, pressure to exclude Japanese newcomers began to build. The Asiatic Exclusion League and trade unions urged federal action. When the San Francisco school board segregated Japanese pupils in 1906, President Theodore Roosevelt was confronted with a diplomatic problem. Not wanting to offend Japan, but willing to see immigration halted, Roosevelt persuaded the board to change its order and the Japanese government to stop giving visas to Japanese laborers. Koreans, whose numbers were small in the United States, were also included under the ban because Korea was under Japanese domination.

Japanese wives of the immigrants could still come to Hawaii and the United States. Some were "picture brides," women who married by proxy Japanese male immigrants they had never met. Congress finally ended this flow in the 1920s when it barred further Japanese immigration. Japan and some American officials had suggested a quota, such as that given to Europeans, but the legislators rejected this proposal. According to the 1870 naturalization act the only immigrants who were eligible to become citizens were whites and persons of African descent. In 1922 the Supreme Court held that white meant "Caucasian" and that Japanese immigrants were not Caucasians. Congress simply banned all persons ineligible for naturalization. Moreover, Californians passed discriminatory laws against the Asian immigrants. In 1913 California by a three to one vote barred these Japanese nationals from owning or leasing land. . . .

Anti-Catholicism, Antisemitism, and Racism

Because the number of Asians was very small compared to Europeans, the exclusion of Asian immigrants did little to dampen the growing flow of immigrants coming to America, which reached record numbers between 1900 and 1914. These numbers were anxiously watched by those Americans who remained opposed to Jewish and Catholic immigrants. Playing upon the fears of Catholicism Wilbur Franklin Phelps founded a magazine called *The Menace* in 1911. Historian John Higham reports that its circulation reached one million within three years. Another fanatical anti-Catholic periodical was *Watson's Magazine*, published by the former Georgia Populist leader Tom Watson. As in the past anti-Catholic zealots portrayed the Roman Catholic Church as a threat to American values. . . .

As the anti-foreign voices grew in the late 19th and early 20th centuries, they found a new argument to restrict Europeans: racism. While prior objections had been based on economics, crime, health, morality, religion and fear of radical alien ideas, now the restrictionists argued that the peoples of southern and eastern Europe were distinct races who were inferior to the so-called races of northern and western Europe.

A variety of politicians, patriotic groups and scholars endorsed these ideas. Madison Grant's *The Passing of the Great Race* (1916) warned against "race" mixing and the threat of continued immigration. The Immigration Restriction League declared in 1910, "A considerable proportion of immigrants now coming are from races and countries, or parts of countries, which have not progressed, but have been backward, downtrodden, and relatively useless for centuries. If these immigrants 'have not had opportunities,' it is because their races have not made the opportunities; for they have had all the time that any other races have had."

The latest newcomers, ran the argument, simply could not fit into American society. Harvard graduate and Boston Brahmin Prescott F. Hall, executive secretary of the Immigration Restriction League, told Congress in 1919, "The Italians, however fitted intellectually, have certain traits that unfit them for coming to our country for years to come because of certain traits known to all, that unfit them to receive the ballot or to be in any case recipients of American citizenship." . . .

Congress . . . finally passed a literacy test on the eve of America's entry into World War I. President Woodrow Wilson vetoed the bill but Congress overrode the President and it became law. Now newcomers would have to be literate in order to pass through Ellis Island.

The Effect of World War I

Immigration dropped substantially, but this was mainly due to the interruption of commerce caused by the outbreak of

World War I in August, 1914. Immigration had fallen steadily since that date; hence the precise impact of the test was unknown during the war. While the war itself cut the immigrant trade, it also fostered increased pressure to halt immigration and end potential disloyalty. Former President Theodore Roosevelt was particularly outspoken in favor of 100 percent Americanism. Hysteria broke loose on German Americans, and any "hyphenated" Americans considered potentially disloyal. Roosevelt put it, "We are convinced that today our most dangerous foe is the foreign-language press and every similar agency, such as the German-American Alliance, which holds the alien to his former associations and through them to his former allegiance. We call upon all loyal and unadulterated Americans to man the trenches against the enemy within our gates."

It seemed as if the war against Germany in Europe had degenerated into a "War against German America." Germans, who had won the admiration of many other Americans because of German science, music, literature and intellectual achievements, now were viewed with hostility. German submarine warfare and atrocities in Belgium received much unfavorable coverage in American newspapers, and German Lutheran churches were viewed with suspicion if they used the German language and if their ministers refused to support the sale of war bonds. To dispel fears of disloyalty, many Lutheran churches switched to English and individual pastors proclaimed their loyalty to the United States and their support of the war effort. Many German Americans Anglicized their names, bought liberty bonds and publicly denounced Germany. Some parochial schools stopped teaching the German language, and German-language publications switched to English. Such professions of loyalty were not enough for Governor William L. Harding of Iowa. In May, 1918, he issued a proclamation "that prescribed English as the sole medium of instruction in public, private, and denominational schools and as the sole means of communication in public addresses and conversations in public places, on trains, and over the telephone. Persons who did not understand or speak the English language were instructed to conduct religious worship services in their homes.". . . .

The issue in the 1920s was how not whether to radically restrict immigration and complete 50 years of federal regulation. In 1921, when over 800,000 immigrants arrived, it appeared that the literacy test would not seriously interfere with migration to America. Moreover, there were rumors that millions more wanted to come to America. A Congressional committee told Congress that "between 2,000,000 and 8,000,000 persons in Germany alone wanted to come to the United States." And another committee claimed, "If there were in existence a ship that could hold 3,000,000 human beings, the 3,000,000 Jews of Poland would board it to escape to America." Moreover, growing numbers of southern and eastern Europeans were literate, which meant that a test originally designed in the 1890s was insufficient as a deterrent in the 1920s.

After the war a revived Ku Klux Klan (KKK), which attacked Roman Catholics, claimed millions of members; part of its credo was immigration restriction. Writers [warned] against the "danger which Nordic America faced from Mediterraneans and Alpines." Antisemitism received new life from Henry Ford's newspaper, *The Dearborn Independent*, which thundered against an alleged international Jewish plot to dominate the world. In this climate the demand for cutting immigration from southern and eastern Europe became overwhelming.

The American Federation of Labor; patriotic societies; the newly formed American Legion; the Immigration Restriction League; the National Grange; the Junior Order, United American Mechanics; and intellectual racists and eugenicists were more respectable than the KKK, and they had more influence in Congress. They differed in their views, with some using racist arguments and the American Federation of Labor claiming, "If the products of our mills and factories are to be protected by a tariff on articles manufactured abroad, then by the same token, labor should be protected against an unreasonable competition from a stimulated and excessive immigration." Business groups such as the National Association of Manufacturers and the U.S. Chamber of Commerce still wanted a supply of cheap labor, but even some business leaders were won over to immigration restriction. Nor could friends of immigrants, such as social workers and the Immigrant Protective League of Chicago, stem the nativist tide.

Introducing a Quota System

The inability of prior restrictions, including the literacy test, to halt mass immigration from southern and eastern Europe prompted Congress to find a new formula. It was found in the national origins quotas, which radically reduced immigration. In passing the acts of the 1920s Congress drew upon the expertise of eugenicists and others who believed that the peoples of northern and western Europe, called "Nordics" or "Anglo-Saxons" were superior. In 1920 the House Committee on Immigration and Naturalization had made Harry Laughlin, a prominent eugenicist, its "expert eugenics agent." Representative Albert Johnson, one of his followers and an admirer of eugenic thinking, led the charge in Congress for reductions in immigration and favoritism for northern and western European nations.

The first quota law, that of 1921, set a total of about 360,000 for European nations. Each European nation received a quota of that figure based on its proportion of the foreign-born population in the 1910 census. This gave northern and western European nations slightly over half the visas. The law was meant to be temporary, and although it cut European immigration substantially, restrictionists wanted the numbers reduced further, especially for southern and eastern European nations. Congress obliged and cut the total and pushed the year back to 1890, which worked to the disadvantage of those nations sending large numbers after that date. This change, too, was temporary and finally another system, the national origins quotas, was put into effect in 1929. Congress fixed the total at approximately 150,000 with the national origins quotas giving each European country a proportion equal to its share of the white population according to the 1920 census. While basing the quotas on the total white population and not just the foreign born gave southern and eastern European nations a greater share than did basing them on the foreign-born population as of 1890, it still drastically cut their allotments from their virtual open immigration before World War I.

Those who protested against the new system represented urban districts with high proportions of immigrants, immigrant organizations, immigrant aid societies, and spokesmen for business and agricultural interests. But the pressure to reduce immigration was too strong for these groups to defeat it.

No doubt fears of immigration's alleged adverse impact upon American workers played a role in the enactment of legislation in the 1920s. So did the belief that the United States was being overrun by radicals, the diseased, criminals and morally unfit immigrants and that too many Jews and Catholics were arriving. But the triumph of the national origins quotas coupled with Asian exclusion demonstrated that Washington wanted the nation's ethnic make up to remain as it was in 1920. Italians had averaged 158,000 annually in the early 20th century, but Italy now had a quota of only 5,802. Greece fared even worse, with an allotment of 307.

There was no reason to believe that President Calvin Coolidge, reflecting the national mood, would not sign the law. He had written, "There are racial considerations too grave to be brushed aside for sentimental reasons. . . . The Nordics propagate themselves successfully. With other races, the outcome shows deterioration. . . . Quality of mind and body suggests that observance of ethnic law is as great a necessity to a nation as immigration law." The President signed the act.

Restricting Immigration Was Good for America

Roy Beck

The huge numbers of immigrants who came to the United States between the 1880s and 1920s were simply unnecessary, according to Roy Beck, the Washington, D.C., editor of the *Social Contract* magazine and a frequent commentator on immigration and population issues. Moreover, he claims, many Americans opposed widespread immigration throughout this era, although the federal government and big business paid little attention.

By 1900 the United States stretched from the Atlantic to the Pacific, and consequently the frontier no longer existed. Furthermore, the nation's industrial economy had matured. In this new atmosphere, Beck argues, large numbers of immigrants were no longer needed. Indeed, the continual arrival of immigrant ships held other Americans back by depressing wages and keeping certain groups, particularly southern blacks, out of industrial jobs. Perhaps even worse, Beck notes, immigrants fostered instability. Not only was America unable to absorb the newcomers quickly, but the presence of these newcomers also encouraged racism and anti-Semitism.

We have heard much about the warm personal stories of ancestors who came to America a century ago, but the hard realities and conflict brought by immigration must be restored to the picture if we are to learn anything helpful from the Great Wave experience. First, we must recognize that the Great Wave drew opposition from the beginning; there never was a period of broad public approval.

In 1880, the volume of annual immigration more than doubled over what it had been during each of the previous four years. And it was more than double the annual average of the previous sixty years. The Great Wave had begun. There was no fanfare or official declaration. Only later did Americans realize that something unprecedented was happening. There had been a surge like this in 1872–73 and back in 1854. But this surge was different. The 457,000 level of immigration in 1880 was not a peak but something of a floor for much of the next 44 years.

Many Americans agitated against the increased immigration almost immediately. Their anger was understandable. Manufacturers, such as the shoemaker Calvin T. Sampson of North Adams, Massachusetts, were importing foreign workers to fight the growing pressure from U.S. workers for an eight-hour workday and for other improvements in working conditions. Sounding remarkably like the pro-immigration forces of the 1990s, the industrialists of that time justified their actions on the basis of protecting an unfettered free-market system. They condemned labor organizing and strikes for better working conditions as violations of the "eternal laws of political economy," according to the historian Eric Foner.

Although American workers resented immigrants from both Europe and Asia, they gained their first success in 1882 with the Chinese Exclusion Act. The legislation and anti-immigrant hostilities leading to it included ugly racial overtones. But the special animus against the Chinese immigrants also was driven by the egregious use of them for several years as strikebreakers. In California, the imported Chinese workers had come to make up a quarter of the wage force even before the Great Wave began.

The pressure to cut immigration did not stop with the action against the Chinese. By 1885, Congress was persuaded to move against some of the immigration from Europe. The Alien Contract Law halted the practice of companies contracting to transport immigrants who then were legally bound to work in indentured servitude for at least a year and often for several years.

Misunderstanding the Statue of Liberty

Those measures knocked the numbers down some. But the volume remained high. [Historian] John Higham says there was widespread public demand for more curbs on immigration in 1886, the year of the dedication of the Statue of Liberty. Many otherwise well-informed people today have misconstrued that event, suggesting that the statue was placed in New York City's harbor as a sign of welcome to the new wave of immigrants. In fact, the statue and its symbolism had absolutely nothing to do with immigration, as the museum inside the statue makes abundantly clear. It was only coincidence that the statue was placed at a time and place where millions of immigrants were entering the United States. Given the deep opposition to the increased immigration

---

Protecting American Workers

In 1902 American labor leader Samuel Gompers explained why he thought immigrant workers were a threat to American ones.

The strength of this country is in the intelligence and prosperity of our working people. But both the intelligence and the prosperity of our working people are endangered by the present immigration. Cheap labor, ignorant labor, takes our jobs and cuts our wages.

The fittest survive; that is, those that fit the conditions best. But it is the economically weak, not the economically strong, that fit the conditions of the labor market. They fit best because they can be got to work cheapest. Women and children drive out men, unless either law or labor organization stops it. In just the same way the Chinaman and others drive out the American, the German, the Irishman.

The tariff keeps out cheap foreign goods. It is employers, not workingmen, that have goods to sell. Workingmen sell labor, and cheap labor is not kept out by the tariff. The protection that would directly help the workers is protection against the cheap labor itself.

Oscar Handlin, *Immigration as a Factor in American History*. Englewood Cliffs, NJ: Prentice Hall, 1959.

numbers at the time, it is doubtful that the people of New York would have contributed the money to build the pedestal if they had thought the statue, which officially was entitled *Liberty Enlightening the World*, had been intended as *America Inviting the World*.

While the rapid industrialization of the northern economy created openings for many new wage earners, the country did not require hundreds of thousands of foreign workers to meet that need. Large numbers of rural Americans, especially white and black workers in the war-ravaged South, could have taken many of those new northern jobs. But most were shut out of the opportunity by the Great Wave immigrants from Europe. The economist Joshua L. Rosenbloom of the University of Kansas found that immigrants were able to use ethnic networking as a means to fill job openings with workers from their own nationality groups. Like many employers in the 1990s, once northern companies learned that they could easily fill their jobs through immigrant networking, they made few efforts to attract new supplies of American workers. "Only when European immigration was cut off during the First World War were concerted efforts undertaken to develop the machinery necessary to attract low-wage southern workers," Rosenbloom concluded.

Immigrants Prevented Americans from Finding Better Jobs

The most tragic result of the manufacturers' preference for immigrant labor was a half-century postponement of opportunity for most of the freed slaves to seek higher-paying jobs outside of the South. That left a large percentage of them dependent for jobs from the very class of southerners that previously had enslaved them. The Great Wave began just as the federal government had abandoned Reconstruction and had withdrawn federal troops from the South. With the immigration-filled northern industries having no need of their services and the federal government no longer willing to protect their rights, many black workers were trapped in the South where most of their political and economic gains since the Civil War were stripped away.

Meanwhile, native-born white Americans in the North and West were feeling their own effects of the greatly expanded pool of labor. One reason the industrialists were so eager to enlarge the labor supply was to try to flatten American wage rates, which were far higher than wages in Europe. Because of an abundance of underutilized natural resources (especially open land) and a relatively small population, the New World in 1870 paid wages that were 136 percent higher than in the heavily populated Old World. But by 1913, American workers had lost almost half that pay advantage, after decades of massive additions of foreign workers. Immigrant labor depressed wages for native labor by competing directly on almost equal terms, according to the economists Timothy J. Hatton and Jeffrey G. Williamson, in their book *Migration and the International Labor Market 1850–1939*. They state that the immigrants "marginalized" most native women and black workers, keeping them out of the mainstream of industrial jobs.

Adding to Americans' concerns about the labor competition from immigrants was the psychological shock of being informed in 1890 by the U.S. Census Bureau that so many people had settled in the West that the frontier, under the Census definition, no longer existed. Williamson has written that, around that time, the absorptive capacity of the American labor market declined; thereafter, immigration dragged down wages even more than it had during the early part of the Great Wave.

At that point, it didn't matter what proportion of the population immigration had once been; conditions had changed. The country had reached a level of maturity that no longer needed or could handle immigration at the old proportions or numbers. Frederick Jackson Turner, the most famous of the country's chroniclers of the closing of the frontier, found immigration much more threatening than during a time of open land. He wrote in the *Chicago Record-Herald* for 25 September 1901:

> The immigrant of the preceding period was assimilated with comparative ease, and it can hardly be doubted that valuable

contributions to American character have come from this in-
fusion of non-English stock into the American people. But
the free lands that made the process of absorption easy have
gone. The immigration is becoming increasingly more difficult of assimilation. Its competition with American labor
under existing conditions may give increased power to the
producer, but the effects upon American well-being are dangerous in the extreme.

A heightened sense of urgency drove Americans to insist
on decisive action in Washington. On 9 February 1897, the
U.S. House of Representatives began a dramatic series of
legislative events: (1) The House voted 217 to 36 to approve
an immigrant literacy test. That test would have significantly
curtailed the immigration of the next decades. (2) A week
later, the Senate voted 34 to 31 to send the immigration restriction bill to President Grover Cleveland. (3) Cleveland
vetoed it on March 2. (4) The next day, the House overrode
the veto by 195 to 37. (5) The Senate—having earlier approved it by such a narrow margin—did not bother to attempt a two-thirds override of the veto. Thus the Great
Wave narrowly escaped being shut off after only seventeen
years and before it grew to its greatest strength.

Many Americans Wanted to Restrict Immigration

Restrictionism had failed for the moment. There were no
public opinion polls to record the actual attitudes of the
American people. But the majority of their representatives in
Congress worked for the next twenty-seven years to reduce
legal immigration levels. That suggests a large segment of
Americans who wanted to substantially change the spectacle
on Ellis Island where hundreds of thousands of immigrants
a year lined up to be processed into the U.S. labor force.

The restrictionist issue carried over to the next presidential
election. William McKinley, running on a platform that supported restriction, was victorious; this time there would be no
presidential veto protecting the foreign influx. But while the
Senate voted 45–28 in 1898 to stop the Great Wave, a recon-
stituted House narrowly defeated the restriction, 104 to 101.

If two members had switched from "no" to "yes," the Great Wave would have lost much of its volume. And the peak decade for Ellis Island never would have occurred.

One branch or the other of Congress was in nearly constant motion during the next two decades, trying to stop the Great Wave. The majority of the members of the U.S. House of Representatives voted to restrain immigration in 1897, 1902, 1906, 1912, 1913, 1915, 1916, 1917, 1921, and 1924. The Senate did the same in 1897, 1898, 1912, 1915, 1916, 1917, 1921, and 1924. But for years, the supporters of high immigration always were able to persuade a president to veto restrictionist legislation and managed to win just enough votes in one of the houses of Congress to prevent a two-thirds vote to override a veto. Industrialists lobbied hard to protect their supply of cheap labor. And leaders of growing blocs of newly naturalized immigrant citizens were influential in making sure immigration continued to add more people to their ethnic power bases.

The country paid high costs for the delay in enacting restrictions. John Higham—who continues to believe that immigration generally has strengthened the American character—has warned defenders of the current wave of immigration that they risk repeating the disastrous mistakes of those who early this century insisted on keeping the Great Wave going. "The inescapable need for some rational control over the volume of immigration in an increasingly crowded world was plain to see, then as now," he wrote. But the business interests, the immigrant leaders, and the traditionalists who feared any increase in the powers of government blocked all reform and allowed problems to fester and grow. As another 14 million immigrants entered between 1897 and 1917, the social fabric frayed, as exemplified by the upheaval in Wausau, Wisconsin. Frustrations among Americans overflowed. America endured a nationwide spread of intense anti-Semitism, anti-immigrant hysteria, and the heyday of the new Ku Klux Klan as a "nationwide, all-purpose vigilante movement," according to Higham.

It was that extreme reaction to the extreme volume of immigration that has tended to cause immigration restriction-

ists today to be suspect as right-wing racists. But Otis Gra-
ham of the University of California, Santa Barbara, has noted
that "Restrictionism attracted some of the best minds in
America, including many liberal clergymen, spokesmen for
organized labor and the black community, and socialists."

Part of the concern of the liberal restrictionists was the
abominable conditions for many immigrants. A congressional study found that new arrivals were three times more
likely than natives to be on welfare in 1909; immigrants
comprised more than half the people on welfare nationwide.
Chicago was especially hard-hit; four out of every five welfare recipients at that time were immigrants and their children. Foreign-born residents constituted a third of the pa-
tients in public hospitals and insane asylums in the country.
The situation was worse in New York City, where the president of the board of health said that almost half the expen-
ditures were for the immigrant poor.

A national commission studied the impact of immigration
for five years and concluded in 1911 that it was contributing
to low wages and poor working conditions. It was not until
1917, however, that immigration restrictions finally were
enacted into law as the House (287–106) and the Senate (62–
19) overrode President Wilson's second veto.

In the public's view, the 1917 action did not block enough
immigrants. Another act in 1921 set a numerical ceiling for
the first time. And then in 1924, Congress decisively gave
the American people the respite they so long had sought.
The "Great Aberration" was over, after forty-four years.

To criticize the Great Wave—or any period of immigration—is not to criticize the individuals who were part of it.
Often through no fault of their own, the immigrants were
used by certain Americans to undercut the wages and power
of other groups of Americans.

World War I Encouraged Immigration Restrictions

John Higham

American participation in World War I began in 1917, although the war had been raging in Europe and elsewhere since 1914. America fought on the side of the English, French, and their allies. The opponents were the Germans and their allies. World War I was an intensely nationalistic conflict in which the participants believed that their national survival was at stake. In this context many people were concerned about any possible threat to national unity, such as those represented by immigration or by the presence of large foreign communities.

In the following selection, history professor John Higham of the University of Michigan asserts that World War I shifted America drastically in the direction of restricting immigration. The war effort required, Higham notes, the creation of an atmosphere of national unity, of a sense of "100 percent Americanization." Many thought that the time had come for America to stop accepting so many newcomers, and to "Americanize" those already here. As early as 1917, in fact, the government required all new immigrants to pass a literacy test to prove they would not be an undue burden on the nation. These attitudes, Higham claims, were the culmination of several decades of milder anti-immigrant sentiment.

The general terms of the great immigration restriction laws of the early twenties stare up at us from the pages of every textbook in American history. We realize that these measures brought to culmination a legislative trend extending back to the 1880s. It is not so obvious perhaps that they belonged equally to a cascade of anti-foreign statutes that began during the war [World War I]. From the passage of the Espionage Act in 1917 through the tribal reaction of the twenties, state and national governments legislated almost ceaselessly against the successive dangers that seemed to arise from America's foreign population. Immigration restriction marked both the climax and the conclusion of an era of nationalistic legislation.

During the war and its immediate aftermath, interest focused not on the old objective of restriction but rather on new policies of repression, Americanization, and deportation. By 1920, however, about as much official coercion as the United States would tolerate had been undertaken; for some time to come further attempts to impose internal conformity would rest more completely in private hands. By 1920, also, the policies of Americanization and deportation, as massive ventures, were suffering general discredit. Political nativism shifted again toward its traditional goals, by the same maneuver that turned nativist thinking back into racial and religious channels. With new momentum the two main prewar trends in legislation revived: economic discriminations against aliens, and immigration restriction. In respect to the former, the early twentieth century movement to exclude aliens from a wide range of white-collar jobs went forward again as soon as the war ended, and in the first half of the 1920's these proscriptions accumulated more rapidly and extensively than ever before. Licensing acts in many states barred aliens from practicing medicine, surgery, chiropractic, pharmacy, architecture, engineering, and surveying, from operating motor buses, and from executing wills. These state enactments paralleled the adoption by Congress of a more general kind of restriction: a human blockade sufficiently drastic to be generally considered at the time a permanent solution of the immigration question. And, in truth, the principles then adopted remain the foundation of our immigration law.

World War I Required National Unity

The whole atmosphere in which the new restriction acts took shape was different from the atmosphere of similar debates in earlier decades. From the establishment of federal regulation in the 1880's until the World War, the main division in attitudes lay between those who wanted a general qualitative and quantitative restriction and those who held to essentially unrestricted European immigration. A large but diminishing middle group remained indifferent or undecided. The restrictionists won only with the enactment of the literacy test on the eve of American entry into the war. Then the new nationalism of 1917 and 1918 changed the terms of discussion. At least in native American opinion, the issue after the armistice no longer concerned the desirability of restriction but simply the proper degree and kind. The war virtually swept from the American consciousness the old belief in unrestricted immigration. It did so, very simply, by creating an urgent demand for national unity and homogeneity that practically destroyed what the travail of preceding decades had already fatally weakened: the historic confidence in the capacity of American society to assimilate all men automatically. And with the passing of faith in the melting pot there perished the ideal of American nationality as an unfinished, steadily improving, cosmopolitan blend. Once almost everyone except immigrant spokesmen tacitly conceded that immigration might overtax the natural processes of assimilation, supporters of a "liberal" policy retired from grounds of fundamental principle to an uneasy, relative position.

After the war, the dwindling company of progressive intellectuals played curiously little part in restriction controversies. Most of them wearily agreed with the popular demand for a more stable, homogeneous ethnic pattern. As early as 1916, the leading journal of progressive opinion, *The New Republic*, made the momentous confession: "Freedom of migration from one country to another appears to be one of the elements in nineteenth-century liberalism that is fated to disappear. The responsibility of the state for the welfare of its individual members is progressively increasing. The democracy of today . . . cannot permit . . . social ills to be aggravated by excessive immigration." Sometimes progressive intellectuals criticized specific restrictive proposals as irrational or prejudiced; more often, they simply avoided the issue.

Both Liberals and Business Leaders Moved Toward Restrictions

The one real effort on the part of liberals to define a clear-cut alternative to the main drift of postwar restriction revealed the distance that American opinion had traveled in a few short years. The Reverend Sidney L. Gulick, a former Protestant missionary in Japan, had advanced in 1914 a "nondiscriminatory" quota scheme designed to eliminate differential treatment of the Japanese by applying a uniform principle to all immigrant nationalities. Briefly, he proposed quotas for each nationality proportionate to the number of naturalized citizens and their American-born children already drawn from that nationality. Each year a federal commission would fix the total allowable immigration at a certain percentage, 10 or less, of those first and second generation citizens. In adopting the rate of naturalization as a standard, Gulick admitted that some nationalities were assimilated more easily than others and argued: "The proved capacity for genuine Americanization on the part of those already here from any land should be the measure for the further immigration of that people." This criterion would substantially reduce the new immigration, as Gulick pointed out. In support of this plan he organized in 1918 a National Committee for Constructive Immigration Legislation, which was endorsed by a variety of respectable people. . . .

While native-born progressives surrendered to the restrictionist trend, big business maintained a tenacious opposition. Rooted in self-interest, the industrialists' clamor against increasingly stringent legislation continued well into the twenties. After the war manpower shortage, corporations looked forward greedily to a revival of heavy immigration, expecting that it would beat down an inflated wage scale and curb the increased power of the unions. Through the Inter-Racial Council, the National Association of Manufacturers, and other trade organizations, business leaders even advocated repeal of the literacy test. Nevertheless, they too had actually retreated some distance from their prewar views. Wartime emotions had worked upon their national consciousness, and the Red Scare frightened many of them at least temporarily. While few industrialists favored more rigid limitations on immigration, most of them now acknowledged the importance of some restrictive controls, on patriotic grounds. The National Association of Manufacturers confessed that immigration might endanger the nation and agreed with the nativists that policy must rest on "the needs and interest of America first." The *Commercial and Financial Chronicle* looked about for a middle ground that would satisfy business needs but also ensure both racial preservation and "protection against the poisonous agents and agencies of anarchy."

These alterations in progressive and business thinking left the immigrants themselves pretty much isolated as uncompromising enemies of any general limitation on transatlantic movement. Doggedly, the immigrants set themselves to keep the gates of America as open as possible for their fellow countrymen. Still, the golden Irish voice of Bourke Cochran rose in the House of Representatives to oppose all restriction except on the criminal, the diseased, or the imbecile. Still, scrappy little Adolph Sabath, renowned in the greenhorn sections of every American city as the immigrant's Congressman, protested in Bohemian accents at any modification of a historic American principle. On this issue the immigrant vote continued to outweigh the labor vote in major urban centers; toward the end of the struggle twenty out of the twenty-two members of the New York state Democratic delegation in the House of Representatives issued an angry declaration excoriating the pending legislation.

Immigrants' Opinions

Meanwhile immigrant writers appealed constantly to the democratic and cosmopolitan strains in the American heritage. Franz Boas continued to lead the attack on ideas of racial superiority. Some minority spokesmen still described the American people as an ever evolving, composite nationality, or America as a home of the oppressed. There was much rhapsodizing over "immigrant gifts," with the Knights of Columbus sponsoring a series of books on the "racial contributions" of various immigrant groups. One Jewish intellectual, Horace Kallen, developed a radically new theory of American nationality in defense of minority cultures. Reacting violently against the dominant 100 per cent American outlook, Kallen argued that true Americanism lay in the conservation and actual fostering of group differences, not in melting them down or "contributing" them. At the time, his doctrine of cultural pluralism made little impression outside of Zionist circles. Indeed, the whole immigrant counteroffensive hardly dented the massive phalanx of native American opinion. Nor did the outcries of the new immigrants rouse any appreciable sympathy among their brethren from northern Europe. The Germans, by the end of 1920 once more restored to favor through another swift reversal of judgment, were doubtless relieved that the lightning struck elsewhere. The Scandinavians showed their undiluted Americanism by joining in the cry for higher bars against the new immigration.

If the enfeeblement of the opposition illustrates the new temper of discussion, the radical demands of postwar restrictionists bring us to the heart of the revolution in opinion. Agitation for legislation did not await the events of 1920; it burst forth immediately upon the signing of the armistice in 1918. And from the very first, the new drive for restriction had a drastic quality inconceivable in the decades before the war. Nativists now demanded nothing less than total suspension of all immigration for periods ranging from two to fifty years.

Appendix of Documents

Document 1: What Is an American?

In the late 1700s, a French writer who had spent a number of years in the British colonies of North America, Michel St. Jean de Crevecoeur, wrote that the American was a different person from the European from which he or she was descended. Although in fact most Americans were British in their background, St. Jean de Crevecoeur thought that America would produce "a new race of men."

What attachment can a poor European emigrant have for a country where he had nothing? The knowledge of the language, the love of a few kindred as poor as himself, were the only cords that tied him: his country is now that which gives him land, bread, protection, and consequence: *Ubi panis ibi patria* ["Where I find bread, there is my country"], is the motto of all emigrants. What then is the American, this new man? He is either an European, or the descendant of an European, hence that strange mixture of blood, which you will find in no other country. I could point out to you a family whose grandfather was an Englishman, whose wife was Dutch, whose son married a French woman, and whose present four sons have now four wives of different nations. *He* is an American, who leaving behind him all his ancient prejudices and manners, receives new ones from the new mode of life he has embraced, the new government he obeys, and the new rank he holds. He becomes an American by being received in the broad lap of our great *Alma Mater* ["Fostering Mother"]. Here individuals of all nations are melted into a new race of men, whose labours and posterity will one day cause great changes in the world. Americans are the western pilgrims, who are carrying along with them that great mass of arts, sciences, vigour, and industry which began long since in the east; they will finish the great circle. The Americans were once scattered all over Europe; here they are incorporated into one of the finest systems of population which has ever appeared, and which will hereafter become distinct by the power of the different climates they inhabit. The American ought therefore to love this country much better than that wherein either he or his forefathers were born. Here the rewards of his industry follow with equal steps the progress of his labour; his labour is founded on the basis of nature, *self-interest*; can it want a stronger allurement?

Wives and children, who before in vain demanded of him a morsel of bread, now, fat and frolicsome, gladly help their father to clear those fields whence exuberant crops are to arise to feed and to clothe them all; without any part being claimed, either by a despotic prince, a rich abbot, or a mighty lord.

Michel St. Jean de Crevecoeur, *Letters from an American Farmer*. New York: Foxx, Duffield, 1904.

Document 2: A Welcome for Immigrants

In 1886 the Statue of Liberty was dedicated in New York harbor. On the base of the statue was enscribed a poem by Emma Lazarus. The poem seemed to be a welcome to emigrants from older lands seeking freedom in America.

> Not like the brazen giant of Greek fame,
> With conquering limbs astride from land to land
> Here at our sea-washed, sunset gates shall stand
> A mighty woman with a torch, whose flame
> Is the imprisoned lightening, and her name
> Mother of Exiles. From her beacon-handed
> Glows world-wide welcome; her mild eyes command
> The air-bridged harbor that twin cities frame
> "Keep, ancient lands, your storied pomp!" cries she
> With silent lips. "Give me your tired, your poor,
> Your huddled masses yearning to breathe free,
> The wretched refuse of your teeming shore.
> Send these, the homeless, tempest-tost to me,
> I lift my lamp beside the golden door!"

Emma Lazarus, "The New Colossus," from *Poems*. Boston, 1889.

Document 3: The Potato Famine in Ireland

In 1845 and 1847, Ireland's potato crop was ruined by blight. Since the potato was the basic food of Ireland's peasant farmers, and since no other food was available to them, Irish farmers suffered terribly. Many died of starvation. Others immigrated to America. Many of those who were able sent money back to the poor in Ireland, as this article from the New York Tribune *reported.*

Jacob Harvey states in *The Courier* that he has taken the pains to call upon all the houses [banks] in this city who are in the daily practice of drawing small drafts on Ireland, and has received from them an accurate return of the amounts received for these small drafts for the entire year 1846, and also during the last sixty days.

The result is so creditable to his own countrymen that he cannot avoid publishing it as an incentive to those who have as yet done nothing to go and do likewise.

Total amount remitted by labouring Irish, male and female, during 1846 from New York, $808,000, of which there were in November and December $175,000. These remittances are sent to all parts of Ireland, and by every packet; and we may judge of the relief afforded to a very large number of poor families in a year when they are cut short of their usual food, the potato. It has required no public meetings, says Mr Harvey, no special addresses, to bring forth these remittances from the poor, nor do they look for any praise for what they have done. It is the natural instinct of the Irish peasant to share his mite—be it money or potatoes—with those poorer than himself; and he thinks he has but done a Christian duty, deserving of no special applause.

It is fitted to exalt our estimate of human nature to record such a proof of the self-sacrifice and severe self-denial through which alone such a sum as is here stated, $808,000, could in one year be remitted from their savings by the Irish at labour and at service in and around this city. Of what other people in the world under like circumstances can such a fact be truly stated?

"The Irish Heart," *New York Tribune*, January 9, 1847.

Document 4: The Thoughts of a German "Forty-Eighter"

Some German emigrants came to America after a series of revolutions in 1848 failed to bring democracy to Germany. Carl Schurz, who went on to become a general in the American Civil War, wrote to a friend at home on March 25, 1855, that he believed the prospects for freedom were better in the United States than in Germany.

As long as there is no upheaval of affairs in Europe it is my firm resolve to regard this country not as a transient or accidental abode, but as the field for my usefulness. I love America and I am vitally interested in the things about me—they no longer seem strange. I find that the question of liberty is in its essence the same everywhere, however different its form. Although I do not regard the public affairs of this country with the same devotion as those of our old home, it is not mere ambition nor eagerness for distinction that impels me to activity. My interest in the political contests of this country is so strong, so spontaneous, that I am profoundly stirred. More self-control is required for me to keep aloof than to participate in them. These are the years of my best strength. Shall

I devote myself wholly to the struggle for existence while I have hopes that I may soon be independent in that respect? I venture to say that I am neither avaricious nor self-indulgent.

If I now seek material prosperity, it is only that I may be free to follow my natural aspirations. Or shall I again subject myself to that dreary condition of waiting, which must undermine the strongest constitution when it is the only occupation? We have both tasted its bitterness; and I am burning with the desire to be employed with visible, tangible things and no longer to be bound to dreams and theories. I have a holy horror of the illusory fussiness which characterizes the life of the professional refugees. My devotion to the cause of the old Fatherland has not abated but my expectations have somewhat cooled; I have only faint hopes for the next few years. Even if the revolution should come sooner than I expect, I do not see why I should not utilize the intervening time. I feel that here I can accomplish something. I am convinced of it when I consider the qualities of the men who are now conspicuous. This inspires me, and even if the prospects of success did not correspond with my natural impulses, I should suddenly find that I had involuntarily entered into the thick of the fight. In these circumstances, why should I wish to return to Europe? I am happy that I have a firm foothold and good opportunities.

After my return from Europe I expect to go to Wisconsin. I transferred some of my business interests there when on my last trip to the West. The German element is powerful in that State, the immigrants being so numerous, and they are striving for political recognition. They only lack leaders that are not bound by the restraints of money-getting. There is the place where I can find a sure, gradually expanding field for my work without truckling to the nativistic elements, and there, I hope, in time, to gain influence that may also become useful to our cause. It is my belief that the future interests of America and Germany are closely interwoven. The two countries will be natural allies as soon as a European upheaval takes place. However different the two nations may be in character, they will have the same opponents, and that will compel them to have a corresponding foreign policy. American influence in Europe will be based on Germany, and Germany's world-position will depend essentially on the success of America. Germany is the only power in Europe whose interests will not conflict with those of America, and America is the only power in the civilized world that would not be jealous of a strong, united Germany. They can both grow without being rivals, and it will be to the interest of each to keep the adversaries of the other in check. Americans will realize this as soon as the Emperor of Austria and the King of Prussia need no longer be considered, and the Germans will become convinced of it as soon as they consider a national foreign policy.

Moses Rischin, ed., *Immigration and the American Tradition*. Indianapolis: Bobbs-Merril, 1976.

Document 5: Norwegian Emigrants See the Fruits of Their Labors

Many Scandinavian emigrants left for America between 1840 and 1880 to escape the poverty of their home villages. A sizable number home-steaded farms in the Midwest and Great Plains states. They found the land there more productive and their prospects better than their relatives' who stayed home.

The soil here is as fertile as any you can find in America, and our daily food consists of rye and wheat bread, bacon, butter, eggs, molasses, sugar, coffee, and beer. The corn that grows on large cobs is rarely eaten by people; it is not tender enough for that, but is used as fodder for the animals. Thus you can understand that we have had no trouble making a living and have not had to ask others for help. My brothers and sisters and I have all acquired land, and we are happy and content. This year we have produced so much foodstuff that we have been able to sell instead of having to buy, and we all have cattle, driving oxen, and wagons. We also have children in abundance. Gunild has given birth to two girls, Sigri and Anne, and I have also had two here, a boy called Terje and a girl called Sigri. But Ole and Joraand have no children.

Our old father, who is in good health, received the $200 in June. My sister Sigri worked for twenty-five weeks in a town forty miles from here and got $25 for that. Guro has traveled thirty-five miles from here down to Koshkonong Prairie to be confirmed; she will not return till next spring.

Since I love you, Tellef, more than all my other brothers and sisters, I feel very sorry that you have to work your youth away in Norway, where it is so difficult to get ahead. There you can't see any results of your labor, while here you can work ahead to success and get to own a good deal of property, even though you did not have a penny to begin with. I wish that you would sell the farm now for what you can get for it and come here as fast as possible. I and all the others with me believe that you would not regret it. Our old father would tell you the same thing. He has heard that you do not feel like leaving, and he says that you are so young and inexperienced that it may be best for you to try your luck in Norway first. Then later you will be very glad to come here. If you do come, we hope that you will not be so foolish as to go to the warm Texas. It is true that Reiersen praises it highly, but when my mother asked him how conditions were in Texas, he himself told her that it was so hot there that if you put a pan with bacon out on the street, it fries by itself. Then, of course, we were frightened at the thought of such a hot climate and were afraid to go there. And when they say in Texas that a man can get a completely satisfying meal out of a cob of corn, we conclude that this must be because the people there are so sickly and unhealthy that they cannot eat very much. We are to blame for not having written about this before, but the reason was that we had not expected that our brothers and sisters would want to go to Texas. We are a little surprised to see that our relatives do not seem to love us so very much, since they want to travel to such a remote place, as if they were afraid of meeting us again. But it is just the same to us; if they can get along without us, we can get along without them, but I do know that none of us would have acted in this way. We have talked to a man by the name of Kjøstel, from Holt, who had traveled far into Texas with Jørgen Hasle, but when he saw the way people lived there he returned. They have neither wheat bread nor butter there, only the coarse corn foodstuff, but we here in Wisconsin would not be satisfied with such hog's feed.

Theodore C. Blegen, ed., *The Land of Their Choice: The Immigrants Write Home.* Minneapolis: University of Minnesota Press, 1955.

Document 6: The Chinese Exclusion Act of 1882

The Chinese were the first group to be forbidden to immigrate to the United States. Many Chinese had come to California after the Gold Rush of 1849. Other Californians were able to convince the government that Chinese people could never assimilate into American life. The federal government responded with the following legislation.

An act to execute certain treaty stipulations relating to Chinese.

Whereas, in the opinion of the Government of the United States the coming of Chinese laborers to this country endangers the good order of certain localities within the territory thereof: Therefore,

Be it enacted by the Senate and House of Representatives of the United States of America in Congress assembled, That from and after the expiration of ninety days next after the passage of this act, and until the expiration of ten years next after the passage of this act, the coming of Chinese laborers to the United States be, and the same is hereby, suspended; and during such suspension it shall not be lawful for any Chinese laborer to come, or, having so come after the expiration of said ninety days, to remain within the United States.

Sec. 2. That the master of any vessel who shall knowingly bring within the United States on such vessel, and land or permit to be landed, any Chinese laborer, from any foreign port or place, shall be deemed guilty of a misdemeanor, and on conviction thereof shall be punished by a fine of not more than five hundred dollars for each and every such Chinese laborer so brought, and may be also imprisoned for a term not exceeding one year.

Sec. 3. That the two foregoing sections shall not apply to Chinese laborers who were in the United States on the seventeenth day of November, eighteen hundred and eighty, or who shall have come into the same before the expiration of ninety days next after the passage of this act, and who shall produce to such master before going on board such vessel, and shall produce to the collector of the port in the United States at which such vessel shall arrive, the evidence hereinafter in this act required of his being one of the laborers in this section mentioned; nor shall the two foregoing sections apply to the case of any master whose vessel, being bound to a port not within the United States, shall come within the jurisdiction of the United States by reason of being in distress or in stress of weather, or touching at any port of the United States on its voyage to any foreign port or place: *Provided,* That all Chinese laborers brought on such vessel shall depart with the vessel on leaving port.

Andrew Gyory, *Closing the Gate: Race, Politics, and the Chinese Exclusion Act.* Chapel Hill: University of North Carolina Press, 1998.

Document 7: Immigrant Labor in Urban Sweatshops

Many of the emigrants who came from eastern Europe after 1880 first worked in sweatshops. In this account, reporter John DeWitt Warner describes not only the business process but also the poor working conditions of immigrant laborers in New York City in 1895.

Two years since it was my duty, as chairman of a Congressional committee, to investigate the so-called "sweating system," New York being one of the several cities visited. The "sweating system" is practically the process by which ready-made clothing is manufactured in tenement-houses.

Conditions have radically changed during the last twenty-five years. Formerly the women of each household made up the greater part of its clothing, the rest being supplied by the local tailor, and made up on his premises. The "ready-made" business has developed new economies, especially in divisions of labor and the method of its employment. Middlemen have been given a place between the "manufacturer" and the actual operative, processes have been cheapened and labor degraded.

The materials are cut and "bunched" for each garment by the manufacturer. They are then distributed in large lots to special jobbers, known as "contractors," each a specialist in his line. For example, one makes coats, another cloaks, another pantaloons, while some make special grades or sizes. With this distribution the wholesaler washes his hands of the business, his ignorance of how and where his goods are actually made up being as ideal as intentional.

Not far from one-half of the goods thus distributed are made up in the contractors' factories. As to the other half, the first contractor sublets the work to a "sweater," whose shop is generally one of the two larger rooms of a tenement flat, accommodating from six to fifteen or twenty "sweating" employees—men, women, and children. In the other large room of the flat are his living, sleeping, and cooking arrangements, overflowing into the workroom. Employes whom he boards, who eat at their work, and who sleep on the goods, frequently complete the intimate connection of home and shop. One-fourth of our ready-made and somewhat of our custom-made clothing are thus put together.

The people engaged are those whose families are most prolific, whose sense of cleanliness is least developed, who comprehend no distinction between living and work rooms, whose premises are dirty to the point of filth, and who are found in the most densely populated portions of the city.

But this is not the worst. Single families, inhabiting one or more rooms, generally having a family as sub-tenants, or a number of lodgers or boarders, subcontract work from the tenement "sweaters." Thus by tenement "home-workers" are made another one-fourth of our ready-made clothing and a much larger proportion of our children's clothing. The homes of these home-workers include many of the most wretched in which human beings exist among us. The conditions of squalor and filth are frequently such as to make even inspection impossible, except by one hardened to the work, while the quarters in which this work is centred are those into which tend the most helpless of our population.

From the wholesale manufacturer, handling each year a product of millions, through the contractor to the "sweater," and on to the "home-worker," the steps are steadily downward—of decreasing responsibility, comfort, and compensation. The profit of each (except the wretch at the bottom) is "sweated" from the next below him.

The contractors' shops are much like other factories—the large proportion of foreign labor and a tendency toward long hours being their main distinctions. In the tenement "sweat shops" unhealthy and unclean conditions are almost universal, and those of filth and contagion common. The employes are in the main foreign-born and newly arrived. The proportion of female labor is large, and child labor is largely used. Wages are from a fourth to a third less than in the larger shops. As to hours, there is no limit except the endurance of the employees, the work being paid for by the "task," and the task so adjusted as to drive from the shop any employee who, whenever he is given a bench, will not work to the limit of physical endurance, the hours of labor being rarely less than twelve, generally thirteen or fourteen, frequently from fifteen to eighteen, hours in the twenty-four.

The lot, however, of these "sweat-shop" workers is luxury compared to that of those engaged in tenement home work. The home-worker is generally a foreigner just arrived, and frequently a woman whose husband is dead, sick, or worthless, and whose children keep her at home. Of these tenement home-workers there are more women than men, and children are as numerous as both. The work is carried on in the one, two, or three rooms occupied by the family, with its subtenants or boarders. No pretence is made of separating shop work from household affairs. The hours observed are those which endurance alone limits. Children are worked to death beside their parents. Contagious diseases are especially prevalent among these people; but even death disturbs from their occupation only the one or two necessary to dispose of the body.

As to wages in this "tenement home-work," there is nothing which can properly be so called. The work is secured by underbidding of tenement sweat shops, and is generally piece-work, one process of which may be attended to by the head of the family, and the rest by its other members according to their capacity. Those engaged are so generally compelled to accept rather than to choose their work that it is taken without reference to the possibility of gaining a livelihood therefrom, the miserable workers earning what they can, begging to supplement it, and dying or being supported as paupers when they fail.

A large proportion—nearly, if not quite, one-half—of all the clothing worn by the majority of our people is thus made under conditions revolting to humanity and decency, and such as to endanger the health of the wearer.

John DeWitt Warner, "The 'Sweating System' in New York City," *Harper's Weekly*, February 9, 1895.

Document 8: Adjusting to the American Labor Market

After 1880, as huge numbers of European emigrants crossed the Atlantic, the United States enjoyed rapid industrial expansion. Many of the immigrants found work in industry easily, especially since they were willing to accept lower wages than long-standing Americans or even earlier immigrants would. A federal immigration commission published the following report on immigrant workers in 1910.

A large proportion of the southern and eastern European immigrants of the past twenty-five years have entered the manufacturing and mining industries of the eastern and middle western States, mostly in the capacity of unskilled laborers. There is no basic industry in which they are not largely represented and in many cases they compose more than 50 per cent of the total number of persons employed in such industries. Coincident with the advent of these millions of unskilled laborers there has been an unprecedented expansion of the industries in which they have been employed. Whether this great immigration movement was caused by the industrial development, or whether the fact that a practically unlimited and available supply of cheap labor existed in Europe was taken advantage of for the purpose of expanding the industries, can not well be demonstrated. Whatever may be the truth in this regard it is certain that southern and eastern European immigrants have almost completely monopolized unskilled labor activities in many of the more important industries. This phase of the industrial situation was made the most important and exhaustive feature of the Commission's investigation, and the results show that while the competition of these immigrants has had little, if any, effect on the highly skilled trades, nevertheless, through lack of industrial progress and by reason of large and constant reinforcement from abroad, it has kept conditions in the semiskilled and unskilled occupations from advancing.

Several elements peculiar to the new immigrants contributed to this result. The aliens came from countries where low economic conditions prevailed and where conditions of labor were bad. They were content to accept wages and conditions which the native

American and immigrants of the older class had come to regard as unsatisfactory. They were not, as a rule, engaged at lower wages than had been paid to the older workmen for the same class of labor, but their presence in constantly increasing numbers prevented progress among the older wage-earning class, and as a result that class of employees was gradually displaced. An instance of this displacement is shown in the experience in the bituminous coal mines of western Pennsylvania. This section of the bituminous field was the one first entered by the new immigrants, and the displacement of the old workers was soon under way. Some of them entered other occupations and many of them migrated to the coal fields of the Middle West. Later these fields also were invaded by the new immigrants, and large numbers of the old workers again migrated to the mines of the Southwest, where they still predominate. The effect of the new immigration is clearly shown in the western Pennsylvania fields, where the average wage of the bituminous coal worker is 42 cents a day below the average wage in the Middle West and the Southwest. Incidentally, hours of labor are longer and general working conditions poorer in the Pennsylvania mines than elsewhere. Another characteristic of the new immigrants contributed to the situation in Pennsylvania. This was the impossibility of successfully organizing them into labor unions. Several attempts at organization were made, but the constant influx of immigrants to whom prevailing conditions seemed unusually favorable contributed to the failure to organize. A similar situation has prevailed in other great industries.

Like most of the immigration from southern and eastern Europe, those who entered the leading industries were largely single men or married men unaccompanied by their families. There is, of course, in practically all industrial communities a large number of families of the various races, but the majority of the employees are men without families here, and whose standard of living is so far below that of the native American or older immigrant workman that it is impossible for the latter to successfully compete with them. They usually live in cooperative groups and crowd together. Consequently, they are able to save a great part of their earnings, much of which is sent or carried abroad. Moreover, there is a strong tendency on the part of these unaccompanied men to return to their native countries after a few years of labor here. These groups have little contact with American life, learn little of American institutions, and aside from the wages earned profit little by their stay in this country. During their early years in the United

States they usually rely for assistance and advice on some member of their race, frequently a saloon keeper or grocer, and almost always a steamship ticket agent and "immigrant banker," who, because of superior intelligence and better knowledge of American ways, commands their confidence. Usually after a longer residence they become more self-reliant, but their progress toward assimilation is generally slow. Immigrant families in the industrial centers are more permanent and usually exhibit a stronger tendency toward advancement, although, in most cases, it is a long time before they even approach the ordinary standard of the American or the older immigrant families in the same grade of occupation. This description, of course, is not universally true, but it fairly represents a great part of the recent immigrant population in the United States. Their numbers are so great and the influx is so continuous that even with the remarkable expansion of industry during the past few years there has been created an over supply of unskilled labor, and in some of the industries this is reflected in a curtailed number of working days and a consequent yearly income among the unskilled workers which is very much less than is indicated by the daily wage rates paid; and while it may not have lowered in a marked degree the American standard of living, it has introduced a lower standard which has become prevalent in the unskilled industry at large.

U.S. Immigration Commission, *Reports*, 61st Cong., 3d sess., 1910, S. Doc. 747.

Document 9: A Third-Generation Immigrant Remembers

Many immigrants accepted work in the United States that was completely unfamiliar to them simply to survive. Della Adler remembers how her immigrant grandfather took to peddling, but even then his family, when they arrived in America in 1870 to join him, had difficulty making ends meet.

Grandfather—Jacob H. Mayerberg—came to this country in 1867, from a small place in Lithuania called Volkovisk. His original mission was a business one, and he expected to return. Destiny decided otherwise.

He had heard that the U.S.A., especially New York City, was perishing from a need for *seforim*—Hebrew books of learning. So, the idea was to come here with a stock of books, sell them at a good profit, and return.

Poor Grandfather! On the way over, every book—plus all else he possessed—was stolen, and he arrived in Castle Garden, destitute.

He did what he was totally unequipped for—physically and by

nature—he peddled. What with, I do not know, but I do know he peddled through New York State in deep, drifted snow and icy winds and finally reached Buffalo and settled down as a *melamed*, a Hebrew teacher. The late Willard Saperston was one of his *talmidim*, his students. He thus eked out a pathetic living in bleak, dreary surroundings, and there Grandmother Hennie and their four children found him when they arrived in this country some three years later.

Grandma's comment on first seeing him was, "Yankov Hirsch, what happened to you? In three years you have become an old man." He was then forty-seven years old.

Grandmother was not one just to sit and do nothing. Her first effort was to find respectable living quarters. To pay the rent, she sold her most valuable possession, six silver spoons. The day came when there was no money to pay another month's rent, and Yankov Hirsch and Hennie assumed a "the Lord will provide" attitude; and the Lord, blessed be He, did provide.

Came a knock on their door, one fine day. A man of friendly mien stood there and asked—did they have one large or two small rooms to rent to six men who peddled in the country and came home just for *Shabbos* [the Sabbath]? There were five married men whose wives were awaiting the necessary *Schiffskarten* to come to America, and there was one twenty-one year-old unmarried youngster who was being petted and spoiled by the older men. Each Thursday, one of the six came home to cook for *Shabbos*. The other five came home on Friday.

The Mayerbergs could, and did, rent them rooms, and this miraculously solved the rent problem for them, until they could scramble to their feet. The single man, Louis Rubenstein, married the eldest daughter of the Mayerbergs, Kate—Chayeh—and they became my parents.

This all happened in the very long ago. Both the Mayerbergs and my parents prospered in a very modest way, and thereafter needed no crutch.

Today, I am the last living member of the Louis Rubenstein family, and the memory of the six silver spoons still lingers.

Abraham J. Karp, ed., *Golden Door to America: The Jewish Immigrant Experience*. New York: Viking, 1976.

Document 10: Making His Way in an Unfamiliar Language

Not all immigrants were comfortable in the sizable immigrant communities they often inhabited, where the language of the old country was spo-

ken and where old customs were practiced. In the following letter, a Polish emigrant looks forward to learning English and finding a well-paying job.

I am polish man. I want be american citizen—and took here first paper in 12 June N 625. But my friends are polish people—I must live with them—I work in the shoes-shop with polish people—I stay all the time with them—at home—in the shop—anywhere.

I want live with american people, but I do not know anybody of american. I go 4 times to teacher and must pay $2 weekly. I wanted take board in english house, but I could not, for I earn only $5 or 6 in a week, and when I pay teacher $2, I have only $4—$3—and now english board house is too dear for me. Better job to get is very hard for me, because I do not speak well english and I cannot understand what they say to me. The teacher teach me—but when I come home—I must speak polish and in the shop also. In this way I can live in your country many years—like my friends—and never speak—write well english—and never be good american citizen. I know here many persons, they live here 10 or moore years, and they are not citizens, they don't speak well english, they don't know geography and history of this country, they don't know constitution of America—nothing. I don't like be like them I wanted they help me in english—they could not—because they knew nothing. I want go from them away. But where? Not in the country, because I want go in the city, free evening schools and lern. I'm looking for help. If somebody could give me another job between american people, help me live with them and lern english—and could tell me the best way how I can fast lern—it would be very, very good for me. Perhaps you have somebody, here he could help me?

If you can help me, I please you.

I wrote this letter by myself and I know no good—but I hope you will understand whate I mean.

"Letter of an Anonymous Polish Immigrant to the Massachusetts Commission on Immigration, August 1914," Report of the Commission on the Problem of Immigration in Massachusetts, Boston, 1914.

Document 11: A Public School in New York City

The millions of immigrants who came to the United States after 1880 turned many American cities into immigrant cities, with residents from all over the world. In this excerpt, journalist A.R. Dugmore claims that at a New York high school he investigated, immigrant children from different backgrounds got along well.

At the corner of Catharine and Henry Streets in New York is a large white building that overlooks and dominates its neighborhood. Placed in the middle of a region of tawdry flathouses and dirty streets, it stands out preëminent because of its solid cleanliness and unpretentiousness. It is the home of Public School No. 1. In it are centred all the hopes of the miserably poor polyglot population of the surrounding district—for its pupils the scene of their greatest interest and endeavor, and for their parents an earnest of the freedom they have come far and worked hard to attain.

The child of American parentage is the exception in this school. The pupils are of the different nationalities or races that have their separate quarters in the immediate neighborhood. If they were to be divided according to their parental nationality, there would be twenty-five or more groups. The majority of the pupils, however, are Swedes, Austrians, Greeks, Russians, English, Irish, Scotch, Welsh, Rumanians, Italians, Poles, Hungarians, Canadians, Armenians, Germans and Chinese. The Germans, Russians and Polish predominate, for there are a very large number of Jewish pupils.

The most noticeable thing in the school is the perfectly friendly equality in which all these races mix; no prejudice is noticeable. The different races are so scattered that there is no chance for organization and its attendant cliques and small school politics. This is particularly interesting in the face of the fact that the one thing more than any other which binds the boys together is their intense common interest in party and city politics. All political news is followed and every question is heatedly debated in and out of class. This interest in politics and the training in argument and oratory it brings is probably due in large measure to the parents. To them this opportunity for political discussion is an evidence of the freedom of the new country which has replaced the tyranny of the old. The lack of organization and the lack of prejudice is shown by the fact that the "captain" or elected leader of a class composed with one exception of Jewish lads is the solitary exception—an Irish boy. In another class the "captain" is Chinese.

A.R. Dugmore, "New Citizens of the Republic," *World's Work*, April 1903.

Document 12: Newspapers in the Old Language

In 1924 a Jewish scholar, Mordecai Soltes, writing for the American Jewish Year Book *noted how Yiddish newspapers served numerous purposes for Jewish immigrants. While many immigrants spoke Yiddish, the language of eastern European Jews, few could read until they took up Yiddish newspapers. This helped them acquire English-language skills as well.*

Moreover, newspapers helped the community remain well-informed.

The simplification of the Yiddish tongue has helped to spread the Yiddish newspapers among the Jewish masses, the vast majority of whom had not had the benefits of a secular education and had not read any journals in the lands from which they emigrated. The Yiddish press proceeded to develop a generation of readers. Therein lies one of the fundamental reasons for the unusual influence which it exerts upon the mind-content of its large family of readers. It is practically the only source of information to which most of them have access. It guides them in the early stages of their process of adjustment to the new and complex American environment. It has educated the large majority of the immigrant Jews up to the point where they would be in a position to appreciate and read the newspaper as an easy, direct means of keeping in touch with important events which occur in this country as well as throughout the world. To the extent to which it has aroused in the immigrant Jews the demand for Yiddish newspapers, the latter have practically developed their own reading public, and have indirectly prepared their readers for an appreciation of the native press.

The facility and readiness with which the various influences of American life are assimilated by the immigrant in transition, are evident in the manner in which the Yiddish press handles the different features, particularly the news. The utilization of emphatic news headings, frequently bordering on the sensational; the human interest treatment of daily events; the promptness with which the leaders detect changes in conditions and the eagerness with which they adapt themselves to the newly-ascertained desires and interest of their readers; the care, skill and ability with which the newspapers are edited, the spirit of enterprise which characterizes their method of conducting the various departments,—all reflect direct influences of the native press.

In their general features the Yiddish daily newspapers are essentially journals for the masses. Their tendency is towards popularization, with sensationalism as the inevitable culmination. On the other hand, one of the distinctive features of the Yiddish press is the disposition to devote an unusually large proportion of its space to solid reading material such as does not usually find its way into the American newspaper, but which goes rather into the American magazine. The reason for this phenomenon becomes clear when we remember that the Yiddish newspaper is very frequently the only source of information and guidance which the reader has. It is therefore not merely a conveyor of news, but also a sort of literary and popular scientific journal, which deals with a wide range of subjects, supplies a large proportion of miscellaneous reading matter and caters to the needs and interests of the reader of magazine-stuff.

Mordecai Soltes, "The Yiddish Press," *American Jewish Year Book XXVI*, 1924.

Document 13: Opinions About "the Japanese Problem"

By the early twentieth century a number of Japanese emigrants had settled in America, primarily on the West Coast. They were to face prejudice and calls to restrict Japanese emigration. The government ultimately responded to anti-Japanese activists, stopping most Japanese emigration in 1907. The author of the following passage, Sidney Gulick, was sympathetic to the Japanese and wanted to summarize the prejudices against them in hopes of creating a more favorable opinion.

The belief is almost universal in California that Japanese racial characteristics are such as to render them unassimilable. Those who urge this point usually admit, however, that, all in all, the Japanese are not inferior to Americans, even in matters of morality. Such disputants are often ready to admit that exceptional cases of immorality have been exaggerated and generalized.

These contestants claim, however, that even though, for the sake of argument, Japanese may be allowed to be superior to Americans in every way, the sufficient ground for strict Japanese exclusion is the unquestioned fact that he belongs to a different race. He is brown; we are white; and this difference, they insist, carries with it such psychological, social, and civilizational differences that any attempt to live together is sure to be disastrous. The further deduction is that the only hope of safety, the only means whereby the friendship of our two nations can be maintained, is to agree to keep apart, each living in the land God has given us.

This position is presented in many forms and with considerable variety of emphasis.

Japanese, it is stated, are so completely Japanese that they are always and everywhere Japanese. Contrary to the average run of mankind, every Japanese thinks of his race and country first and only later of himself. It is claimed that his patriotism, therefore, is of such an intense nature that it is absolutely impossible for him to expatriate himself and become a loyal citizen of another land; that, even if he should do so in form, it would be in form only; he could not possibly become a sincere American; he would still be seeking to promote the interests of his native land and his Emperor and would inevitably be a source of danger to us in case of war with Japan.

Moreover, Japanese are so different from us, it is asserted, that mutual understanding is impossible; their social customs are the very opposite of ours; they are stolid in appearance and stoical in spirit. In a word, they are "inscrutable" and "mysterious"; they are impelled by motives we do not and cannot understand, and doubtless we appear the same to them.

It follows, as a matter of course, that they are not assimilable. They do not wish to become Americans and we do not wish to have them. Even though they may adopt our modes of clothing, housing, and eating, and many of our social habits, the change is only superficial and for a purpose; down in their hearts they are the same unchanging Asiatics, smiling and deceitful.

Because of all this, intermarriage between Japanese and whites is particularly obnoxious. How can oil and water mix?—or brown and white? The offspring is "neither Japanese nor American"; what is it but a fearsome monstrosity?

Specific illustrations are cited. It is charged that in such places as Vacaville and Florin Japanese have established entirely Japanese communities; they have possessed themselves of large consecutive areas and constitute so large a majority of the population that the children threaten to swamp the schools. In consequence, the white population is moving out, for they do not like the Japanese and do not wish their children to associate with them. This still further aggravates the difficulty, for it leaves compact Japanese colonies, with their national customs and Buddhist religion, cankers in our body politic.

Sidney Gulick, *The American Japanese Problem*. New York: Charles Scribner's Sons, 1914.

Document 14: Mexican American Life

Many Mexicans, who began to immigrate to the United States in large numbers in the early twentieth century, experienced a life that incorporated both cultures, as this interview shows.

In Mazatlan my father was the owner of one of the best hotels of the place. Europeans, Americans and prominent persons in Mexico were almost the only ones who went to stay at that hotel as they went through Mazatlan. At seventeen years of age I married an American mining engineer with whom I became acquainted at that hotel; he had been introduced to me by my father. My sister married a partner of my husband. Until I was sixteen I attended a private school of Mazatlan where I studied a lot of English, for my father had the idea of sending me to the United States to study. Once married, I traveled with my husband almost all over the Mexican Republic. We went to the Southern and the Central States and to all those where there are mines. He was very good to me in every way. He gave me everything that I wished and which was within his reach. We were married five years and it was almost one continuous honeymoon. But my husband died of fever and I was left a widow and without money. As I had practiced English a lot with him, and besides had made a trip to this country before he died, I decided when I found myself left alone to go and live in Nogales, Arizona. There, as I was still young (in 1917 I was twenty-two years old), I went around a lot with young Americans and Mexicans from Nogales, Arizona, and Nogales, Sonora. I got a job selling stamps in the American post-office of Nogales and got pretty good pay. . . .

I established a store in Nogales and there I fell in love with a young American who is now my husband. He is a mechanic, much younger than I. He speaks Spanish perfectly for he was brought up on the border. We decided to come and settle in Los Angeles and we have now been here several years. My husband earns six dollars a day and as that isn't enough for I like to dress well, etc., I rent two rooms of our house with which I help to pay the rent. I also work in a real estate office where I earn $15.00 a week for being there in the morning and also two per cent on the houses or land which I am able to sell. Besides, since I have an automobile and know the city well, I hire it with myself as chauffeur to honorable persons, and especially to Mexicans. I do every kind of business that I can, the thing is to earn something to help my husband. Once I even worked as an extra in a moving picture studio where I earned five dollars a day.

I get up in the morning at seven and make breakfast for my husband and myself. This consists of mush, eggs, milk and coffee. I also prepare his lunch and take him to his work in the automobile which we have bought and then I go to mine. At noon when I come home I make ham and eggs or anything for lunch or take my lunch in a restaurant. I come early in the afternoon if I don't have anything to do, and after I have fixed and swept the house, I get supper ready. That is our big meal, as it is with the Americans. I make Mexican stews, vegetables and American side dishes, chocolate, milk and coffee, *frijoles*, etc. I buy pies and sweets and we have a good supper. Then we go out to a movie or some dance hall or riding in the automobile. We are almost always on our way back by ten at night and then go to bed.

We always buy the daily, the *Los Angeles Examiner* and we read the principal items. I don't read the Mexican newspapers, because I am hardly at all interested in Mexico anymore, for my family is almost all here. I am thinking of going back but I don't know when, that depends on when the country gets in peace. When it is in peace my husband and I will go and we will establish a modern garage for the sale of oil and gasoline and the repair of automobiles, for I think good money can be made in that business.

I am Catholic and my husband is also but we hardly ever go to church. I pray at night on going to bed and in the morning when I get up but we don't make confession.

I think that the American women have good taste in dressing, perhaps better taste than the Mexican women of the capital, and as I like to dress well I always buy stylish dresses.

I have never had any trouble with the Americans; they have always treated me well. Once when I was introduced to an American family they asked me if I was Spanish and when I said I wasn't, that I was Mexican, they then said that the Mexicans weren't as clean nor as white as I; but I told them that in Mexico there are people as white and blonde, as intelligent and clean as in any other country of the world.

I have never believed in witches nor do I know of any here. There are probably some among the Mexicans who live on the East Side. Although I like my people very much I don't want to live with them, especially on the East Side, because they are very dirty there; there are many robberies and one can't live comfortably.

I think of myself as a very modern woman, following the American style but I am not extreme like the American women. For example I never bathe myself in the beaches or other public places because there all the people can see one's body and I wouldn't like that.

All the furniture of my home is American. I have my gas stove and gas heater also. I have my piano so that I can play it when I want. I also have a radio to listen to the concerts and news. I have always liked to buy everything for cash but I have purchased a few things on installments.

Wayne Moquin and Charles van Doren, eds., *A Documentary History of the Mexican Americans*. New York: Praeger, 1971.

Document 15: The Immigrant Threat to Racial Purity

By the early 1900s nativist sentiment had grown widespread. Sometimes, as in the following passage from Madison Grant's The Passing of the

Great Race, nativism was based on blatantly racist ideas. Grant believed that immigration from nations outside of northern and western Europe would water down America's genetic "stock."

The native American by the middle of the nineteenth century was rapidly becoming a distinct type. Derived from the Teutonic part of the British Isles, and being almost purely Nordic, he was on the point of developing physical peculiarities of his own, slightly variant from those of his English forefathers, and corresponding rather with the idealistic Elizabethan than with the materialistic Hanoverian Englishman. The Civil War, however, put a severe, perhaps fatal, check to the development and expansion of this splendid type, by destroying great numbers of the best breeding stock on both sides, and by breaking up the home ties of many more. If the war had not occurred these same men with their descendants would have populated the Western States instead of the racial nondescripts who are now flocking there.

The prosperity that followed the war attracted hordes of newcomers who were welcomed by the native Americans to operate factories, build railroads, and fill up the waste spaces—"developing the country" it was called.

These new immigrants were no longer exclusively members of the Nordic race as were the earlier ones who came of their own impulse to improve their social conditions. The transportation lines advertised America as a land flowing with milk and honey, and the European governments took the opportunity to unload upon careless, wealthy, and hospitable America the sweepings of their jails and asylums. The result was that the new immigration, while it still included many strong elements from the north of Europe, contained a large and increasing number of the weak, the broken, and the mentally crippled of all races drawn from the lowest stratum of the Mediterranean basin and the Balkans, together with hordes of the wretched, submerged populations of the Polish Ghettos.

With a pathetic and fatuous belief in the efficacy of American institutions and environment to reverse or obliterate immemorial hereditary tendencies, these newcomers were welcomed and given a share in our land and prosperity. The American taxed himself to sanitate and educate these poor helots, and as soon as they could speak English, encouraged them to enter into the political life, first of municipalities, and then of the nation.

The result is showing plainly in the rapid decline in the birth rate of native Americans because the poorer classes of Colonial stock, where they still exist, will not bring children into the world to compete in the labor market with the Slovak, the Italian, the Syrian, and the Jew. The native American is too proud to mix socially with them, and is gradually withdrawing from the scene, abandoning to these aliens the land which he conquered and developed. The man of the old stock is being crowded out of many country districts by these foreigners, just as he is to-day being literally driven off the streets of New York City by the swarms of Polish Jews. These immigrants adopt the language of the native American; they wear his clothes; they steal his name; and they are beginning to take his women, but they seldom adopt his religion or understand his ideals, and while he is being elbowed out of his own home the American looks calmly abroad and urges on others the suicidal ethics which are exterminating his own race.

Madison Grant, *The Passing of the Great Race*. New York: Charles Scribner's Sons, 1916.

Document 16: A President Supports Immigration

In 1917, as the World War I–era calls for "100 percent Americanism" grew louder, President Woodrow Wilson vetoed a bill that would have required immigrants to pass a literacy test. The veto was overridden by Congress, which had first proposed such a test in 1897, and the bill became law.

In two particulars of vital consequence this bill embodies a radical departure from the traditional and long-established policy of this country, a policy in which our people have conceived the very character of their Government to be expressed, the very mission and spirit of the Nation in respect of its relations to the peoples of the world outside their borders. It seeks to all but close entirely the gates of asylum which have always been open to those who could find nowhere else the right and opportunity of constitutional agitation for what they conceived to be the natural and inalienable rights of men; and it excludes those to whom the opportunities of elementary education have been denied, without regard to their character, their purposes, or their natural capacity.

Restrictions like these, adopted earlier in our history as a Nation, would very materially have altered the course and cooled the humane ardors of our politics. The right of political asylum has brought to this country many a man of noble character and elevated purpose who was marked as an outlaw in his own less fortunate land, and who has yet become an ornament to our citizenship and to our public councils. The children and the compatriots of these illustrious Americans must stand amazed to see the representatives of their

Nation now resolved, in the fullness of our national strength and at the maturity of our great institutions, to risk turning such men back from our shores without test of quality or purpose. It is difficult for me to believe that the full effect of this feature of the bill was realized when it was framed and adopted, and it is impossible for me to assent to it in the form in which it is here cast.

The literacy test and the tests and restrictions which accompany it constitute an even more radical change in the policy of the Nation. Hitherto we have generously kept our doors open to all who were not unfitted by reason of disease or incapacity for self-support or such personal records and antecedents as were likely to make them a menace to our peace and order or to the wholesome and essential relationships of life. In this bill it is proposed to turn away from tests of character and of quality and impose tests which exclude and restrict; for the new tests here embodied are not tests of quality or of character or of personal fitness, but tests of opportunity. Those who come seeking opportunity are not to be admitted unless they have already had one of the chief of the opportunities they seek, the opportunity of education. The object of such provisions is restriction, not selection.

If the people of this country have made up their minds to limit the number of immigrants by arbitrary tests and so reverse the policy of all the generations of Americans that have gone before them, it is their right to do so. I am their servant and have no license to stand in their way. But I do not believe that they have. I respectfully submit that no one can quote their mandate to that effect. Has any political party ever avowed a policy of restriction in this fundamental matter, gone to the country on it, and been commissioned to control its legislation? Does this bill rest upon the conscious and universal assent and desire of the American people? I doubt it. It is because I doubt it that I make bold to dissent from it. I am willing to abide by the verdict, but not until it has been rendered. Let the platforms of parties speak out upon this policy and the people pronounce their wish. The matter is too fundamental to be settled otherwise.

I have no pride of opinion in this question. I am not foolish enough to profess to know the wishes and ideals of America better than the body of her chosen representatives know them. I only want instruction direct from those whose fortunes, with ours and all men's, are involved.

Moses Rischin, ed., *Immigration and the American Tradition*. Indianapolis: Bobbs-Merrill, 1976.

Document 17: Immigration Quotas Are Justified

The American government ended the era of open immigration with a series of laws passed in the 1920s. These laws placed quotas on emigration from specific countries as well as a cap on the total number of immigrants to be allowed annually. The quotas favored emigrants from northern and western Europe, which made complete sense to Congressman William Vaile, who made the following statements.

We would not want any immigrants at all unless we could hope that they would become assimilated to our language, customs, and institutions, unless they could blend thoroughly into our body politic. This would be admitted, I suppose, by the most radical opponent of immigration restriction. In fact, it is one of the stock arguments of these gentlemen that, although the immigrant himself may be assimilated slowly, his children, born here, become Americans in thought, action, speech, and character. That statement, often splendidly true, must nevertheless be accepted with many qualifications; but at least it is clear enough that the second generation will be assimilated quicker than the first—whatever may be the effect in many cases of such assimilation upon the United States. It would seem still clearer that the third and subsequent generations will be still more American than their predecessors.

It is also one of the stock arguments of the antirestrictionists that the immigrant has taken an important part in the building up of the country. Surely his children and grandchildren, both in numbers and in the quality of their work, have taken a still more important part.

Now, it seems rather illogical for gentlemen who vaunt the assimilability and the work of alien groups in our population to claim that those who have been for the shortest time in the process of assimilation and in the work of the Republic should have greater or even equal consideration because of this very newness. It would seem if those who came to the work at the eleventh hour are to have a penny, then at least those who have "borne the heat and burden of the day" should not be put off with a farthing.

It is a fact, not merely an argument, that this country was created, kept united, and developed—at least for more than a century of existence—almost entirely by people who came here from the countries of northern and western Europe. That people from southern and eastern Europe did not begin to come in large numbers until after 1890 certainly proves that those who came before them had built up a country desirable enough to attract these late comers.

Shall the countries which furnished those earlier arrivals be discriminated against for the very reason, forsooth, that they are represented here by from 2 to 10 generations of American citizens, whereas the others are largely represented by people who have not been here long enough to become citizens at all?

If there is a charge of "discrimination," the charge necessarily involves the idea that the proposed quota varies from some standard which is supposed to be not "discriminatory." What is that standard? From the arguments of those opposed to the bill it would appear that the census of 1910 is now regarded as not "discriminatory," or at least as less "discriminatory" than the census of 1890. It will be remembered that the census of 1910 was adopted as a base for emergency legislation, legislation not expected to be permanent, legislation not claimed to be exact, but intended to answer the purpose of an urgently needed restriction of the total volume of immigration. It has answered that purpose fairly well, but with some unnecessary hardships obviated by the present bill. The number admitted under it, however, has been far too great, and it is now proposed to cut the quota more than one-half.

But it is not the cut in the total which is so bitterly complained of. It is the change in the proportions, and it is interesting to note that those who violently opposed the passage of the 3 per cent law now with equal violence demand the retention of its proportions in the present legislation. But at least we can say that it has not been in operation long enough to have become an established and inviolable principle of distribution if some more equitable basis could be devised.

Moses Rischin, ed., *Immigration and the American Tradition*. Indianapolis: Bobbs-Merrill, 1976.

Discussion Questions

Chapter 1: The First Great Wave: European Emigration from 1830 to 1880

1. Leonard Dinnerstein and David M. Reimers argue that economic conditions and the availability of land were the major motives for European immigrants between 1830 and 1880. How did the United States offer immigrants an escape from poverty and starvation? What conditions in the United States would tend to discourage immigration?

2. According to Carl Wittke, immigrants were encouraged to come to America by both earlier arrivals and various businesses. What reasons could earlier immigrants give to either emigrate or stay home? What kinds of businesses stood to gain from increased traffic in immigration, and how?

3. Europeans emigrated for a wide variety of political, cultural, and economic reasons, according to Maldwyn Allen Jones. What conditions in Europe helped to both inspire and facilitate emigration? What role did political or religious discontent play?

4. The vast territorial and economic expansion of the United States in the mid-1800s created many opportunities for immigrants, according to Maxine Sellers. Why did certain immigrants seek to homestead new lands while others stayed in industrial cities? Which immigrants had an easier time adapting to their new lives?

5. Roger Daniels argues that Roman Catholic immigrants from Germany and Ireland faced a great deal of prejudice in the United States. Why might Americans have felt threatened by these newcomers? What forms did this prejudice take?

Chapter 2: The Second Great Wave: European Emigration from 1880 to 1924

1. John F. Kennedy argues that the European immigrants of 1880 to 1924 made huge contributions to American life. Which areas of Europe did these immigrants come from, and why were they inspired to leave home?

2. According to Georges Perec, Ellis Island was not a particularly welcoming arrival point for new immigrants. Why might the American government have felt the need to process new immigrants on Ellis Island? What questions and other challenges did immigrants face on Ellis Island?

3. Many of the immigrants who came between 1880 and 1924 settled in cities rather than rural areas. Why, according to Sean Dennis Cashman, did most immigrants avoid farming? What opportunities did cities offer them instead?

4. According to Richard Krickus, a strong movement arose to "Americanize" new immigrants quickly. Why did Americans feel the need to assimilate newcomers as quickly as possible? What forms did this "Americanization" process take?

5. New immigrants had to adapt to more than a new homeland, according to Philip Taylor. What other challenges did they face? What strategies did immigrants use to adjust to their new communities, neighbors, and jobs?

Chapter 3: Emigration from Asia

1. Ronald Takaki argues that Asian immigrants came largely to fill the labor needs of the expanding United States. What countries did these new immigrants come from? Why did American employers want Asian workers?

2. According to Robert A. Wilson and Bill Hosokawa, Chinese and Japanese immigrants tended to build institutions that strengthened their communities but which also remained separate from mainstream American life. Why did Asian immigrants adopt this approach?

3. Chinese immigrants originally came to the United States during the California Gold Rush, according to Jack Chen. Did the Chinese succeed as gold miners? What other occupations did they seek? What contributions did they make to the society of early California?

4. According to Thomas Sowell, Japanese immigrants tended to be better educated than most other immigrants, as well as better-off financially. Why did the Japanese government allow such people to emigrate? What work did Japanese immigrants perform?

5. Immigrants from the Philippines, an American possession, followed those from China and Japan. Why did American em-

ployers seek Filipino laborers, according to H. Brett Melendy? Did they enjoy the rights of American citizens?

Chapter 4: Emigration from Mexico

1. Many Mexicans became automatic Americans after the Mexican-American War of 1846. How were these new citizens treated, according to James Diego Vigil? What rights and protections had they been promised?

2. According to Lawrence Fuchs, many Mexican immigrants were in fact sojourners, crossing the border regularly. What impact did this have on both their job opportunities and their treatment in the United States?

3. Mexican immigrants were often caught in between Mexican and American culture, according to Richard Griswold del Castillo and Arnoldo De León. How did their actions reflect this status? Why did loyal Mexicans emigrate?

Chapter 5: The Open Door Closes

1. According to Ellis Cose, Chinese were the first to have their immigration restricted by federal law. Why did other Americans, often other immigrants, want to restrict the Chinese? What arguments did they use?

2. Why, according to David M. Reimers, did Americans want to restrict immigration across the board in the late 1800s and early 1900s? What specific groups did restrictionists target?

3. According to Roy Beck, restricting immigration was the proper thing for the American government to do in the 1920s. What arguments does he use? How did immigrants increase instability in America?

4. American participation in World War I was a major factor in restricting immigration, according to John Higham. Why did many people feel that "one-hundred percent Americanization" was necessary? What measures did the federal government take in response to such attitudes?

Chronology

1600s
Englishmen settle the eastern seaboard from Maine to Georgia; they are joined by smaller communities of Scots, French, Dutch, Spanish, Germans, and Swedes.

1607
England establishes the first permanent European settlement in the future United States at Jamestown, Virginia.

1700s
Large numbers of English, Scots, and Scots Irish immigrants settle in America; fewer come from other European countries.

1776
The United States declares its independence from Great Britain.

1818
Regular sailing services between New York and Liverpool, England, begin; many emigrants from England, Ireland, and Germany embark from Liverpool.

1830
Large-scale emigration from Europe to the United States begins; between 1830 and 1880, nearly 7 million Europeans immigrate to America; most come from Ireland, Germany, or the Scandinavian nations of Denmark, Norway, and Sweden; aside from the requirement that immigrants be counted, no federal laws about immigration exist.

1840
Regular steamship service between England and the United States begins, making immigration even easier.

1845
The American Party, an anti-immigrant party later known as the Know-Nothings, is founded.

1845–1847
The Irish Potato Famine initiates heavy emigration from Ireland.

1846
Crop failures in Germany and Holland encourage emigration.

1846
The Mexican-American War ends, transferring much of the Southwest to American control; in those areas, seventy-five thousand Mexicans automatically become Americans.

1848
Revolutions in Germany cause political and economic uncertainty; some Germans choose to leave for the United States.

1848
Gold is discovered at the settlement of a German immigrant, John Sutter, in California; the Gold Rush of 1849 follows.

1850s
The Taiping Rebellion, the promise of easy wealth, and the efforts of labor contractors encourage Chinese men to leave for California.

1850
The German Jewish immigrant Levi Strauss opens a dry-goods business in Sacramento, California, to serve the gold miners.

1854
The Know-Nothing party achieves its greatest electoral successes, with victories in local elections in several states.

1855
Castle Garden on New York City's Manhattan Island is opened as an immigration reception center.

1861–1865
The American Civil War restricts most new immigration; immigrants are heavily represented in both the Union and Rebel armies.

1862
The Homestead Act is passed by the U.S. government to encourage the settlement of the West; it offers 160 acres of free land to anyone who settles and farms the land for five years.

1865–1869
The transcontinental railroad is built; many of the laborers are immigrants, either Irish in the East or Chinese in the West.

1868
The Fourteenth Amendment to the Constitution guarantees American citizenship to all people born on American soil.

1869

The first group of Japanese immigrants arrives in the United States; many more come after 1886, when the Japanese government lifts its restrictions on emigration.

1870

Several Midwestern states stage a National Immigration Convention in Indianapolis, Indiana; their goal is to encourage further immigration of European farmers; an American Naturalization Act establishes that only "white persons and persons of African descent" can be American citizens.

1875

The United States passes the first federal immigration restriction, which forbids the importation of foreign convicts or prostitutes.

1880

With vast numbers of Irish, Germans, and Scandinavians still arriving, the second wave of mass immigration begins with new groups from southern and eastern Europe; they are joined by newcomers from Japan, the Philippines, and Mexico.

1881

The government of Russia begins to oppress its large Jewish community with legal restrictions as well as pogroms.

1882

The Chinese Exclusion Act effectively ends Chinese immigration to the United States; the act is the first attempt by the American government to prevent the immigration of a particular national group.

1886

The Statue of Liberty is dedicated in New York Harbor.

1892

Ellis Island in New York Harbor is opened as the new immigration reception center; by 1932 Ellis Island had welcomed 12 million immigrants.

1894

The Immigration Restriction League is formed in Boston; its members seek to limit the immigration to peoples of Nordic or northern European descent.

1897
Congress passes a bill requiring all new immigrants to pass a literacy test; the bill is vetoed by President Grover Cleveland.

1898
The United States annexes the Hawaiian Islands, the original destination of many emigrants from Asia; victory in the Spanish-American War awards the Philippines, among other territories, to the United States.

1901
President William McKinley is assassinated by Leon Czolgosz, the child of naturalized immigrants from Poland; anti-immigrant sentiment grows.

1901–1910
The decade of the heaviest immigration to the United States until the 1980s; new arrivals include over 2 million emigrants from Italy, over 2 million from Austria-Hungary, 1.5 million from Russia, and 167,000 from Greece; many of the emigrants from Russia and Austria-Hungary are either Polish or Jewish.

1904
Italian immigrant Amadeo Giannini opens the Bank of Italy in San Francisco; later, Giannini's institution becomes known as the Bank of America.

1907
The Gentleman's Agreement is reached between the governments of the United States and Japan; the agreement stops Japanese immigration, except for the wives of Japanese men already here and prospective brides.

1910
The Mexican Revolution begins, sending hundreds of thousands of Mexicans across the border into the United States; according to the census, over a half million Jewish immigrants live in one and a half square miles of Manhattan's Lower East Side.

1913
California passes the Alien Land Law, which makes it illegal for noncitizens to purchase land; it is directed at the Issei, the first generation of Japanese Americans.

1914–1918
World War I curtails emigration from Europe; American partici-

pation in the war in 1917–1918 inspires more calls to restrict immigration due to the danger of "foreign" influences.

1916

Madison Grant's *The Passing of the Great Race*, which claims that America is in danger of racial dilution, is published.

1917

Over President Woodrow Wilson's veto, Congress passes an immigration law that requires all immigrants over age sixteen to be literate; it also bans all emigration from Asia.

1921

The Emergency Immigration Act is passed; it establishes broad-based immigration restrictions based on national quotas; only 3 percent of the foreign-born population of each nationality, according to the 1910 census, are to be allowed annually.

1924

The Johnson Reed, or National Origins, Act reduces the quotas to 2 percent of the foreign-born as of the 1890 census, thus tilting new immigration heavily in favor of Britain, Ireland, Germany, and Scandinavia; a total cap of approximately 160,000 is also established.

1929

Further modifications of the National Origins Act take effect, moving immigration quotas still further in the direction of northern and western European countries.

1952

The McCarran-Walter Immigration Act gives immigration preferences to people with relatives in America or with special skills.

1965

Congress passes the Immigration Act of 1965, which ends the system of national quotas; a total of 170,000 immigrants are to be allowed under the new system, but numerous groups are exempt from that total, including political refugees, those with close relatives in the United States, and those with needed occupations; these exemptions raise immigration totals to heights not seen since the early 1900s.

For Further Research

Books

Taylor Anbinder, *Nativism and Slavery: The Northern Know-Nothings and the Politics of the 1850s*. New York: Oxford University Press, 1992.

Thomas J. Archdeacon, *Becoming American: An Ethnic History*. New York: Free, 1983.

Marion Bennett, *American Immigration Policy: A History*. Washington, DC: Public Affairs, 1963.

Jerome Blum, *The End of the Old Order in Rural Europe*. Princeton, NJ: Princeton University Press, 1978.

John Bodnar, *The Transplanted: A History of Immigrants in Urban America*. Bloomington: Indiana University Press, 1985.

David M. Brownstone, Irene M. Frank, and Douglas L. Brownstone, *Island of Hope, Island of Tears*. New York: Rawson, Wade, 1979.

Carlos Bulosan, *America Is in the Heart: A Personal History*. Seattle: University of Washington Press, 1973.

Roger Daniels, *Asian America*. Seattle: University of Washington Press, 1988.

Charlotte Erickson, *American Industry and the European Immigration*. New York: Russell and Russell, 1967.

Richard Gambino, *Blood of My Blood*. New York: Doubleday, 1974.

Nathan Glazer and Daniel P. Moynihan, *Beyond the Melting Pot*. Cambridge, MA: MIT Press, 1970.

Susan A. Glenn, *Daughters of the Shtetl: Life and Labor in the Immigrant Generation*. Ithaca, NY: Cornell University Press, 1990.

David Gutierrez, *Walls and Mirrors: Mexican Americans, Mexican Immigrants, and the Politics of Ethnicity*. Berkeley and Los Angeles: University of California Press, 1995.

Oscar Handlin, *Boston's Immigrants*. New York: Atheneum, 1968.

———, *The Uprooted*. Boston: Little, Brown, 1973.

Edward Hutchinson, *Immigrants and Their Children, 1850–1950*. New York: Wiley, 1956.

Harry Kitano, *Japanese Americans: The Evolution of a Subculture*. Englewood Cliffs, NJ: Macmillan, 1969.

Dale T. Knobel, *"America for the Americans": The Nativist Movement in the United States*. New York: Twayne, 1996.

Alan Kraut, *The Huddled Masses: The Immigrant in American Society, 1880–1921*. Arlington Heights, IL: Harlan Davidson, 1982.

———, *Silent Travelers: Germs, Genes, and the "Immigrant Menace."* New York: BasicBooks, 1994.

Michael LeMay, *From Open Door to Dutch Door: An Analysis of U.S. Immigration Policy Since 1820*. New York: Praeger, 1987.

Huping Ling, *Surviving on the Gold Mountain: A History of Chinese American Women and Their Lives*. New York: State University of New York Press, 1998.

Frederick C. Luebke, *Bonds of Loyalty: German Americans and World War I*. DeKalb: Northern Illinois University Press, 1974.

Carey McWilliams, *North from Mexico*. New York: Greenwood, 1968.

Charles H. Mindel and Robert W. Hamerstein, eds., *Ethnic Families in America*. New York: Elsevier, 1976.

Eva Morawska, *For Bread with Butter*. Cambridge, England: Cambridge University Press, 1985.

Walter Nugent, *Crossings: The Great Transatlantic Migrations, 1870–1914*. Bloomington: Indiana University Press, 1992.

Moses Rischin, *The Promised City: New York Jews, 1870–1914*. Cambridge, MA: Harvard University Press, 1962.

Ole Rolvaag, *Giants in the Earth*. New York: Harper, 1929.

Maxine Seller, *Immigrant Women*. Albany: State University of New York Press, 1994.

Mary J. Shapiro, *Gateway to Liberty: The Story of the Statue of Liberty and Ellis Island*. New York: Vintage Books, 1986.

Harry Shih-Shan Tsai, *The Chinese Experience in America*. Bloomington: Indiana University Press, 1986.

Mark Wyman, *Roundtrip to America: The Immigrants Return to Europe, 1880–1930*. Ithaca, NY: Cornell University Press, 1993.

Joseph Wytrwal, *America's Polish Heritage*. Detroit: Endurance, 1961.

Periodicals

Emory Bogardus, "American Attitudes Toward Filipinos," *Sociology and Social Research*, September 1929.

Katherine Neils Conzen, "Immigrants, Immigrant Neighborhoods, and Ethnic Identity: Historical Issues," *Journal of American History*, December 1979.

Marcus Lee Hansen, "The History of American Immigration as a Field for Research," *American Historical Review*, 1926–1927.

Morell Heald, "Business Attitudes Toward European Immigration," *Journal of Economic History*, 1953.

John Higham, "Another Look at Nativism," *Catholic Historical Review*, 1958.

Simon Kuznets, "Immigration of Russian Jews to the United States: Background and Structure," *Perspectives in American History*, 1975.

Oliver MacDonough, "The Irish Famine Emigration to the United States," *Perspectives in American History*, 1976.

Paul M. Ong, "Chinese Labor in Early San Francisco: Racial Segmentation and Industrial Expansion," *Amerasia*, 1981.

David Sonder, "Rogues, Whores, and Vagabonds," *Social History*, 1978.

Index